Constitutional Interpretation

D1562208

To Charles L. Black, Jr.

Constitutional Interpretation

Philip Bobbitt

BLACKWELL
Oxford UK & Cambridge USA

First published 1991

Basil Blackwell Ltd
108 Cowley Road, Oxford, OX4 1JF, UK

Basil Blackwell, Inc.
3 Cambridge Center
Cambridge, Massachusetts 02142, USA

British Library Cataloguing in Publication Data

A CIP catalogue record for this book is available from the British Library.

Library of Congress Cataloging in Publication Data

Bobbitt, Philip.
    Constitutional Interpretation / Philip Bobbitt.
        p.   cm.
    Includes index.
    ISBN 0-631-16484-7 – ISBN 0-631-16485-5 (pbk.)
      1. United States—Constitutional law—Interpretation and
construction.   I. Title.
KF4550.B6   1991
342.73'02--dc20
[347.3022]   90-45109
                                         CIP

Typeset in 11 on 12.5 pt Garamond by Photo-graphics, Honiton, Devon
Printed in Great Britain by T.J. Press Ltd., Padstow, Cornwall.

τίς δὲ μηδὲν ἐν δέει καρδίαν ἀνατρέφων
ἢ πόλις βροτός θ᾽ ὁμοίως ἔτ᾽ ἂν σέβοι δίκαν;

μήτ᾽ ἀνάρχετον βίον μήτε δεσποτούμενον αἰνέσῃς.
παντὶ μέσῳ τὸ κράτος θεὸς ὤπασεν,
ἀλλ᾽ ἄλλα δ᾽ ἐφορεύει.

ξύμμετρον δ᾽ ἔπος λέγω,
δυσσεβίας μὲν ὕβρις τέκος ὡς ἐτύμως.
ἐκ δ᾽ ὑγιείας φρενῶν ὁ πάμφιλος καὶ πολύευκτος ὄλβος.

Aeschylus, *Eumenides*, 522–37

> Whether city or man,
> Is one who ignores conscience
> Likely to revere justice?
>
> Speak in praise of neither an ungoverned existence
> Nor one that is determined by a single rule.
> God gave the rule that mediates in all things
> And He oversees different things in different ways.
>
> I advocate mutual concern:
> Irrationalism is actually the product of disregard,
> But the well-adapted life we very much desire
> Is born from the health of the soul.

(trans. L. E. Chronis)

Contents

Preface

A Preface is inevitably an acknowledgment; I am pleased to make this one explicitly so. There may be readers who skip Prefaces and Acknowledgments, Forewords and the like, and go straight to those pages that are numbered in arabic numerals. I am not one of these. Such passages are not merely apéritifs. They acknowledge the role of others, usually not named elsewhere, in the creative product; and they often disclose the motive of the author in publishing.

This work completes an undertaking begun by an earlier book, *Constitutional Fate*, which presents the materials for constitutional analysis in a way that accounts for the legitimacy of constitutional decisionmaking. The present book, *Constitutional Interpretation*, had to be written once the earlier work was published although I did not realize that at the time and there have been many occasions in the interim when I have concluded that I was not the person to do so. *Constitutional Fate* propounded a solution to the problem of the legitimacy of judicial review, which arises from the claim that the overturning of legislative and executive acts by the judiciary, on constitutional grounds, is undemocractic (the so-called Countermajoritarian Objection). That solution is to some extent incomplete, however, unless the further questions regarding justice and justification, that solution raises are addressed.[1]

Constitutional Fate was written, and largely published in a law review, in 1979. At that time I went into the government and subsequently into a kind of exile from constitutional commentary. I believed that I had essentially solved the problem of the Countermajoritarian Objection and judicial review. I had done this by developing a system that specified six forms of constitutional argument that permitted one to map any constitutional proposition onto a field of legitimacy. Just as Cartesian geometry allows one to algebraicize geometry – or gödel numbering allows one to associate logical propositions with numbers – so one could associate any legitimate constitutional argument with one of the interpretive principles of *Constitutional Fate*. (For example: "the Fifth Amendment requires that compensation be paid when the government takes private property for its use" can be associated with the form of textual argument; "the Fourteenth Amendment requires that counsel must be made available to an indigent defendant" can be associated with doctrinal argument, and so on.) This method permits one to translate all the asserted statements in a well-formed judicial opinion into a series of constitutional arguments. Using this system to characterize whether a particular proposition in constitutional law was true or false (e.g., "the Constitution requires a trial by jury in all criminal cases" is true because it can be associated with a form of legitimate argument), I then argued that there existed a number of constitutional propositions whose truth or falsity could not be determined. And the examples I gave of these were the six interpretive principles themselves. This I believed exploded the prevailing project of attempting to enshrine these principles or any particular interpretive principle as determinative of both the legitimacy and justification of a constitutional decision to overturn (or uphold) an act of government.

The occasion for the present work was an invitation to write up three lectures on the United States Constitution, delivered in 1987 as the Mellon Lectures at Oxford University. I do not think that, but for the incidence of the lectures, this book would have come into being, at least in its present form, and for this invitation I must thank Professor Byron Shafer and the trustees of the Mellon Foundation. 1987 was the 200th anniversary, or Bicentennial, of the signing of the American constitution in Philadelphia by the delegates to the Convention that proposed the ratification of that historic covenant. For most of the year I found myself again in Washington where I had re-entered the government. I only returned to Oxford in late December, barely arriving within the calendar anniversary, possibly the last of many commemoratives of the Bicentennial Year. Subsequently a meeting was arranged with Mr Sean Magee, an engaging and lively editor with Basil Blackwell, who offered to publish the lectures, under the unusual constraints I requested.

The publisher graciously agreed to reprint virtually an entire U.S. Supreme Court opinion as the end-paper to the volume, a costly but useful and helpful device. This enables the reader to unfold the opinion, whose paragraphs and sentences are numbered, and follow along the commentary within the volume, line by line. An equally generous gesture was the promise to publish hardcover and paper editions simultaneously, a move that publishers understandably resist but one which, for an author whose goal is to get his ideas out to as large and as anonymous an audience as possible, is highly desirable. As publishers of most of the Wittgenstein corpus, Blackwell Publishers have an especial appeal to me. They have been patient, encouraging, indulgent and supportive throughout. Ms Jill Landeryou and Mr Simon Prosser continued to believe in the project even when there was no evident reason to conclude that they would ever, in fact, see page proofs.

The following Spring, I returned to Oxford to resume my college fellowship. I nevertheless had some doubts as to whether the lectures should be published. During this time I had occasion to review work that reflected this schema I had described. Some of this was merely a replay of much of the initial reaction to *Constitutional Fate*, in which reviewer after reviewer assumed that I had to be advocating a privileged role for ethical argument, despite my numerous disclaimers to the contrary. One even complained that the sub-title "Theory of the Constitution" had confused him; shouldn't it be "The Theory of the Constitution", he asked?

But much of this work was more ambitious. And I came to realize that I had, to some extent, perhaps incited the very errors that so grated on me, for in my description of the six modalities of argument as legitimating I had not addressed the issue of what to do if the forms disagreed, e.g., if textual argument led to one conclusion and historical argument to another. By invariably adopting one of the forms to criticize the others subsequent critics had inadvertently focussed on this dilemma. Thus they were led to repeat – at the level of the interpretive principles or forms – the very error they wished to escape from at the level of the individual propositions about law. The fact that this analysis sometimes came from the political left was only ironic.

For it was the assault on American constitutional institutions commenced by the American right wing in the 1950s and 60s that had prompted my reaction in the late 1970s. This attempt to discredit the legitimacy of our legal institutions was taken up by the cultural left in the early 1980s and, one might say, the current work is a reaction to this development. At present the activities of the left have had one significant political impact: they have enabled the right wing to lever a number of dubious propositions into respectability because they seem, by contrast, common-sensical and even unavoidable. One consequence of the extravagant claim that "all sex within marriage is rape" for example, is to provide support for an indefensible reluctance to pass laws addressing violence against women. These assaults are a depressing aftermath to the great triumphs of American law that brought civil rights and civil liberties within reach of all the American people, and the principles of human rights to international recognition at Helsinki. Lee is supposed to have said that "Duty is the sublimest word in the English language." To explicate and defend these institutions, where they are explicable and defensible, is a duty I inherited, as most of us come into title with things, partly by the obligation of background and partly by the obligation of training.

It was my conviction, expressed in *Constitutional Fate*, that what the right and left share in this debate is a fundamental epistemological mistake. Each of these perspectives assumes that law-statements are statements about the world (like the statements of science) and thus must be verified by a correspondence with facts about the world. Confronting the unavoidable observation that law-statements (such as "the First Amendment's protection of free speech does not permit government to impose spending limits on the contributions of individuals to their own political campaigns") often do not correspond to any facts asserted in the Constitution (e.g., the First Amendment does not mention campaign finance), these commentators set about constructing external referents to which such statements could correspond. Since the Constitution *per se* did not appear to resolve many of the hard questions put to it in law cases, it seemed undeniable to them that people who interpret the Constitution must look to something else in order to accomplish this interpretation. (This accounted, in part, for the vitriolic way in which sitting judges who denied any such resort to extra-legal principles, were attacked. These denials seemed laughably disingenuous.) Not surprisingly, these commentators did not agree on what constituted a legitimate external referent; interestingly, they inevitably seemed to have chosen one or another of the archetypal forms of argument as the source for an ideologically constructed hierarchy. Many on the right settled on historical forms of argument as the sole legitimating form. Thus historical facts: what did the framers and ratifiers intend the First Amendment to apply to? or historical hypotheticals informed by facts: how might the Framers have reacted to the notion of restricting campaign expenditure? were thought required if the legal conclusions of these arguments were to have status as law (and not merely political opinion made law by virtue of the power of the decider). On the left, many enshrined prudential argument as the sole source of legitimating fact. The question always became: does this interpretation produce an acceptable result (where the impact of the decision was the factual referent)? Thus many on the left called for more empirical work to be done to determine the real-world effects of constitutional decisions. "What is the actual effect of First Amendment jurisprudence in protecting political dissent in America? Did *Roe* v. *Wade* really protect women's decisions regarding childbirth, or did it actually create a formidable political force opposed to abortions while dividing and deflecting the women's movement?"

These commentators and critics ignored the one fact about the world that might have been relevant: that once a form of argument, a modality of understanding and decisionmaking, was transformed into an external and ideological referent, it lost the legitimating force it hitherto contributed. This added to the virulence of the debate, since both sides could now claim, with equal merit, that the other had abandoned the Constitution as law. A critic on the left might say: "it is illegitimate to act as if the Constitution and the original understanding are the same thing. The Constitution does not say that it should be interpreted in accordance with the original understanding. The proposal that we should follow the original understanding must be justified on substantive grounds." To which a critic on the right would reply: "to assess the legitimacy of an interpretive principle by reference to substantive political preferences is to abandon what is distinctly legitimating about legal decisions, i.e., that they are not governed by political factors."

During the ensuing decade following the publication of *Constitutional Fate* I watched this debate, intermittently and from afar. Because I felt that the question of legitimacy was fundamental for this debate, and because I believed that the analysis of *Constitutional Fate* was correct, I went on to other work.

You see, I formerly believed – and still do – that understanding the forms of constitutional arguments as the *way* in which a constitutional proposition is true rather than the reason it is true can account for their legitimating force and allows one to avoid many of the contradictions one encounters in extracting from them the satisfaction of expectations we would rightly have about scientific observations. What I did not see was that the possibility of conflict between forms would resuscitate the debate over legitimacy and encourage an eager resort to "ideologizing" preferred modalities to provide the external referent that such legitimacy was, mistakenly, thought to require.

This is how the argument went: Everyone agrees the Constitution is law. Therefore the Constitution does not just mean what particular people want it to mean. If it did, it would not be law. The problem is that it is not always clear what the Constitution means, how it is to be applied/interpreted. Reasonable people disagree about what it means. Some people think that a Constitution that guarantees "the equal protection of the laws" requires race conscious affirmative action policies in order to remove the effects of past and present discrimination (a prudential argument); other people think that a state that engages in affirmative action is violating that same guarantee (a textual argument). In hard cases, two or more legitimate modalities will conflict. Since the Constitution itself does not direct how it is to be interpreted – does not say which modality is to be used – it seems undeniable that, at least in hard cases, people who interpret the Constitution have to look to something other than the various legitimating forms of argument. This means that the interpretation of the Constitution must inevitably be based on principles that are external to the words of the Constitution itself. Those principles have to be created rather than found: the Constitution does not contain the instructions for its own interpretation.

This argument concedes that the Constitution could not, however, mean just anything at all, that it is not wholly "indeterminate" regarding its appropriate interpretation. After all, sometimes resort to interpretive principles admits only one answer. Additionally, what the Supreme Court thinks, and what it will say about questions not yet decided but likely to arise soon, can be predicted with considerable accuracy. Moreover, some interpretations are better than others, i.e., only some correspond to the various legitimating modalities. Some interpretations of ambiguous provisions are flawed, e.g., will produce an unacceptable increase in judicial discretion (prudential); will leave politically weak groups at the mercy of the state (structural); will make liberty too fragile (ethical); will be insufficiently respectful of the claims of original intent (historical). So constitutional interpretation is not indeterminate even though it does not always yield unique answers.

How shall we choose, however, among good interpretations? "Constitutional law," concludes the critic whose remarks I have paraphrased, "must be able to be confident that good reasons, rather than mere preferences, support certain views about the relationship between state and society. Here it is necessary for constitutional law to develop interpretive principles by confronting squarely, and in the context of the broad frameworks set out by constitutional commands, the question of what sorts of consequences the legal rules under attack have for constitutional liberty and equality (including the constitutional commitment to a form of self-government)."

In other words: Constitutional law must be able to provide good reasons, rather than mere preferences, for choosing among the alternative outcomes generated within the frameworks of the modalities. The author quoted above comes out for "liberty and equality". Yet even these broadly-subscribed-to objectives raise the troubling point: why these objectives, indeed why objectives at all? What is the legal basis for this, i.e., why is it legitimate? It may be that we cannot, in fact, give good reasons that explain our choice of one legitimate outcome over another, equally legitimate, one if by "good" reasons we mean legitimate ones.

In this book I will offer a resolution of this issue. This is not easy because, as I will show, the resolution favored by those whose argument I have just summarized – a resort to an external referent – would sacrifice the legitimacy of the method.

I will show how the United States has developed the six forms of constitutional argument to which I have referred. I will show how the operation of these forms maintains legitimacy. This is Book I.

Then I will ask the reader to work through three case studies: an Opinion of the U.S. Supreme Court, a description of the Iran-Contra Affair, and the nomination proceedings of Judge Robert Bork for elevation to the Supreme Court. The skills gained in these exercises amount to a sort of auto-experiment. This is Book II. The reader can then judge for himself or herself as to the claims made for the various modalities of argument.

Then I will attempt to answer the problem posed above: how can we choose among competing modalities without sacrificing either legitimacy or justice when the method of assuring legitimacy does not tolerate additional argumentative resorts and, at the same time, concededly does not ensure justice? This is Book III. I will try to show that our customary ways of approaching this problem are structured by expectations about meaning and choice that are in fact unnecessary; I will demonstrate that these customary approaches generate reforms that are actually harmful to the legitimacy and justice of the system. I will show how the system, as I understand its functioning, can be defended as just. (This is undertaken in Chapters 3, 4, and 5 of Book III, respectively.)

The argument I have paraphrased above demands that "Constitutional law must be able to provide good reasons, rather than mere preferences, for choosing among the alternative outcomes generated by the operation of the various forms of argument." But is this reasonable sounding demand really necessary? I think it depends upon a frequent confusion between how we know that we know something (the subject of epistemology) and what in fact we know when we know something (the subject matter of ontology). From an epistemological point of view it is obvious that any justification for a particular choice is grounded in the context of the choosers: thus they may be motivated by prejudices, habits, whims, unarticulated convictions, and so on. To say that such choices are a matter of "judgment" is often to say that there may not be any special reason that accounts for the decision. But it does not follow from that concession, if such it be, that the decision taken is unjustifiable.

The argument to the contrary arises from a suspicion that the decisions made are made for the wrong reasons, or for ulterior purposes or at least not for right reasons. The critic focusses on the mind of the decider and demands: when making a decision, how does the decider know that the process of his or her judgment is right and conflates this issue (which is of interest to the psychologist) with: is the decision that is made justifiable? (a question of interest to law.) I will attempt to show, in Chapter 3 of Book III, that the apparent basis for this demand is ill-founded.

The demand for "right reasons" as a condition that must precede right decisions has many consequences. For one, it tends to make education into an instrument of social transformation whereby the "right" rules are inculcated. One sees this, in varying degrees, from both sides in the curriculum debate that currently rages in some American universities: the canonical right v. the multicultural left. Here, as elsewhere, both sides are united in the assumption that we are what we know, and that what we know are propositions about the world. It is easy enough to see this in the right wing with its required reading lists and its purged texts. But it is sometimes just as easy to miss it in the left.

It is not, as some would argue, that the cultural left does not believe in objectivity. If they were so skeptical, they would also be skeptical of the conclusion that the history of Western institutions is predominantly one of oppression, colonialism, exploitation, etc. That is, they would attribute the source of these impressions to their own groundedness in unhappy childhoods, colonial cultural warps, logocentric high schools, and so on. Rather they very much believe in, indeed hunger for, objectivity. They simply think it exists first in theory. That is why Stalinists were always referring to the most monstrous lies as "objectively" true.

There are, of course, consequences for legal education in the views that are urged in the present work. Familiarity with the modalities of argument is as important to legal thought as familiarity with the languages of art, literature, philosophy, physics, and biology is to humanist thought. But while such knowledge and dexterity are essential to one working with constitutional materials from a legal point of view, they do not substitute for conscience. The habits of conscience can be cultivated – sensitivity to the arguments of others, distrust of one's own motives, patience in not deciding too soon and courage in making one's decisions clear when it is time – but the soul of one's conscience is not manipulable. Very simple, ignorant people often have shining consciences; highly educated and very moral people often seem to have little conscience at all. I have no recommendations; I will make only this observation: there is no conscience without faith for without faith there is only expediency. Without faith, there are no tragic choices; there are only choices.

In June of 1990 I again rejoined the government. During these months I found it very difficult to work on the typescript of the book. On August 2 Iraq invaded Kuwait, presenting the United States Government with a number of consequential international and constitutional legal issues. It was easy not to turn to proofreading.

Only after the American counter-attack and victory did I find myself able to resume work on this book. It is now a week in a cold winter and it is many springs since that first Mellon Lecture in North Schools. The war has made my insistence on the points presented herein even greater: how hollow would the rather patronizing claims of much of the professoriat have sounded if journalists and politicians and citizens generally could have resorted to constitutional analysis on their own without the intimidating but often ludicrous claims made for "the consensus of opinion of constitutional lawyers"! (Though of course the conclusions reached by such analysis might, or might not, have agreed with mine.)

I have learned a great deal writing this book. And I have learned much from the commentary on this work. Acknowledging their help scarcely discharges the debts I have incurred to many persons. Among those persons are: Hans Linde, Geoffrey Marshall, Mark Sagoff, Barbara Aldave, Akhil Amar, Robert Post, Jefferson Powell, Sanford Levinson. They thoughtfully gave me comments on the typescript of the original lectures. Guido Calabresi and Gilbert Harman were helpful too at a later stage, as was my colleage Michael Young.

Ms Caroline LeGette has been an indefatigable and ingenious research assistant in the preparation of footnotes. My fine secretary, Ms Lisa Chronis, has worked extremely hard to produce the pages in typescript that preceded this text. A summer grant from the Law School Foundation of the University of Texas, for which I was recommended by Deans Mark Yudof and Michael Sharlot, relieved me of the necessity to teach the summer term in the final weeks of work. Parts of Book III were originally published in the Stanford Law Review in the essay "Is Law Politics?" I am grateful to the editors of that Review, especially Mr Brian Wildenthal. Susan Poneman was of inestimable help to me in the proofreading of galleys, at that stage at which the author simply no longer sees the words on the page. Finally, to S. W. B. (as she was once), who sacrificed more for this work than I realized at the time, my pointless gratitude.

The more acute of my readers will see what a seriously American problem is faced in this book, and placed right in the center of American hopes, as a vortex and turning point. Some will be unable to take seriously ideas that implicitly disavow the most fundamental assumptions of our age about progress and justice on what might be sarcastically called *philosophical* grounds. But others will learn how

to work with constitutional materials for the first time to reach a
validation, or instance, of the very point of view I am urging. Let
such readers know that I am convinced that these tasks represent
the highest art, in the sense of that man to whom, as my sublime
predecessor on this path, I have dedicated this book.

Note

1   Very roughly, *Constitutional Fate* showed that the legitimacy of
judicial decisions was maintained by adherence to certain conventional methods of constitutional construction; without judicial
review this adherence would be impossible; hence the charge that
judicial review undermined the legitimacy of judicial decision was
nonsensical. This solution, however, severed legitimacy from justification (legitimacy was, so to speak, its own reward) and this raised
another question in its place: if these methods of interpretation
maintained legitimacy but did not, however, ensure justice, how
could the system be justified without sacrificing legitimacy (since
legitimacy precluded us from going outside these methods for rules
of decision)?
   Because this solution resembles, with respect to the distinction
between legitimacy & justification, the view of legal positivists with
respect to law and justice, it may attract the charge that Ronald
Dworkin levelled against legal positivism, namely that of "anti-
realism" (following Dummett). In this context, "realism" is the view
that legal statements possess an objective truth-value by virtue of
some objective reality. The anti-realist believes, by contrast, that
law statements are true or false only by reference to the sort of
evidence we conventionally regard as determinative. (For the anti-
realist, the modalities of constitutional law are instead overriding
interpretive principles). I fear that some who stop reading at this
Preface may think I am simply re-stating the conflict between those
who believe in natural justice (which perforce determines legitimacy)
and those who doubt such a belief and think that law's legitimacy
(and its sense of justice) are a matter of human construction alone
– that law, like power, grows out of the barrel of a gun, or the point
of a pen.
   As I stated in *Constitutional Fate*, however, I reject both of these
positions, and indeed believe them to be united in an unspoken
expectation that the meanings of legal propositions are given by the

conditions that render them true or false. Richard Rorty has recently characterized such a rejection as anti-representationalist, rather than anti-realist, because it rests on an objection to the very supposition that the utility of a term is a result of its standing in a particular relation, or correspondence, to something else. R. Rorty, *Objectivity, Relativism, and Truth*, 3–4 (1991).

BOOK I

CONSTITUTIONAL INTERPRETATION IN THE UNITED STATES

1

THE WRITTEN CONSTITUTION

Every society has a constitution. That is like saying "every vertebrate has a spine." To *be* a society is to be constituted in some particular way, and so every society, the Holy Roman Empire and the Boy Scouts, la Cosa Nostra and the Quakers, the inmates of a prison and the local garden club, all have constitutions. Very few societies, however, are governed by *written* constitutions,[1] which we have come to associate with states.

Yet the earliest written constitutions governed societies that were not states. While many ancient societies have had written constitutions – one thinks of Hippocrates' followers[2] or of the medieval Knights Templar[3] or the Poor Clares[4] – it was not until the end of the eighteenth century, that is rather recently, that a state was governed according to a written constitution. The United States was the first state to attempt a written constitution. Why?[5] When St Francis gave Clara di Scifi a *"forma vitae"* for the society of nuns she had founded, this constitution, for so it was, was written. And when the pilgrims signed the Mayflower Compact, they signed a written constitution.[6] Why did it take states so very long to adopt this useful approach?

What may seem useful to us did not always appear to be so. It took a change in the way people thought about things – in this case, the way they thought about the state – before a written legal instrument would actually *seem* appropriate. To understand this, we must first recall the purposes of legal writing, or rather the purposes of reducing legal arrangements to writing. As every lawyer knows, a written instrument is employed to reduce the discretion of the

parties. A contract, for example, sets a certain price, precisely
because that price would otherwise fluctuate with the market. The
sovereign consumer (like the sovereign producer-seller) is thus constrained by agreement. On account of just such purposes, however,
it was long presumed that a written constitution was incompatible
with the sovereignty of a state. A state irrevocably bound would no
longer *be* sovereign once it agreed to be constrained by a supreme
written instrument. On similar grounds, it was once argued that
every treaty, for example, could be renounced by its signatories
(whether or not it contained terms purporting to forbid renunciation)
because any state irrevocably setting limits regarding the exercise of
its own power would have rendered itself something less than a
sovereign state. The consent of a state to such terms would thus call
into question the very validity of the treaty itself.[7]

What had to come about in legal minds, therefore, before a written
constitution could appear a natural thing, was a view of the state
that separated it from sovereignty.[8] The American innovation was
not the writing *per se*, but rather the political theory whereby the
state was objectified and made a mere instrument of the sovereign
will that lay in the People.[9] That, in turn, made a written constitution
possible. And a written constitution made limited government possible.

To put this in a lawyerly way: a written constitution is like a trust
agreement. It specifies what powers the trustees are to have and it
endows these agents with certain authority delegated by the settlor
who created the trust. If the trustees were identical with the settlor,
they would be at liberty to alter the trust agreement and thus alter
the limits of their authority. A written constitution too is not only
a set of rules; it is a way of creating rules. And thus, like the trust
agreement, a great deal turns on the distinction between the
endowing sovereign and the limited agent-trustees. If the sovereign
is distinct from the government, then the instruments of state can
be limited in their authority. Thus the distinction, the *non*identity
as it were, between the sovereign and the organs of state, which
seemed so absurd to minds before the eighteenth century, was a
necessary idea both for a written constitution, and for achieving the
objectives of such a constitution. For precisely this latter reason,
Jefferson wrote that "Our peculiar security is in the possession of a
written constitution."[10] The principal drafter of the Declaration of
Independence held the view – indeed was the architect of its
expression, for the Declaration is the political basis for the idea of

the constitution – that the state was the creation of sovereign power, not the other way around.[11] This is what is meant by the word *inalienable* in the Declaration – memorized by countless schoolchildren who must wonder what their "inalienable rights" are. The People, on this view, cannot alienate, that is sell or trade, their rights because to do so would render them less than sovereign. It is the parallel, with respect to the People, of the renunciability of treaties with regard to sovereign states. For someone of such views, a written constitution to govern a state is quite a natural idea.

Many important features of the United States Constitution arise from this distinction between sovereign and state. Indeed the very nature of representative democracy and its embodiment in Article I of the US Constitution, as well as the unique division of authority so misleadingly called "the separation of powers," may be seen as solutions to the problems of legitimacy posed when sovereignty resides in the People and not in their government. When sovereignty is thus lodged, there must be a way to educate and keep the interest of a mass of persons not accustomed or trained to the responsibilities of power; and there must be a way of certifying their transfer of this power to their agents in the government. Article I, as we shall see, is devoted to the solution of this problem. Another of the constitutional innovations made possible by the American approach is the unique role it provides for judicial review, i.e., the necessity for courts to review acts by the organs of government for their *legality*.

By relying upon a written instrument to perfect the constitutional understanding, the framers of the United States Constitution introduced the modalities of legal argument into the politics of the state. This has had a profound importance for constitutional interpretation. Since the Constitution was a written law, it had to be *construed*, and this was to be done according to the prevailing methods of legal construction. The ways in which Americans interpret the Constitution could have been different; indeed the forms of constitutional discourse are very different in other societies. For Americans, however, these ways have taken the forms of common law argument, those forms prevailing at the time of the drafting and ratification of the US Constitution. Thus the methods hitherto used to construe deeds and wills and contracts and promissory notes, methods confined to the mundane subjects of the common law, became the methods of constitutional construction once the state itself was put under law.

2

THE PROBLEM OF LEGITIMACY

Judicial review is the means by which a court assures itself that the
acts it has been asked to undertake – to enforce a statute, or imprison
a felon, or award damages to a person who has been libelled, and
so on – are in fact lawful, that is, that they are authorized and
permitted by the Constitution.

In a series of lectures in 1979,[1] I addressed the familiar question
of the *legitimacy* of judicial review and the problem posed by the
Countermajoritarian Objection to that legitimacy. This Objection
may be stated as follows:

A Supreme Court decision that strikes down a statute on grounds of its
unconstitutionality effectively casts a virtually unchallengeable veto against
the acts of elected officials, despite the fact that the Court's members have
not themselves been elected to do so nor have been authorized by the
Constitution to do so. By thwarting the will of the prevailing majority it
exercises an essentially anomalous role in a democracy.[2]

In other words, some critics question whether judicial review itself
is "authorized and permitted by the Constitution." Sometimes this
attack is supplemented with a story that purports to explain how
such a travesty could occur in the American democracy. I wince to
think how often the following account, or something like it, has
been told to unsuspecting civics students.

Following the Jeffersonian victory in 1800, the lame duck Federalist Congress conspired with the defeated Federalist President to create numerous
federal judgeships, and fill them with Federalist appointees. The "Midnight

Judges" Act gave President Adams a number of judicial posts to fill; among them was that to which he nominated William Marbury who was duly confirmed by the Senate. Adams's Secretary of State, John Marshall, to whom the signed commission had been sent for delivery to the appointee, neglected however to actually send the commission. Thus Jefferson's Secretary of State, James Madison, found it and other undelivered commissions upon taking office. He declined to deliver the commissions. Marbury sued under a federal statute providing that writs of mandamus (extraordinary orders directing government officials to perform specific acts) could be issued by the Supreme Court after a hearing held pursuant to the Court's original – as opposed to appellate – jurisdiction.

The entire country awaited the outcome of the decision. John Marshall was now the Chief Justice of a Court on which sat a Federalist majority. Would he order the President to deliver the commission? If he did, would Jefferson obey? A constitutional crisis hovered above the awaited decision.

In the opinion *Marbury v. Madison*, Marshall declined to rule on the petition, thus avoiding a collision with the Executive, by holding that the statute attempting to give original jurisdiction to the Supreme Court in order to issue writs of mandamus unconstitutionally augmented the jurisdiction of the Court by exceeding that provided for in Article III.

Thus (the story goes) did the wily John Marshall befuddle the Jeffersonians who had sought a confrontation while at the same time claiming for the judiciary the profound power of judicial review. By doing so while appearing to *decline* power, and in the context of an intense but irrelevant and distracting dispute, Marshall got away with seizing a power of "dubious legality."[3] This ploy is the source of the Supreme Court's authority to declare statutes unconstitutional.

Let me say at once that there is *nothing* to the final, absurd paragraph of this story. Even a cursory glance at the historical and legal materials will reveal[4] that the exercise of judicial review by the Court was widely noticed and virtually nowhere objected to in the press sympathetic to either party.[5] In the very midst of the generation that ratified the Constitution, Marshall's exercise of the power of judicial review was explicitly and universally taken as appropriate. Moreover, the Federalist Papers,[6] available legal precedent,[7] action by the First Congress[8] and all the other conventional sources of legal argument conclusively establish that such review is an integral part of the constitutional structure, was intended to be so, and has been confirmed as such countless times. In the words of John Marshall, which so often evoke a sophomoric snicker nowadays as the punchline for the narrative I have summarized above:

The question of whether an Act repugnant to the Constitution can become the law of the land is a question deeply interesting to the United States; but, happily, not of an intricacy proportioned to its interest. It seems only necessary to recognize certain principles, supposed to have been long and well-established, to decide it.[9]

Actually, judicial review *is* one of those by no means rare issues in constitutional law that presents an easy case. Nevertheless this odious little anecdote lives on, as a way of accounting for the otherwise puzzling persistence of what, according to the Countermajoritarian Objection, is a highly dubious, indeed monstrous anomaly. That Objection was avidly picked up by those partisans whose political programs have made them anxious to discredit the federal courts, first in the 1930s and more recently in the 1970s and 1980s,[10] but there is more to it than simply politics.

It is perhaps obvious that *Marbury* v. *Madison* does not "establish" judicial review, if by that term it is meant that the case holding the judiciary to have the power to review statutes for their constitutionality legitimates that practice by setting a precedent for it. Of course *setting* a precedent cannot legitimate the initial exercise of such an authority because there is no precedent to legitimate *that* precedent. One cannot establish the legitimacy of judicial review by citing the case about to be decided. But what may be less obvious is that none of the conventional legal approaches in addition to precedent that support the constitutionality of judicial review can establish its legitimacy, because each depends on assumptions about the appropriate form of argument that can only be validated as a consequence of constitutional review. There is an excellent textual argument for the judicial review of state statutes:[11] that is why it presents an "easy" case. But one is only persuaded, for example, that the text of the Supremacy Clause provides an authoritative grounding for the judicial review of state acts if one has first been assured that recourse to the text is constitutionally justified. Thus the Objection persists despite what ought to be definitive replies, for it goes to the heart of *how* we legitimate our decisions by implying that only "majorities" can accomplish this.

It was the attempt to meet this Objection that generated my description and discussion of six *modalities* of constitutional argument. These, I argued, maintained the legitimacy of judicial review in the United States. None of the modalities I identified, taken singly or together, justify judicial review. Judicial review is, rather, a practice by which constitutional legitimacy is assured, not endowed.*

My conclusions precipitated other questions. How was legitimacy then distinguished from justification? For if the modalities of argument could not justify judicial review, then surely arguments and, opinions that followed these modalities could not justify their outcomes. Were there other practices of constitutional review outside the judiciary that might also employ these modalities to reach legitimate constitutional decisions? And above all, what if the conscientious adherence to these modalities resulted in contradictory outcomes? That is, suppose an historical argument led to one conclusion in the construction of the Eleventh Amendment and whether it barred the citizens of one state from suing another state, and the text led in exactly opposite directions to another holding.[12] If both were legitimate, as it seemed, which was right? These sorts of questions are the next frontier for constitutional jurisprudence.

Rather than addressing these questions, however, the discussions over the legitimate *forms* of constitutional argument and decision have become even more intense. During this time we have all endured the arid, tedious debates about judicial review, debates that the bicentennial of the US Constitution turned into a ceaseless caravan from conference to conference, always navigating by circular arguments. I doubt that a day went by during that year[13] that some constitutional lawyer/scholar did not repeat the same old empty doubts about the legitimacy of judicial review or assert the same familiar and convictionless defenses.[14]

We must put aside our fascination with the mirage of the Countermajoritarian Objection. The doubt it casts on judicial review is an illusion created by the very ideologies that render it impossible to answer. For example, notions of "majoritarianism" are carefully boundaried in the constitution; not every group can declare itself a constituency and hold an election. Therefore the short answer to the Objection is that insofar as judicial review preserves the legitimacy of the constitution, it preserves, not threatens, the operation of democratic representation. The use of the six forms of constitutional argument is the way we decide constitutional questions in the American legal culture. The practice of judicial review is compelled by

---

* Those readers wishing to pursue the subject of the Countermajoritarian Objection are directed towards my *Constitutional Fate*.

such methods. There is no more to say about the legitimacy of such review.

Accepting (if only provisionally) that the analysis in *Constitutional Fate* resolves the problem of judicial review, let us turn to the problems that resolution poses. If legitimacy is maintained by the modalities, what if the modalities conflict? And this question will eventually lead us to the others, the practice of constitutional interpretation by other branches and the distinction between legitimacy and justification. If a legitimate system does not ensure justice, how can it be justified? And if following the methods of legitimacy does not provide justification, then how can the system be said to be just?

3

THE MODALITIES OF
CONSTITUTIONAL ARGUMENT

First, what is a *modality*? It is the *way* in which we characterize a form of expression as true.[1] For instance, a *logical* modality may be attributed to a proposition, "*p*," by saying that it is logically necessary or contingent or logically impossible, that "*p*." This is to say that from a logical point of view, the dimension of possibility[2] is critical to engage the inexorable force of inference while other dimensions of the proposition are from this point of view irrelevant. To say that it is known or unknown or known that it is not true that "*p*," is to employ an *epistemic* mode. That is to say that from an epistemological point of view, the role of knowledge engages the force of logic, while other features of "*p*," are irrelevant. And so on for other modalities. To say that it is obligatory, permissible or forbidden, that "*p*," is to mark a *moral* or *deontic* mode. To say that it is now or will be or was the case that "*p*," attributes a *temporal* modality. By contrast, simply to say "that *p*," or "it is *de fide* true that p," does not characterize the way in which "*p*," is true.

To see the difference among modalities, consider the following propositions with respect to a *logical* modality: it is necessarily the

---

What follows in this chapter does not claim to offer whatever original contributions may be part of this book. Rather it reviews material first stated in my book *Constitutional Fate*, to which I have referred. It seemed worse to assume that the reader had already read that book or must now go out and buy a second book to be able to read this one, than simply to summarize the concepts in that work that are necessary to this one.

case that a professor's husband is a married man; it is possible that a professor could be a married man; it is impossible that a professor's wife could be a married man. The way in which these propositions are true, from a logical point of view, is determined by the relationship between the facts they assert and the possibility of those facts (principally the fact that "a husband is a married man" is necessarily true, i.e., it is impossible that it could be false). There are rules that will determine the truth or falsity of a proposition in this modality; these rules construe the facts stated by the proposition according to the standards of the modality, in this case, the logical possibility of the facts stated. Now consider instead the proposition: "all professors should be unmarried men." Whether this is true or not cannot be determined by our knowing the extent to which this state of affairs is possible. It might be true even if it were impossible; it might be false even if it were absolutely necessary (as once was the case at some universities). Thus we must apply the standards of a different modality – a moral or deontic mode – to determine the truth of the facts asserted.

To see the difference between a modal statement and an ordinary proposition, consider these two statements: (1) "One can never know whether another person is telling the truth;" and (2) "You are lying" or "I believe you are lying to me." To determine whether or not (1) is true requires an inquiry into the conditions of knowledge: what counts as knowing, what are grounds for doubt and so on. But to determine the truth of (2) we need to find out something in the world (although it is not always clear precisely what, particularly in taking testimony from one whose word you doubt!). That is, (2) asserts the truth *of* a particular statement about the world while (1) asserts a truth *about* a statement, namely, that it cannot be known.[3]

I will be speaking of *constitutional modalities* – the ways in which legal propositions are characterized as true from a constitutional point of view. In my earlier work I identified six such modalities. Of course, these might be divided or recategorized in different ways, but this particular array has been accepted, I think, by persons working in this area.[4] These six modalities of constitutional argument are: the historical (relying on the intentions of the framers and ratifiers of the Constitution); textual (looking to the meaning of the words of the Constitution alone, as they would be interpreted by the average contemporary "man on the street"); structural (inferring rules from the relationships that the Constitution mandates among the structures it sets up); doctrinal (applying rules generated by precedent); ethical (deriving rules from those moral commitments of the American ethos that are reflected in the Constitution); and prudential (seeking to balance the costs and benefits of a particular rule). Now let us look at some examples, and a somewhat more formal statement of each form of argument.

Consider the question whether a state may validly enforce a law that makes it a crime to procure an abortion. An *historical* modality may be attributed to constitutional arguments that claim that the framers and ratifiers of the Fourteenth Amendment intended, or did not intend, or that it cannot be ascertained whether it was their intention, to protect pregnant women from a state's coercion, through threats of fines and imprisonment, to bear children. Similarly, a historical modality might approach the abortion question as: did the framers and ratifiers of the Fourteenth Amendment intend to countenance, or to overturn by means of the Amendment, or are their intentions unclear as to the effect of the Amendment regarding, those state laws that existed at the time of ratification that prohibited abortions?

Oftentimes this modality is confused with textual argument since both can have reference to the specific text of the Constitution.[5] Historical, or "originalist" approaches to construing the text, however, are distinctive in their reference back to what a particular provision is thought to have meant to its ratifiers. Thus, when Justice Taney in the *Dred Scott* case was called upon to construe the scope of the diversity jurisdiction in Article III, which provides for suits "between citizens of the several states,"[6] so that he might decide whether a slave could seek his freedom in a diversity suit before a federal court, he wrote:

It becomes necessary to determine who were the citizens of the several states when the constitution was adopted. And in order to do this we must recur to the governments and institutions of the colonies. We must inquire who at the time were recognized as citizens of the states, whose rights and liberties outraged by the English government and who declared their independence and assumed the powers of government to defend their rights of arms. We refer to these historical facts for the purpose of showing the fixed opinions concerning the Negro race upon which the statesmen of that day spoke and acted.[7]

Now consider the same question – who are the "citizens" of the phrase that provides for suits in federal court "between citizens of different states" ("diversity" suits) – from another point of view. A *textual* modality may be attributed to arguments that the text of the Constitution would, to the average person, appear to declare, or deny, or be too vague to say whether, a suit between a black American citizen resident in a state and a white American citizen resident in another state, is a "controversy between citizens of different states." I would imagine that the contemporary meaning of these words is rather different than that which Taney found them to mean to the framers and ratifiers of 1789. One should not be tempted to conclude, however, that textual approaches are inevitably more progressive than originalist approaches. Sometimes the text can be a straitjacket, confining the judge to language that would have been different if its drafters had foreseen later events. Thus consider whether wiretapping is prohibited by the Fourth Amendment, which guarantees "the right of the people to be secure in their persons, houses, papers and effects against unreasonable searches and seizures."[8] Here is Chief Justice Taft in a case in which incriminating information was largely obtained by federal prohibition officers intercepting messages on the telephones of the conspirators:

The amendment itself [he says] shows that the search is to be of material things – the person, the house, his papers or his effects. The amendment does not forbid what was done here for there was no seizure. The evidence was secured by the sense of hearing and that only. There was not entry of the houses. The language of the amendment cannot be extended and expanded.[9]

By contrast, a later court had no trouble finding that wiretapping came within the Amendment. It simply relied upon historical argument – the intentions that animated the adoption of the amendment – and concluded that:

The purpose of the . . . Fourth Amendment [is] to keep the state out of constitutionally protected areas until it has reason to believe that a specific crime has been or is being committed.[10]

Consider another constitutional question: can a court issue a subpoena (or should it enjoin some other subpoena) for the disclosure of the President's working notes and diaries? To say that the institutional relationships promulgated by the Constitution require or are incompatible with or tolerate a particular answer to this question is to use a *structural* mode of argument. There are many recent, celebrated examples of this form of argument to be found in the cases of the US Supreme Court; indeed the 1980s were particularly notable for the Court's focus on structural issues.[11] But structural argument is hardly a recent invention. *McCulloch* v. *Maryland*, the principal foundation case for constitutional analysis, relies almost wholly on structural approaches. In determining whether a Maryland tax on the Federal Bank of the United States could be enforced, Chief Justice Marshall studiedly refuses to specify the particular text that supports his argument, and explicitly rejects reliance on historical arguments, preferring instead to state the rationale on inferences for the structure of federalism. Such a structure could not be maintained, he concluded, if the states, whose officials are elected by a state's constituency, could tax the agencies of the federal government present in a state and thereby tax a nationwide constituency. The constitutional structure would not tolerate such a practice.

In the following passage, taken from an 1884 case,[12] we may observe another typical example. In this case the defendant and others were convicted in a federal court for having conspired to intimidate a black person from voting for a member of Congress, in violation of federal statutes. The question was: does Congress have the power to punish violations of election laws under the Constitution since the text nowhere provides such a power? Justice Miller wrote for the Court:

That a government whose essential character is republican . . . has no power by appropriate laws to secure this election from the influence of violence, of corruption, and of fraud, is a proposition so startling as to arrest attention and demand the gravest consideration. . . . The proposition that it has no such power is supported by the old argument often heard, often repeated, and in this court never assented to, that when a question of the power of Congress arises the advocate of the power must be able to place his finger on words which expressly grant it. . . . It is not true, therefore, that electors for members of Congress owe their right to vote to the State law in any sense which makes the exercise of the right to depend exclusively on the law of the State. . . . It is as essential to the successful working of this government that the great organisms of its executive and legislative branches should be the free choice of the people as that the original form of it should be so. . . . In a republican government like ours . . . the temptation to control these elections by violence and corruption is a constant source of danger.[13]

Structural arguments are a little less intuitively obvious than arguments from the text or history of the Constitution, so perhaps it would be well to briefly outline their characteristic form. Usually, arguments in this modality are straightforward: first, an uncontroversial statement about a constitutional structure is introduced [for example, in the case above, the statement that the right to vote for a member of Congress is provided for in the Constitution]; second, a relationship is inferred from this structure [that this right, for example, gives rise to the federal power to protect it and is not dependent on state protection]; third, a factual assertion about the world is made [that, if unprotected, the structure of federal representation would be at the mercy of local violence]. Finally a conclusion is drawn that provides the rule in the case. (A second example is provided in the notes.)[14]

Consider whether the state can require mandatory testing for the AIDS virus antibodies. To say that it is wise, or unwise, or simply unclear on the present facts whether or not it is wise to permit such testing is to propose an evaluation from a *prudential* point of view. In the first half of this century, this mode of constitutional argument was principally associated with doctrines that sought to protect the political position of the courts.[15] But the dramatic national crises of depression and world war soon provided ample reason to introduce the practical effects of constitutional doctrine into the rationales underpinning doctrine. For example, one such case arose when, in the depths of the midwestern farm depression, the Minnesota legislature passed a statute providing that anyone who was unable to pay a mortgage could be granted a moratorium from foreclosure. On its face such a statute not only appeared to realize the fears of the framers that state legislatures would compromise the credit market by enacting debtor relief statutes, but also plainly to violate the Contracts Clause that was the textual outcome of such concerns. Moreover, the structure of national economic union strongly counseled against permitting states to protect their constituents by exploding a national recovery program that depended on restoring confidence to banking operations. Nevertheless the Supreme Court upheld the statute, observing that:

An emergency existed in Minnesota which furnished a proper occasion for the exercise of the reserved power of the state to protect the vital interests of the community.[16]

Very simply, the Court recognized the political expediency of the legislature's action and acquiesced in it. Another national crisis framed the background of the *Bowles* case, ten years later. Congress had passed the Emergency Price Control Act providing for administrative action to freeze or reduce rents for housing accommodations in areas adjacent to defense establishments. The district court held against the government and struck down the Act as unconstitutional, but the Supreme Court reversed the decision in language that is frankly prudential:

We need not determine what constitutional limits there are to price-fixing legislation. Congress was dealing here with conditions created by activities resulting from a great war effort. A nation which can demand the lives of its men and women in waging of that war is under no constitutional necessity of providing a system of price control on the domestic front which will assure each landlord a "fair return" on his property . . . Congress has done all that due process under the war emergency requires.[17]

These cases provide examples of prudential argument, but this approach is by no means confined to the extremes a nation undergoes in emergencies. Of course in such circumstances prudential arguments are likeliest to be decisive. But, as one of prudentialism's most eloquent practitioners argued, such an approach has a place in every decision:

The accomplished fact, affairs and interests that have formed around it, and perhaps popular acceptance of it – these are elements . . . that may properly enter into a decision . . .; and they may also enter into the shaping of the judgment, the applicable principle itself.[18]

Prudential argument is actuated by facts, as these play into political and economic policies as to which the Constitution is itself agnostic. The legal rule to be applied is derived from a calculus of costs and benefits, when the facts are taken into account. Accordingly, this often gives rise to a "balancing test" (the balance being a scales, not a tightrope.)

By contrast, when we say that a neutral, general principle derived from the caselaw construing the Constitution should apply, does not apply or may apply, we make an appeal in a *doctrinal* mode. (It should also be observed, in anticipation of material that will be taken up in Book II, that doctrinal arguments are not confined to arguments originating in caselaw; there are also precedents of other institutions, e.g., the practices of earlier Presidents as well as the various corollaries incident to fashioning rules on the basis of precedent.)

To familiarize oneself with this form of argument, let us take up this question: to what extent can a state constitutionally aid parochial schools? Suppose, for example, that parochial school students whose schools are not on the route of free public school buses are given a cash allowance by the state to provide for their transportation. Does this offend the Establishment Clause of the First Amendment because the state is bearing the burdens of costs that would otherwise be born by churchmembers, in much the way that the government in Great Britain, a country that has an established church, provides funds to supplement the income of the Church of England? A judge confronting such a case would probably begin, not by reading the text of the First Amendment which states a rule in rather general terms[19] but by turning to precedent to find similar cases in which authoritative decisions would govern the present one. Not surprisingly, in the area of Establishment jurisprudence there is a great deal of constitutional doctrine, developed in many cases. The standards these cases develop and apply can be stated as legal rules; the case "on point" – that is, whose facts are similar in those aspects that are relevant to the legal question being posed – is probably *Everson* v. *Board of Education*, which sustained the power of local authorities to provide free transportation for children attending church schools.[20] In *Everson* the Supreme Court treated the provision of transportation as a form of public welfare legislation, noting that it was being extended by the state "to all its citizens without regard to their religious belief." The Court wrote:

It is undoubtedly true that children are helped to get to church schools. There is even a possibility that some of the children might not be sent to the church schools if the parents were compelled to pay their children's bus fares out of their pockets when transportation to a public school would have been paid for by the State.[21]

Transportation, however, benefited the child in the same way as did police protection at crossings, fire protection, connections for sewage disposal, public highways, and sidewalks. Based on this rationale, subsequent cases have developed a three-pronged test: does the state program have a secular purpose; is its principal effect neither to advance nor inhibit religion; does its administration excessively entangle the state in religious affairs?[22]

Applying this test to the question above, the judge might write: "*Everson* must be distinguished from the instant case because the program in *Everson* provided transportation common to all students, whereas here only some students – the parochial ones – are given cash allowances. While we do not question that the legislature had a secular purpose in mind, we think the evidence indicated that the effect of these allowances was in fact to make the parochial schools more attractive to parents than their secular counterparts, and thereby advance the cause of religious institutions. Moreover, the oversight required of the state to ensure that the allowances are in fact spent on providing a system of parochial school transportation intrudes the administrative apparatus of the state into the affairs of the church schools. This can only lead to the interference with budgets and an insistence on allocations for transportation that will excessively entangle the state in the administration of church affairs. Accordingly the program must be held unconstitutional."

Or a judge might write: "*Everson*, which also involved public transportation to parochial school students, governs this case. Here as there, the state's program provides aid to students and their parents, and not – as in cases that have applied *Everson* and struck down state assistance in this area – direct assistance to church-related schools. Its secular purpose, to provide school transportation at greater efficiency and less cost to the state than expanding its own bus fleets, is apparent. Like school lunches, public health services, and secular textbooks, the transportation provided here confers a benefit on the parochial student that is at parity with what the secular student receives. Thus its effect is neither to advance nor inhibit religion, but rather to avoid exacting a penalty from the parochial student. Finally, whatever state management is required to administer the program will be limited to the oversight of transportation; such involvement as there may be need not, therefore, excessively entangle the state in those religious matters with regard to which it has no role."

In either case, the hypothetical judge has applied a rule derived from the relevant caselaw. The rule is neutral as to the parties; that is, it applies equally to Catholics and Jews and atheist claimants and does not vary depending on who is bringing or defending the suit. And the rule is general, that is, it applies to all cases in which the state is arguably giving assistance to religious institutions, and is not confined to the facts of the original case that gave birth to the rule. One more point, however, should be made about this modality: its operation is not confined to the application of *stare decisis*, that is, the strict adherence to previously decided cases. On the contrary, in the American system one of the principles of doctrinalism is that the Supreme Court may reverse the relevant precedent.[23] This would appear to follow from the family of modalities – that provide alternative legal rules – and the supremacy of the Constitution to the acts of government (including, of course, the judicial branch). The Court is entitled, indeed obligated, to overrule itself when it is persuaded that a particular precedent was wrongly decided and should not be applied.

Finally, let us consider the modality of ethical argument. This form of argument denotes an appeal to those elements of the American cultural ethos that are reflected in the Constitution. The fundamental American constitutional ethos is the idea of limited government, the presumption of which holds that all residual authority remains in the private sphere. Thus when we argue that a particular constitutional conclusion is obliged by, or permitted, or forbidden by the American ethos that has allocated certain decisions to the individual or to private institutions, we are arguing in an *ethical* mode.

Ethical arguments arise as a consequence of the fundamental constitutional arrangement by which rights, in the American system, can be defined as those choices beyond the power of government to compel. Thus structural and ethical arguments share some similarities, as each is essentially an inferred set of arguments. Like structural arguments, ethical arguments do not depend on the construction of any particular piece of text, but rather on the necessary relationships that can be inferred from the overall arrangement expressed in the text. Structural argument infers rules from the powers granted to governments; ethical argument, by contrast, infers rules from the powers denied to government. The principal error one can make regarding ethical argument is to assume that any statute or executive act is unconstitutional if it causes effects that are incompatible with the American cultural ethos. This equates ethical argument, a constitutional form, with moral argument generally.

Let us review a hypothetical example that shows the basic pattern of ethical argument. Note that while the American cultural ethos may encompass cheeseburgers, rock and roll, and a passion for Japanese electronics, the American *constitutional* ethos is largely confined[24] to the reservation of powers not delegated to a limited government.

It was recently reported[25] that a state judge in South Carolina had given the choice of thirty-year prison sentences or castration to three convicted sex offenders. Suppose a convicted man accepted the bargain and was released on probation terms that incorporated this pledge (as by drug-induced impotence). Then suppose that he ceased taking the prescribed drug. If his probation were revoked, a constitutional challenge to the terms of his probation might take this form:

1 The reservation to the individual of the decision to have children is deeply rooted in the American notion of autonomy; there is no express constitutional power to implement a program of eugenics.

2 Moreover, such programs are not a conventionally appropriate means to any express power.

3 Those means denied the federal government are also denied the states.

4 The South Carolina sentence amounted to ordering a man to comply with a eugenics scheme that deemed him ineligible to procreate.

The element of the American ethos at stake is the reservation to individuals and families of the freedom to make certain kinds of decisions. Similar sorts of arguments are to be found in cases in which a state attempted to bar schools from teaching foreign languages;[26] in which a state passed a compulsory education act requiring every school-age child to attend public school (that is, implicitly outlawing private schools);[27] in which a local zoning ordinance was applied to prohibit a grandmother from living with her grandchildren;[28] in which a hospital sought authority to amputate a gangrenous limb from an elderly man who refused his consent;[29] in which a man allegedly suffering from delusions (but concededly harmless) was confined to a mental hospital for almost twenty-five years without treatment.[30] One may test one's mastery of this form of argument by taking each of these examples and stating an ethical argument to resolve it, e.g., (1) There is no express constitutional power to monopolize education; (2) moreover, a statute outlawing private education is not an appropriate means to any express power (such as regulating commerce or providing for armed forces); (3) The decision to educate one's children privately or parochially or publicly is reserved to the family; (4) A statute compelling attendance exclusively at public schools amounts to a scheme to coerce families into a particular educational choice and destroy private educational options.

These then are the six modalities of constitutional argument in the United States. I have argued elsewhere[31] that each of these forms of argument can be used to construct an ideology, a set of political and practical commitments whose values are internally consistent and can be distinguished, externally, from competing ideologies. I will discuss this relationship in more detail and indeed I will argue in Book III that this move from the modalities to ideology is a mistaken inference of explanation from description. For the moment, however, I am merely concerned that the reader should not conclude that, because of this relationship – because, for example, some persons may believe that one particular modality represents the only legitimate means of interpreting the Constitution (e.g., historical argument) since it is verifiable by a resort to materials (e.g., the intentions of the ratifiers) that are mandated according to a particular political theory of interpretation (e.g. "originalism") – the modalities of argument are no more than instrumental, rhetorical devices to be deployed in behalf of various political ideologies. The modalities of constitutional argument are the ways in which law statements in constitutional matters are assessed; standing alone they assert nothing about the world. But they need only stand alone to provide the means for making constitutional argument.

There is no constitutional legal argument outside these modalities. Outside these forms, a proposition about the US constitution can be a fact, or be elegant, or be amusing or even poetic, and although such assessments exist as legal statements in some possible legal world, they are not actualized in our legal world.

4

THE USEFULNESS OF THIS APPROACH

What is the usefulness of approaching American constitutional law through the study of these modalities? First, it permits the critical reader to describe the ideological and political manipulations of the various grammars of constitutional law without pretending that these ideological and political commitments are somehow "behind" or "beneath" these grammars. It is a flaw of conventional Marxism, and of some contemporary movements in American jurisprudence, that these approaches simply assume an epistemological attitude that is highly controversial, i.e., they undertake to explain events in the world by reference to ideas that allegedly cause such events while maintaining that the explanatory scheme itself is outside the otherwise pervasive causal influence it allegedly describes. No doubt there are many persons who continue to believe that class, or race, or sex or personal history determine "how we see the world" – as though these were spectacles that are put on at a certain age and could be removed, indeed have been removed by the clear-sighted analyst. This is only a modern version of the claim that such influences determine how we behave. But to a growing number this will seem naive. The world is a human idea, inseparable from our perceptions and appreciation of it, and thus something we can apprehend only with the spectacles of humanity firmly in place. Nor are our faculties detachable from the perspectives they enable or the world without which they are disabled.

There is no reason to believe that our faculties are either inductive (gathering unassimilated raw data that sorts itself out into ideas) or deductive (proceeding from first principles that are our genetic inheritance); subjective (and the world therefore capable of complete determination by our individual wills) or objective (and thus determined independent of human apprehension). Although most people may to some extent hold the views that link all these antinomies together – the view, that is, that there *must* be some sublime explanatory mechanism that allows our ideas to interact with the world – there is no reason to think so.

No reason, that is, except that these assumptions appeared to give philosophy the tools for ambitious undertakings. By such dichotomies philosophy sought the refuge of certainty in the individual consciousness, despite the pervasiveness of doubt that one finds at the center of the isolated human heart; it sought the transcendence of understanding despite the fragmentary nature of experience. But this was achieved, in Thucydides no less than in Freud and Weber, at the cost of hypothesizing a kind of ether that was a medium between human practices and the will. Thus for social science, the things that human beings did – like law – they did for a reason, not always the reason they thought, of course, but on account of a cause. This confusion of motive and cause lies at the heart of "explanatory" writing about law. It is a confusion the study of the modalities of argument dispenses with.

Law is something we do, not something we have as a consequence of something we do. Sometimes our activities in law – deciding, proposing, persuading – may link up with specific ideas we have at those moments; but often they do not, and it is never the case that this link must be made for the activities that are law to be law. Therefore the causal accounts of how these inner states come into being, accounts that lose their persuasiveness in contact with the abundance of the world, are really beside the point. If we want to understand the ideological and political commitments in law, we have to study the grammar of law, that system of logical constraints that the practices of legal activities have developed in our particular culture. A study of the modalities gives us such a description. It shows us how people thought without the unnecessary pretense of claiming we know why they thought a certain way, and the discredited assumption that our ways of thinking are separate from, and are instruments of, our preferences for certain values.

Second, the study of constitutional modalities shows how American law permits an ideological presence in law without converting law into politics. Tocqueville was of course correct in saying that "scarcely any political question arises in the United States which is not resolved, sooner or later, into a judicial question."[1] Yet nowadays one might almost take the reverse statement to be the case. A modal approach allows us to distinguish the usually conflated terms of interpretation and ideology and thus shows us what is at stake in the reductionism of law into politics.[2]

Third, this approach, as I have shown in earlier work,[3] reveals the circularity of the usual arguments that attempt to overcome the Countermajoritarian Objection to judicial review. Each of the standard defenses of judicial review turns out, on inspection, to be a defense of a particular modality of argument. Let me give some examples.

"Originalists" in constitutional interpretation assert[4] that it is the duty of the courts to give expression to the original intentions of the framers and ratifiers. To do otherwise jeopardizes the legitimacy of review since, without the restraints imposed on judges and on the authority granted to them on the basis of the original understanding of the constitutional endowment, judges are mere usurpers of power. This, however, is a plea for the use of historical argument by an appeal to its premises. One would not be persuaded by such an argument unless one already believed that the intentions of the framers were responsible for empowering the officials of government.

I noted a few pages ago[5] that a study of the Federalist Papers,[6] and the First Judiciary Act confirm the intention of the framers and ratifiers to endow the courts with the jurisdiction to examine acts of federal and state governments for their constitutionality. Standing alone this reply to the Countermajoritarian Objection is also circular, and for the same reason: it depends upon the assumption that the *intentions* that judicial review is supposed to enforce provide a legitimate basis on which to review (and reverse) the outcomes of the political process.

In the same way, there have been answers to the Objection offered by "textualists."[7] Article VI, in the Supremacy Clause, provides that "This Constitution . . . shall be the supreme law of the land and the Judges in every State shall be bound thereby, anything in the Constitution or laws of any State to the contrary notwithstanding." This would seem to imply that (1) all judges, when asked to apply any law, must do so in conformity with "supreme" law; that is the common import of the word "supreme"; and (2) that the laws and constitutions of the states, even when construed by state judges, must give way to the provisions of the United States Constitution in case of conflict; "giving way" is, I think, the common inference drawn from the use of the term "do as here instructed anything to the contrary notwithstanding;" and (3) that insofar as the same Article also carefully provides that only those federal laws "which shall be made in pursuance" of the Constitution are the law of the land, this language indicates that federal laws that conflict with the Constitution cannot be given effect as law. If I said to an average American, "You may apply only those laws that are made in pursuance of the Constitution," he would be puzzled if I then said, "You may assume that any statute adopted by a majority of both Houses of Congress is necessarily in pursuance of the specified objectives of the Constitution." Surely he would say, "Really? Why?" Moreover, any reason I gave him, in fact my giving him an answer at all, would concede his power of review. But this textual answer to the Countermajoritarian Objection presumes an authority in the text. The average American might very well have stopped me when I said "You may apply only those laws, etc." and at *that* point said "Really? Why?" and the answer "Because it says so" assumes a lot. In fact it assumes the very legitimacy of the interpretive approach it is trying to defend.

The prudential advocate of judicial review[8] urges us that the institution is legitimate because it serves a goal (or goals) with which the advocate associates himself. These goals may be: the protection of minorities;[9] the exercise of vigilance on behalf of civil liberties;[10] the taming of revolution into reform[11] or the fanning of reform into revolt[12] (consciousness raising); and so on. Some prudentialists concede that, in order to respond to the Countermajoritarian Objection, partisans of this approach "have attempted to ground constitutional theory in . . . public values [that] must be different from ones that merely happen to be commonly shared."[13] One has to ask: what legitimates those values? Even if we assume that there is a public interest that is distinct from the aggregate of private interests that majoritarianism is supposed to reflect, the prudential argument for judicial review is only persuasive if one were already persuaded that the usefulness of judicial review was a legitimate criterion by which to measure its legitimacy. In a practical culture like the United States, it must also seem an absurd question. But there are legal cultures in which the very disutility of a decision is thought to enhance its claim to disinterestedness.

There are profound structural,[14] ethical[15] and doctrinal[16] arguments supporting judicial review in the face of a Countermajoritarian Objection. Good examples of these are found in *Marbury* v. *Madison*,[17] the first case in which judicial review is discussed by the Supreme Court. Briefly these are: the majoritarianism of the elected branches can only be legitimated if it is confirmed by an unelected branch which owes its only fidelity to the Constitutional Oath and not to a faction for support (structural);[18] the Court is required to police the boundary between private rights and public power since rights are mainly inferred in the US constitution from the limits on power (ethical);[19] any court, in order to decide a case according to law, must determine the constitutionality of the law it is asked to apply since the Constitution is the supreme law (doctrinal).[20] But Marshall does not – and could not – maintain that these answers justify judicial review. They are the consequence of judicial review; after all, they appear in a case that decides that question. They belong to the modalities of legal argument. If they are justificatory, what justifies *them*?

Treating the archetypal forms of argument as modalities avoids this problem. Since they are not statements about the world, they cannot serve as justifications for judicial review (or anything else). Recognizing their character as *modalities*, however, provides a way of satisfying the requirements of legitimacy without the circularity that inevitably intrudes once we attempt to justify the modes. Once we looked carefully at constitutional argument, it became apparent that the legitimacy of judicial review was maintained by adherence to these forms of argument. An opinion stated in these terms was accepted as legitimate and so also for briefs and oral arguments, whereas other forms of argument, some acceptable in other legal cultures, rendered a decision quite illegitimate (for example, kinship arguments, reliance on religious texts or ecclesiastical authority, decision by chance.) In the American legal and constitutional culture, judicial review *must* occur if the judicial function is to be legitimated because it provides the occasion for decisions based on such arguments.

This is a solution, however, that many will find unsatisfying. It separates legitimation from justification and thus, for those who hunger for a justification of judicial review, this solution famisheth even as it is consumed. On the view that I have urged, judicial review that is wicked, but follows the forms of argument, is legitimately done; and review that is benign in its design and ameliorative in its result but which proceeds arbitrarily or according to forms unrecognized within our legal culture, is illegitimate. Doubtless this is distressing to those who fear that law will thereby be detached from justice;[21] I am sure that the real reason the absurd countermajoritarian debate lasted as long as it did is because the persons who kept it going thought that if they could find a firm foundation for judicial review – even if it was a narrow one – this would assure justice. If the solution I have suggested is accepted, doubtless it will appear to many that we will be in this intolerable dilemma: if law is good, it is not law; if law is law, it is not good. If merely following the forms of argument satisfies the requirements of legitimation, but tells us nothing about justice, how will we know when review is justified? Will we find ourselves instead in Gilmore's hell, where there is "nothing but law, and due process is meticulously observed?"[22] On this subject too, however, I believe my account has something to offer and I will return to this important question in Book III.

Fourth, and most practically among the contributions to be made by an account that explicates the modalities of constitutional argument, the approaches I have depicted in constitutional law retrieve that law from the monopoly currently held by the judiciary. The lawyer-citizen, or even the lawyer-journalist, is unlikely to know the current state of play in most constitutional doctrine. Since only a few of us can devote ourselves to keeping up with the ever-lengthening opinions that comprise constitutional jurisprudence, one becomes easy prey for casuists who assert, in a worldly way, that law is really an irrelevance in *constitutional* law. But if citizens and journalists (and politicians) know the basic modes, the fundamental ways of thinking about the Constitution as law, they can work through current problems on their own.

For example: recently the Supreme Court heard the case of a minor who had been convicted of a capital crime. The issue presented was whether the Constitution prohibited his execution. Counsel for the boy claimed that the execution of a minor violated, among other provisions, the Eighth Amendment's prohibition against cruel and unusual punishment. Well, does it? A good beginning to an answer would track the various modes.

1   Why did the framers of the Eighth Amendment propose, and the public ratify, provisions such as the amendment's bar on punishment that is "cruel and unusual"? What purposes might they have had in mind for such phrasing rather than simply specifying particular tortures they wished to prohibit? It is clear that capital punishment itself was accepted by the framers and ratifiers of the Constitution (and indeed that boys who were scarcely teenaged were executed at the time). Do we conclude from that history that this provision does not therefore apply or perhaps instead that their intention may have had as much to do with the society the founders wished us to become as with the protection of (then) contemporary sensibilities? It may be that they wished us to have the legal authority to enforce humane restraint, however that idea might evolve.

2   What do the words "cruel and unusual" mean to us nowadays? It strikes me as clear enough that a state could not inject a convict with a lethal virus and then leave him to waste away and die; but at the same time, many people appear to think that a lethal injection that acts more or less instantaneously is less cruel than other methods. How precisely does cruelty vary with the age of the person to be executed? It seems cruel to me to punish even an animal that cannot govern its behavior; is a child like that? And if a small child is like that, so that it seems paradigmatic of cruelty to kill a child even when he has committed a terrible act, at what age will we cease holding such a presumption? Does our sense of the words "cruel and unusual" not become more acute with the severity and finality of the punishment; is it not especially cruel (and therefore remarkable, "unusual") to end a life that has hardly begun to appreciate the enormity of taking life? And perhaps less "cruel" to permit a person to mature into that awful recognition, even if it must take place in confinement?

3   Might such executions actually deter other young people from committing murder themselves? Or might a constitutional bar against their execution make teenagers favored as paid killers? What are the facts of cases in which juveniles committed murders but were not tried as adults; did they go on to commit other crimes? How likely are mistakes in such cases?

4   Is it important, to preserve a pluralistic national community such as the United States, that different states be allowed to set the age level of executions as they see fit, perhaps with no very low minimum? Or can it be inferred from the relationship between

citizens and the government they have created, that government may not exact a penalty without a corresponding level of certainty – less for the breathalyzer that takes away a driver's license, more for the process that takes ten years out of a life? And if so, what kind of certainty do we require of a process that takes away all of an adult life because that life will never be commenced?

5   Is it consistent with the priceless value our society places on life that we permit the state to take it by execution? Or would it be inconsistent with that value to permit a murderer to escape execution?

6   And then, but only then, what is the relevant caselaw that a court would apply?

I realize this exercise must seem comparatively superficial when placed alongside the brief and opinion in *Thompson* v. *Oklahoma*.[23] Yet playing such a game ought to give one an idea of how to proceed to answer a constitutional question rather than simply shrugging one's shoulders. Just as importantly, this approach allows legislators and government executives to uphold the Constitution *as law* without simply making them into law clerks for the courts. A President will often consider difficult constitutional issues – I will discuss some of these in Book II[24] – and these may be in areas that the courts have purposefully avoided, or have not yet addressed, or are in disagreement about, or, finally, have taken positions that the President is disinclined to join. The approaches I have described allow us to evaluate constitutional questions from the perspective of a particular office yet nevertheless to remain true to the Constitution as law (even if we disagree with current judicial authority on a particular subject). In a pluralistic political society such as the United States, this is a significant contribution.

Yet putting all this aside, there is a fifth reason that is sufficient in itself: the study of the modalities of constitutional argument makes the analysis of legal reason-giving more perspicuous. This we shall see, I trust, in the examples provided in Book II.

5

THE PROBLEM OF INDETERMINACY

It can be easily shown, I think, that the various "explanations" of the American constitutional process that result from taking one of the modalities and elevating it to a privileged status are unsuccessful in that they do not in fact either explain why courts decide cases in a certain way or why such holdings would be legitimate if they did. It does not, for example, establish the legitimacy of a judicial decision to show that the judge is conscientiously trying to decide the case in the way the framers and ratifiers would have wished. A similar point can be made in regard to the justice of the particular outcomes of such decisionmaking. It can be shown, that is, that a single modality does not assure a just outcome simply because one has devised a theory of justice that depends upon assuming the rightness of a particular method of interpretation. In Book II, we will apply those modal forms to actual constitutional problems.

A single modality cannot be both comprehensive and determinate. If it is determinate – does not generate contradictory outcomes – then there will be some cases it cannot decide; specifically, it will not be able to legitimate the particular method associated with that modality. If the scheme is comprehensive, it will generate inconsistent outcomes; specifically, it will be indeterminate as to which of the conventional modalities is to be applied.

I have maintained that an analysis of the family of modalities of constitutional interpretation can account for the legitimacy of such interpretation. In Book III, I will argue that these practices, taken as a group, also enable justice, not because they are determinate but, as will be seen, precisely because they are *not* determinate, i.e., do not specify unique results. But before we leave the discussion of the single modality masquerading as an all-encompassing explanation, I would like to show its close kinship to what is thought to be its polar opposite, viz, those accounts that conclude that constitutional argument is meaningless because it is indeterminate.

Consider this remark by Professor Sanford Levinson in reply to the question posed by the indeterminacy of constitutional meaning, that is, how we can apply a particular provision objectively when it has no single, determinate meaning:

> There are simply different Constitutions. There are as many plausible readings of the United States Constitution as there are versions of Hamlet, even though each interpreter, like each director, might genuinely believe that he or she has stumbled onto the one best answer to the conundrums of the texts.[1]

This view, and its competitor – that a particular approach determines the correct meaning – are positions held by two contending groups locked in combat over the problem of *indeterminacy*. That they need each other to sustain the argument is perhaps obvious; what is not so clear is that the argument itself arises from a modal confusion that they share. If you think that constitutional argument on a particular matter asserts a proposition about an object in the world (about the Constitution, for example), you may be inclined to believe that such arguments have a truth-functional status like other propositions about the world. If I say Jupiter has five moons, I am saying something that, in principle, can be verified. It is either true or false. In the same way, if a court concludes that "the equal protection clause does not apply to sex discrimination" that is a statement of fact about the world. The clause does not apply from now on to sex discrimination cases. And it is easy to confuse that with another idea, which is, "the Constitution directs that the equal protection clause does not apply to sex discrimination." (Particularly easy since the court that makes the former statement has probably supported it with the latter.) It is tempting to conclude then that this proposition too is a statement about the world. If you did think that, then judges who claimed to be applying the Constitution were also implicitly claiming to discover and verify truths about the Constitution. Indeed such discovery and verification become conditions that establish the acts of judges as law, rather than merely politics. They ground such decisions in the Constitution itself.

At this point, one's temperament and sensibility come into play, because it does not take long to look around and see that authoritative statements about what the Constitution "directs" are the subject of great disagreement. Such statements by the US Supreme Court, who ought to know, can be shown to be contradictory, to have relied on different rationales, changed over time on the same facts, and so on. Some people react to this by saying that most of those decisions must be wrong, and we must tidy up constitutional adjudication. We must rely on those methods that will allow us to verify our propositions. A method, for example, like textual argument offers such verification. How do I know the statement "a state may sue another state" is true, constitutionally speaking? Because it can be verified by reference to the text.[2] Similarly, with respect to historical argument, how can I verify the assertion that the Constitution permits a national intelligence agency? Because it is discussed in the papers of the framers and ratifiers.[3] All the rest of the caselaw that expresses holdings that cannot be verified in this way is simply not law.

The strict constructionists who assert that constitutional interpretation ought to be confined to determining the intentions of the framers and applying that intention are characteristic of this reaction to the chaos of the Reporter system. In Robert Bork's words:

[The] Constitution is not law [if it does not] tell judges what to do and what not to do. [And] the only way in which the Constitution can constrain judges is if the judges interpret the document's words according to the intentions of those who drafted, proposed and ratified its provisions.[4]

Another group of persons, however, saw the same phenomena, the same profusion of contradictory caselaw, and reacted in precisely the opposite way. We might call them the reconstructionists. A good expression of their views might be:

By its own criteria, legal reasoning cannot resolve legal questions in an "objective" manner; nor can it explain how the legal system works or how judges decide cases . . . [L]aw is not neutral: It is a mechanism for creating and legitimating configurations of economic and political power.[5]

There being no determinate rules in constitutional law (and thus the resulting contradictions of the caselaw) it is quickly concluded that there are no real rules at all. Nor is this a bad thing; rather, it exposes the farce. It shows that law is simply politics after all. All law is masked power. Even the propositions that the most single-minded strict constructionists would produce are not "law," because there are no verifiable grounds for such *limitations* and, in any event, these also produce contradictory results and are not uniquely determinate. Historians, after all, disagree.[6] So do textual critics.[7]

I have already noted that these two groups are united by an epistemological assumption that I regard as untenable.[8] I will discuss this at greater length in Book III but I should like to observe here that in either case – the strict constructionist (or partisan of a particular modality) or the reconstructionist – a kind of reduction takes place. Either law is reduced to politics, since this is a fundamental reality and law statements are political statements by extension, or law is reduced to history, or textual construction, etc., since only statements about objective matters are entitled to status as law statements. In either case, a law statement is, in principle, reducible to a statement about the world. Both groups believe that a holding in constitutional adjudication is a proposition that is either true or false. As Owen Fiss reminds us:

The judge . . . seeks not just a plausible interpretation, but an objectively true one. Judges may not project their preferences or their views of what is right or wrong, or adopt those of the parties, or of the body politic, but rather must say what the Constitution requires. The issue is not whether school desegregation is good or bad, desirable or undesirable, to the judge, the parties, or the public, but whether it is mandated by the Constitution. The law aspires to objectivity.[9]

But I have argued that if you believe the holdings of a court, insofar as they are constructions of the Constitution, are not statements about the world, but are moves within a serious game, movements as practised as any classical ballet and yet no less contingent, then reductionism is out of the question. A modality is, I repeat, the way in which a proposition is true; constitutional modalities determine the way in which a constitutional proposition is true. The holding of a court therefore has a different modal status than a scientific statement about an object in the world. Each is validated in the use of its different standards. One's expectations about what constitutes law accordingly change. The epistemological assumption that requires us to have a frame of reference outside the forms of argument comes to seem a needless and troublesome premise. Then, the assumption that meaning must reside in a factual assertion will be dropped and one will no longer be able to declare, or feel the need to declare, that there is no "law" in constitutional law, or that there can only be law if constitutional interpretation is confined to a single mode. What I did not see when I first made this argument, but of which I am now persuaded, is that it was not epistemological naivete alone that accounted for the failures I would ascribe to strict construction and reconstruction. Because there have recently been critics who went beyond the rigidities of strict construction and reconstruction, who were both epistemologically sophisticated and skeptical, who nevertheless were unable to offer truly persuasive alternatives, I have come to believe that an insufficient attention to the characteristics of rules of law as well as to their status of modal statements was responsible. I will give two examples of such sophisticated criticism regarding the subject of indeterminacy.

The first example is Owen Fiss's important essay entitled "Objectivity and Interpretation."[10] Recognizing that the meaning of a constitutional text is not "out there" to be discovered, Fiss argues that law nevertheless requires an independence of our will. True, the Constitutional text is very general – it fails to define many terms and does not address some important issues – and it is also comprehensive, in the sense that it protects a multitude of values, some of which potentially conflict with others. But, Fiss insists "in this regard the Constitution is no different from a poem . . . Generality and comprehensiveness are features of any text."[11]

Such features do not defy interpretation, they "provoke" it.[12] With this statement, Fiss indicates that he does not share the assumption of strict construction and reconstruction that meaning is an object, though he agrees with them that, for an interpretation to be law, it must to some extent be determinate, that is, its correctness must be at least partly independent of the will of the decider.

Fiss proposes that this constraint is imposed by certain "disciplining rules" that determine the correctness of a particular interpretation. The truth of the application of these rules, in turn, is determined by the interpretive community of peers engaged in the enterprise of constitutional interpretation. Fiss recognizes that

The meaning of a text does not reside in the text, as an object might reside in physical space . . . Indeed interpretation is defined as the process by which the meaning of a text is understood and expressed, and the acts of understanding and expression necessarily entail strong personal elements. At the same time, the freedom of the interpreter is not absolute . . . He is disciplined by a set of rules that specify the relevance and weight to be assigned to the material (words, history, intentions, consequence) . . . The disciplining rules may vary from text to text. The rules for . . . contractual interpretation vary from statutory interpretation and both vary from those used in constitutional interpretation . . . [These disciplining rules] constrain the interpreter, thus transforming the interpretive process from a subjective to an objective one, and they furnish the standards by which the correctness of the interpretation can be judged.[13]

This is a considerable advance over the usual debate. What is interesting, however, is the way in which it is no advance at all. For Fiss takes these "disciplining rules" to be something outside the process of adjudication. They can be appealed to, presumably, to settle disputes. Indeed it is precisely because they are outside the forms of argument that require their application that they can be said to be "objective." It is clear from this that he does not recognize his "disciplining rules" as modalities; and thus he simply moves the search for an objective status for legal propositions and holdings, which he rightly criticizes, to these rules. This leads to three errors.

First, lawyers and judges make structural, historical, ethical arguments and the rest, they do not *apply* them. (And only professors discuss them.) The true "disciplining rules" in constitutional law are rather ways of evaluating rules, they are not the rules themselves. They are not rules off to one side, as it were, of the process of applying rules. And indeed how could they be otherwise? For if they were such, they themselves would be subject to interpretation and we would have commenced a regress. To simply say that an interpretive community will validate these rules does not tell us on what basis they will decide and thus why we should respect such a decision. Why should we accept a rule that admits the relevance of historical argument, for example?

Fiss is aware of this regress and his efforts to foreclose it precipitate a second error. He writes:

Other disputes may arise, however, and they may involve a challenge to the very authority or existence of a rule. Some judges or lawyers may, for example, deny the relevance of history altogether in constitutional interpretation. Disputes of this type pose a more serious challenge to the idea of objectivity than those over the application of a rule, for such disputes threaten the source of constraint itself. It should be remembered, however, that in the law there are procedures for resolving these disputes – for example pronouncements by the highest court and perhaps even legislation and constitutional amendments.[14]

But of course a declaration by the US Supreme Court that, henceforth, constitutional argument will confine itself to a single modality – like historical argument – would emphatically not end the debate. Such authority would change practices before jurisdictionally inferior courts perhaps; but whom would it persuade? That it would command the allegiance of those courts and commentators already committed to doctrinal approaches simply underscores the irreducibility of the problem: for how could a court renounce *that* modality, even though this option is, on Fiss's formulation, a necessary possibility?

Thus Fiss repeats the mistake of confusing a statement such as "the Court decided an issue a certain way" with the statement that "the Constitution requires that issues be decided in a certain way." The former has the truth status that Fiss hungers for; the latter has truth or falsity only within a specified constitutional modality.

The essay by Fiss is at once rightly influenced, rightly pulled in the direction of leaving the old debate and its static, self-absorbed dichotomies, and also hopelessly mired in the habits of that debate. The effort to show that indeterminacy cannot be equated with a license to the powerful, and the view that an interpretive community will determine the truth functions of a particular proposition are both surely nods in the right direction. But they are made from an armchair that has not moved, since they are said to promise an "objective" resource of constraint without which, it is implied, we must return to battle with the philistines of both camps. This is the third error: it is to express the hope that either of these fierce disputants, who are locked together by their habits of thought as much as by their combat against each other, could possibly be moved by Fiss's arguments. For the reconstructing nihilist, the disciplining rules are yet another example of unprincipled power, validated by no more than the hierarchical structure of the courts (who are, by definition, a bunch of hegemonists); whilst for the strictly constructing positivist Fiss's argument would support conferring even greater decisional power on the *political* branches. There the interpretive community is at least linked to the electoral franchise, and therefore the constraints it endorses have the legitimacy of the democratic mandate.

A second treatment of the problem of indeterminacy comes from Professor Stanley Fish, the literary critic, who some years ago strayed into the fray of the law professors and has happily lingered there (in part, he says, owing to his astonishment that they should take his insights as novel). Like Fiss, he is dissatisfied with the usual alternatives, whose partisans have dominated the bicentennial celebrations with their antiphonal pairs. He describes them thus:

The wholly mechanical alternative is the view . . . that meaning is a property of – is embedded in – texts and can therefore be read without interpretive effort or intervention by a judge . . . The wholly discretionary alternative is the opposite view . . . that texts have either many meanings or no meanings, and the reader or judge is free to impose – create, legislate, make up, invent, according to his or her own whims, desires, partisan purposes, etc.[15]

Fish's solution rejects rules as "constraints" on interpretation. This, he assures us, should not be too unsettling since there is an internalized order that is necessarily reflected in practice precisely because it is not external to the interpretive enterprise. To be able to do constitutional law, then, one has already been seized by ordering principles that operate as constraints:

The person who looks about and sees, without reflection, a field already organized by problems, impending decisions, possible courses of action, goals, consequences, desiderata, etc., is not free to choose or originate his own meanings, because a set of meanings has, in a sense, already chosen him and is working itself out in the actions of perception, interpretation, judgment, etc. he is even now performing.[16]

This is surely right, and to that extent an advance over Fiss. To be able to judge Fiss's disciplinary rules, one would already have had to master them. But, like Fiss whom he criticizes and with whom he shares a commendable distaste for the standard positions, Fish is also insensitive to the modalities of constitutional law, and thus also unpersuasive in his attempt to solve the indeterminacy problem.

And yet Fish is on the very verge of an appreciation of the forms of constitutional argument when he writes:

When there is a disagreement about the shape or meaning of a sentence, it is a disagreement between persons who are reading or hearing (and therefore constituting) it according to the assumptions of different circumstances . . .

If there are debates about what the Constitution means, it is not because the Constitution "provokes" debate, not because it is a certain *kind* of text, but because for persons reading (constituting) it within the assumption of different circumstances, different meanings will seem obvious and inescapable. By "circumstances" I mean, among other things, the very sense one has of what the Constitution is *for*. Is it an instrument for enforcing the intentions of the Framers? Is it a device for assuring the openness of the political process? Is it a blueprint for the exfoliation of a continually evolving set of fundamental values? Depending on the interpreter's view of what the Constitution is for, he will be inclined to ask different questions, to consider different bodies of information as sources of evidence, to regard different lines of inquiry as relevant or irrelevant, and finally to reach different determinations of what the Constitution plainly means.[17]

This is very well done – it was also brilliantly done by Karl Llewellyn[18] – but it is only half of a strategy: recognizing that there are forms of argument that maintain the legitimacy of the interpretive practice, that they are the ways by which we evaluate various applications of the Constitution, is simply to observe that they are *modalities*. One must then go on to recognize the limits of such legitimation, for here law is very different from literature. The six modalities I have described maintain the legitimacy of constitutional interpretation by officials whose views have legal consequences; these forms of arguments, however, do not justify such consequences, for they are not the animating force behind the conflicts being addressed through argument. It may be that when one reads a novel, one is moved to pick up the book to test one's own views and emotions, to engage in a solitary dialogue with oneself in the quietness and turmoil of the individual engagement with the text. And this may be as true of the child reading a fairy tale or a businessman reading a "thriller" while traveling on an airplane or an aesthete reading Proust. The motive is not important. It is in the consequences for state action that the enterprise of constitutional construction must be distinguished from literary interpretation. Decisions are sought, decisions are required, when their consequences have legal effect, that is, an effect that calls forth actions of the state that must be rationalized in accordance with the decision. As we shall see in Book III, *the requirement of a decision* provides the basis for the interpretive family of modalities.

We will also subsequently see that this requirement not only distinguishes law from literature, but is at the very heart of the

American constitutional system of interpretation. For now it is enough to indicate that this system thrives on a certain sort of indeterminacy, one that is confined to the modalities of assessment. Robert Cover was absolutely right in observing that force and violence underlay legal interpretation in a way that was not case with literature.[19] This observation is more than a mere distinction; it is part of the account of the internal rules of legal analysis. Cases do not arise because the litigants want to test what a particular judge thinks the Constitution is for. Litigants want justice. The recognition of this desire is absent from Fish's analysis.

We might, for example, have a judicial system that carefully observed the forms of argument in the pursuit of inhumane values; the legal system that enforced the return of fugitive slaves was such a system.[20] Or, on the other hand, we might have a system that abandoned the forms of constitutional behavior in pursuit of goodness and righteousness. Perhaps the FBI's pursuit of organized crime has sometimes taken on this character. Perhaps the Salem witch trials were an example of both phenomena in alteration. In such cases, legitimacy is shown to be separate from justification, whereas in literary criticism the forms of evaluation embody the critic's values. To say that *The Grapes of Wrath* exposes the class structure may be an observation laden with significance for critics of a certain school;[21] to say the same thing of *Maher v. Roe*,[22] which denied women a right to abortion financing, may be to say something important, but it is not legal argument and has no legal consequences (though of course it may have important consequences for the law and the respect due it). This distinction is what Fiss has in mind when he refers to "external" perspectives outside the law and gives as an example of someone who is operating on "the basis of some religious or ethical principle . . . or on the gounds of some theory of politics [and concludes that in such instances] the evaluation is not in terms of the law."[23]

Fish does not tolerate such a distinction. He rather harshly criticizes Fiss for saying that political considerations are not legal moves and that to incorporate them into the forms of argument politicizes the process. Indeed he is rather disdainful of Fiss's fears of politicization:

If [an external perspective were brought to bear], it would not be because the structure of the law had been made to bend to the pressure of some moral and political perspective, but because a structure already moral and political had been given another moral and political shape.[24]

Of course law is a political structure and various kinds of political change – amending the Constitution, packing the Supreme Court, tailoring jurisdiction on substantive grounds – do alter the structure. But what Fiss meant – perhaps owing to a greater sensitivity to the distinctly *legal* dimension of constitutional interpretation than Fish – is that the moves within each of the modalities are not political, indeed that a move within a mode is not even legitimate if it cannot be rationalized on a non-political basis, the basis of the particular modality. That is how political questions are transmuted into legal questions in the United States. Not just any argument will do, and a political argument *per se* will never do. Law is a political structure just as a painting is a piece of furniture. But the standards of painting – perspective, figure, composition – are not the standards of interior decorators, and the standards of legal argument – neutrality, generality, consistency – are not the standards of the political operative.

Conflating these genres, Fish finds it impossible to take Fiss's fears seriously. Where Fiss feared that the Constitution, "would be reduced to a mere instrument of political organization,"[25] Fish is avuncularly reassuring: "There is nothing . . . to worry about."[26] Using the Constitution in a way that would call into question the point of constitutional adjudication cannot happen. The very construction of the Constitution by lawyers will prevent this.

I fear this flattering confidence is unwarranted. It is the consequence of not seeing any real point in constitutional interpretation other than interpretation. But consider these possibilities. First, the forms of argument might be used in the pursuit of values that were incompatible with the humane respect for decency and dignity that are pre-supposed by but cannot be guaranteed by the Constitution – the *Korematsu*[27] case (in which the Supreme Court upheld the forced relocation of Japanese-Americans on valid prudential grounds) is one such example. Second, the forms might be turned against each other, de-legitimating the constitutional processes of interpretation, as was for a time the effort of the leadership of the US Department of Justice in its abusive remarks about the Supreme Court. In either case, the mere practice of the forms does not ensure the vitality even of the purposes and institutions they presuppose. The reason this is so resides in their character as modalities; the ways in which statements are true are not, themselves, assertions about the world. They are not true or false and thus cannot serve to determine what is just in the world.

This would upset Fiss; it relaxes Fish. Neither reaction is entirely appropriate. Fiss is, at last, reductivist. His "disciplinary rules" can be reduced to propositions about a community of speakers. Fish, on the other hand, believes in the irreducible nature of every text. There is nothing more to say about the interpretive rules than that they function as they do. That they are neither true nor false is an interesting statement only insofar as it is, itself, something of a paradox.

I have frogmarched these two distinguished commentators onto the stage for a reason other than to criticize them. Indeed, as I have observed, their work reflects a considerable advance over the usual stuff, showing a sophistication that is notably absent in the typical law journal article. Their debate, however, must be counted a failure, for it is hard to see that either man's approach is persuasive: Fiss's defense against reductionism turns out, on inspection, to be a reductionist program; Fish's defense of anti-foundationalism is unable to provide a role for justice. Their positions cannot be the last words of those who would reject foundationalism in epistemology or law. My purpose has been to show that the source of these failures lies in an insufficient attention to the nature of legal rules as incommensurate modalities. If neglect of this description could mislead commentators of such prominence as Fish and Fiss then the subject is worth discussion.

When I have persuaded the reader – if indeed I can – that an attentiveness to the analytical perspectives afforded by a modal view is helpful, then we will shortly have to face the questions such a perspective brings to the fore: how do we choose among the various modalities in any given situation when they indicate different outcomes? How do we justify such a system? Is it just? For it profiteth us not to devise an approach that solves some problems – like the Countermajoritarian Objection to judicial review – if it creates other more important problems and renders them intractable. But first, I must demonstrate convincingly that such approaches are indeed useful. This can only be done with concrete legal materials. Book II will examine some samples of constitutional analysis from the perspective of the modalities.

BOOK II

HOW TO ANALYZE A CONSTITUTIONAL CASE

1

THE CASE METHOD

In this book I aim to defend the thesis that the modalities of constitutional argument provide a useful analytic perspective on the traditional problems of American constitutional law. I propose that we should change our focus from attempts to explain why men and women think and argue as they do in constitutional law, to a description of how they have thought and argued. This description can serve as a means of mastering the techniques that it describes. Moreover, the reader who has mastered these approaches to constitutional interpretation is better suited to understanding its puzzles and the pull of its dilemmas.

In Book I, I endeavored to show that the jurisprudential basis for the modes of American constitutional interpretation lay in the separation of sovereignty and state, a separation that made the written constitution possible. I then reviewed the six modes, or modalities, of such interpretation. I further observed that an attentiveness to the modalities of interpretation resolved a number of anomalies, among them the Countermajoritarian Objection to judicial review, the circularity of justification for that review, and the paradoxes of indeterminacy, for example. And I suggested that such an approach offered a method that was accessible to non-judicial constitutional actors.

In Book II, I will take up this last promise – that is, I will show how such methods can be used by the student or the US President or a member of Congress to analyze a constitutional issue. Then, in Book III, I will consider the principal difficulty posed by such an approach – that it leads to confusion and contradiction when the various modes conflict, and for that reason does not assure justice.

As many readers are no doubt aware, some ruefully so, constitutional law, like other branches of the law, is taught in the United States by reference to the cases applying and construing the Constitution. This was not always so. The developments that brought the American law schools into prominence coincided with the introduction of the case method. The coherence and power of the method have distorted our perception of what it is we actually learn. For once the arguments and holdings of cases were seen to be *facts*, legal education could no longer be content with learning *practices*. That was, at any rate, the conclusion of its chief discoverer, Christopher Columbus Langdell, the first Dean of the Harvard Law School.

> [All] the available materials of that science [that is, law] are contained in printed books. . . . [T]he library is . . . to us all that the laboratories of the university are to the chemists and physicists, all that the museum of natural history is to the zoologists, all that the botanical garden is to the botanists . . .[1]

Two methodological consequences flow from Langdell's "scientific" view of law. First:

> [T]he number of fundamental legal doctrines is much less than is commonly supposed; the many different guises in which the same doctrine is constantly making its appearance, and the great extent to which legal treatises are a repetition of each other, being the cause of much misapprehension. If these doctrines could be so classified and arranged that each should be found in its proper place, and nowhere else, they would cease to be formidable from their number.[2]

and second:

> [T]he cases which are useful and necessary for [the purpose of mastering legal principles or doctrines] bear an exceedingly small proportion to all that have been reported. The vast majority are useless, worse than useless, for any purpose of systematic study.[3]

Thus came the first casebooks and the first case-methods of teaching. It is not surprising that these types of books – collecting the "leading cases" along doctrinal lines – and this type of teaching, asking the student to infer and apply the unifying theories that underlay the rationales of these cases within their doctrinal categories, should also have been applied to constitutional law. For while these methods arose from the formlessness with which federalism threatened the common law (Langdell was a Contracts scholar), the characteristics that made such methods useful in analyzing the common law subjects were also present in American constitutional cases, precisely because the American courts were using common law forms of argument in those cases.

Every significant casebook and law review reflects this approach,[4] though few of their authors and editors would subscribe to Langdell's description of law as a science. Despite such up-to-date agnosticism, however, these authors and editors usually do in fact share the main consequence of Langdell's description, namely that legal holdings are propositions about the world. As such, they can be verified, if they are *law*, by reference to some feature of the world, some fact outside the control of the verifying judge or scholar. And so the "progressive"[5] casebooks add dubious historical and social science materials, while the "conservative"[6] casebooks confine themselves to reprints of notable cases. But whatever the excerpt, one will always find it followed by a set of leading questions designed to elicit the relevant "fact" and to invite the reader to compare that fact with the holding and rationale of the doctrine. In his lecture, the law professor will, by the use of other cases and hypotheticals, adroitly or fecklessly, demonstrate the competing values and rationales at stake. The more vain the professor, the more it will appear that the court's opinion is a hopeless series of ill-conceived assertions that can be effortlessly shown to contradict the past (precedent) as well as the future (those hypotheticals). But suppose we abandoned this style. How might we teach then? What would a class do if it adopted a descriptive analysis of constitutional problems?

I will take three such problems and work through them in a way that is attentive to the modalities of constitutional argument. These three problems are (1) the case of *Missouri* v. *Holland*, which presented the Supreme Court with the questions posed by a statute adopted pursuant to a treaty rather than to the usual Article I bases for Congress's legislative authority; (2) the issues that should have been addressed by the President when he considered whether to develop a quasi-private covert action capability without government funding (the Iran–Contra problem); and (3) the constitutional problem confronting US Senators who were asked to confirm the nomination of Robert Bork on the basis of his views of the proper construction of the Constitution.

2

MISSOURI v. HOLLAND

The United States entered into a treaty with Canada for the protection of migratory birds. In the treaty was a provision that each of the contracting powers undertake to pass laws that forbid the killing, capturing, or selling of the birds except in accordance with certain regulations. Congress enacted such legislation and Missouri brought suit, saying its reserved powers protected by the Tenth Amendment were violated by the act and treaty. Thus runs a standard account of the case.[1]

Mr Holland was a federal game warden. The State of Missouri sued him in a federal district court to enjoin his enforcement of regulations providing for a closed season on hunting certain game birds. These regulations were adopted to enforce the provisions of a statute that, in turn, was enacted pursuant to a treaty between the United States and Canada. Missouri claimed, and the district court agreed, that the Congress had acted unconstitutionally in attempting to legislate with regard to a subject as to which it was given no express power and which was, therefore, presumed to have been reserved to the states.

It is a relatively easy thing to derive various arguments based on the six modalities: the historical, textual, structural, doctrinal, prudential and ethical forms of argument. And, indeed, these were precisely the arguments urged by counsel. Thus the Attorney General for Missouri argued[2] that the federal arrangement depends upon

---

Missouri v. *Holland*, 252 U.S. 346; 40 S. Ct. 382; 64 L. Ed. 641 (1920).

both federal and state authorities that are supreme within their spheres; that the regulation of game was a uniquely state power; that consequently the preservation of federalism could not co-exist with a federal regime of game regulation, no matter how fragmentary (a structural argument);[3] and that the framers had never intended that the states be shorn of their sovereignty in internal affairs, one aspect of which – one that antedated and was continued beyond the adoption of the Constitution, there being no suggestion otherwise during the ratification debates – was the state regulation of migratory game (a historical argument);[4] and that under the common law of England, the absolute control of wild game was held to be an attribute of sovereignty; that the American courts had held states to have retained those sovereign powers not ceded to the federal government (a doctrinal argument);[5] and that the text of the Tenth Amendment expressly reserves to the states those powers not delegated to the federal government, while the text of Article I – which specifies the powers delegated to the federal government – makes no mention of the ownership or control of wild game (a textual argument).[6]

Similarly the Solicitor General, appearing for the United States, argued[7] that the text of Article I does grant to Congress the power to enact such laws as may be plainly adapted to the purpose of giving effect to treaties; this is the import of the Necessary and Proper Clause (another textual argument);[8] that, citing *Cohens v. Virginia*[9] and *The Legal Tender Cases*,[10] it has been held that not only has Congress the power to legislate statutes for the purpose of executing treaties but that the subjects of such legislation are not limited to the subjects with respect to which it is empowered to legislate in domestic affairs (a doctrinal argument);[11] and that the power of the state over game is limited by such norms and prohibitions as are required of the federal government (an ethical argument).[12] These were the arguments put to the Supreme Court on March 2, 1920. On April 19 the Court delivered its opinion, which was read by Justice Oliver Wendell Holmes, Jr.

[A copy of this brief opinion has been provided as a fold-out and is situated between pages 140 and 141. For the remainder of this chapter, the reader should make the opinion available for reference.]

Let me begin by summarizing Holmes's argument. It has three steps. Holmes observes that the prohibitions of the Tenth Amendment – that certain powers are reserved to the states and that the federal government may exercise only its enumerated powers – are prohibitions by negative implication. That is, they take their scope and definition from the limits of the *affirmative* empowerments of the federal government. Thus they are to be distinguished from direct prohibitions, such as those of the Bill of Rights that plainly state specific acts that the federal government may not undertake. Second, Holmes notes that the affirmative empowerment of Congress to pass statutes in order to execute treaties, is pointedly distinguished from the Article I empowerments of Congress by the passage "to make laws necessary and proper to carry into execution . . . all *other* powers vested in the government of the United States."[13] Thus the prohibitory implications of Article I for the Tenth Amendment, which are so fruitful in other contexts, are irrelevant here, since the limits of Article I empowerments cannot in this case be used to imply prohibitions. Third, and finally, Holmes concludes that the limits of the treaty-based statute-empowering provision – that is, the authority of Congress to make laws in order to comply with a treaty – are determined by the limits on the underlying treaty power and not, *a fortiori*, by the limits inferred from the enumerations of Article I powers. Since the nation is empowered to make any treaty on any subject that is necessary, if the necessity is clear then the Tenth Amendment's implied prohibitions will not bar either a treaty or a statute adopted to enforce such a treaty.

It is a close, complex, and careful argument. I have abstracted it into three steps. The opinion, however, proceeds by legal argument, that is, by the modalities I have specified. These forms of argument take the reader through a rich rhetorical strategy, culminating in a doctrinal creation of such polish and finish that the forms barely show. Let us go through the opinion carefully and expose this structure.

[At this point, the reader should read the Opinion and then, keeping it to hand, follow the commentary by referring to the numbered paragraphs and sentences in the Opinion. I have deliberately chosen the slightly excerpted opinion to be found in the most widely used American constitutional law casebook; as will be seen, even here, in the most distinguished of the doctrinal constitutional collections, the editor's elisions reflect a certain insensitivity to the argumentative strategy of the opinion.]

Paragraphs 1–2: Introduction

Paragraph 1 states the facts, and the jurisdictional history of the case. Characteristic of doctrinal judges, the statement of facts by Holmes is rather spare.

Paragraph 2 provides the background to the adoption of the treaty and describes its basic provisions. Holmes carefully notes that the purpose of the treaty is identical with that of the challenged statute, indeed that the treaty expressly provides for a statute that in turn contemplates executive regulations for the enforcement of the treaty's provisions. But he does not dwell on any particular findings of fact about the endangered species that the treaty seeks to protect, and in fact does not even name the species involved. Rather Holmes seeks to escape the impress of particular facts to enable the statement of a doctrinal principle. He writes:

It is unnecessary to go into any details because [the] question raised is the general one whether the treaty and statute are void as an interference with the rights reserved to the States.

This lack of interest in the particular facts of the case is in sharp contrast to the focus of a prudential judge. When Brandeis once pressed Holmes to acquaint himself with the new social realities of industrial New England, Holmes wrote to his old friend Sir Frederick Pollock: "I hate facts. I always say that the chief end of man is to form general propositions."[14]

Paragraph 3: Statement of the Question

Paragraph 3 is a slightly complicated textual argument, made with Holmes's customary economy. I cannot do it in three sentences. It goes this way:

1 The text of the Tenth Amendment, which Missouri urges as a bar to the statute, reserves those "powers not delegated to the United States by the Constitution."

2 The text of Article II, section 2, however, *is* an express delegation specifically providing for the federal power to make treaties.

3 Moreover, the text of Article VI explicitly states that treaties are binding on the states.

4 So, if a treaty is within the federal power to conclude, then the text of Article I, section 8 will suffice to support a statute in support of that treaty, the Tenth Amendment notwithstanding, since this section expressly enumerates the power to pass laws in execution of powers provided for but not otherwise found in Article I.

These four steps, comprising a careful textual argument, set up the question. Now everything will turn on whether the treaty made with Canada is a valid exercise of the treaty power (of Article II, section 2).

Paragraph 4: Missouri's Argument Examined

Thus far Holmes has used a single form of argument to set up the question. Now, in paragraph 4, he deploys five of the forms in a complex interplay that shows *how* the question can be answered. This involves stating Missouri's complaint in the form of a consti-tutional argument (a structural one) and then using virtually the entire array of constitutional arguments to rebut the state's approach. By this strategy, he rejects the attempt to resolve the question on purely structural lines.

[I have numbered the sentences to allow a reading that distin-guishes each of these forms.]

Sentence 1 states the basic, structural argument advanced by Mis-souri. It can be parsed this way: (a) not every conceivable treaty is valid; (b) a treaty is invalid if it is inconsistent with the Constitution; (c) it therefore follows that there must be some constitutional limits to the treaty-making powers; (d) there are well-known constitutional limits to the federal power to make statutes; (e) these limits would be transgressed if Congress could ignore them by relying on the treaty power as an alternative basis for statutory empowerment; (f) therefore one limit on the treaty power is that it cannot serve as the predicate for a statute that Congress otherwise could not adopt. Holmes devotes the rest of paragraph 4 to answering this structural argument. A structural argument is one that deduces particular rules as necessary to, and thus implied by, the requirements of the various constitutional structures of federalism, of the various federal branches, of the representative state, among others, and the relation-ships these structures mandate. To simplify Missouri's argument a bit, I might restate it as: there must be *some* limits to the treaty power or it would contradict the essential limiting structure of a written Constitution of delegated powers; statutes that are beyond the power of Congress to adopt are examples of such contradictions; therefore at least one limit on the treaty power is that it cannot serve as a basis for a statute that would contradict the Constitutional structure.

The balance of the paragraph is a refutation of this argument. Sentence 2 sets up the first line of Holmes's reply by preparing the ground for a distinction between statutes passed pursuant to Congress's Article I enumerated powers and statutes that rely on other grants of Congressional authority. The assault comes in the innocuous form of a doctrinal argument. Here Holmes addresses two cases, *United States* v. *Shauver*[15] and *United States* v. *McCullagh*[16] in which a federal statute purporting to regulate the killing of migratory birds within the states had been struck down by courts relying on *Geer* v. *Connecticut*,[17] which clearly held that migratory birds were owned by the states and that Congress had no power to displace that control. Without reaffirming these cases, Holmes distinguishes them by noting that the Congressional power there asserted was not the treaty power. This is a straightforward doctrinal argument, relying on the principle that a precedent only governs cases to the extent that the case originally decided, and urged now as controlling, presented the argument now to be resolved in the instant case. Despite the broad language in *Geer*,[18] its facts do not permit a holding as encompassing as the rule that Congress has no power to displace state control regarding game, for the *Geer* Court was not considering a statute based on empowerments other than those enumerated in Article I.

Sentence 3 supports this crucial distinction by reference to the language of Article VI. That language reads:

This Constitution, and the Laws of the United States which shall be made in Pursuance thereof; and all Treaties made, or which shall be made, under the Authority of the United States, shall be the supreme Law of the Land; and the Judges in every State shall be bound thereby, any Thing in the Constitution on Laws of any State to the Contrary notwithstanding.[19]

Notice that there is a careful distinction in the text (here marked by a semi-colon) between laws made in pursuance of the Constitution, on the one hand, and treaties made under the authority of the United States, on the other. Notice also, however, the precise weight that the opinion places on this distinction: it is presented in order to distinguish Congress's authority when it relies solely on its enumerated Article I powers, from its authority to pass laws that are necessary and proper for the execution of a national power to make treaties. In so doing Holmes carefully discriminates between the clauses that endow *powers*, on the one hand, and the Necessary and Proper Clause, which applies to *means*, on the other. He thus asserts no more on the basis of his textual argument than that there is a distinction among the powers of government; and he thereby avoids the tempting judicial solecism of augmenting those powers by a resort to the Necessary and Proper Clause as a "power," and relying on that clause to support the statute.[20]

Sentences 4 and 5 consider the construction of the distinction among powers. Sentence 4 questions whether a purely textual interpretation is appropriate, since it might construe the key phrase "the authority of the United States" as no more than the diplomatic formalities that, customarily, employ this phrase. Sentence 5 reminds us instead of the importance of Missouri's structural argument with which the paragraph began, and assures us that the crucial distinction Holmes has drawn among powers by no means obviates the structural argument that *some* limits must exist; it only opens up a question for interpretation distinct from that previously focussed on the limits to *Article I* powers. The limits to the treaty power "must be ascertained in a different way."

Sentence 6 considers a prudential approach to this question. Holmes indicates that he is unwilling to entertain adopting a test that generates rules that might make it impossible for the federal government to act in international affairs as required in times of extremity. If the test proposed by Missouri presumes that the power of sovereignty – for this is the import of the phrase "a power which must belong to and somewhere reside in every civilized government" – can be somehow absent from situations requiring national action, then the test is an unrealistic one and must be treated with skepticism.

In this passage Holmes refers to a fundamental matter I discussed at the beginning of Book I, the separation between national sovereignty and the organs of the state. To say, as I have, that the written US Constitution presumes such a separation is not to say that therefore sovereignty dissipates. Holmes forthrightly rejects such an implication: "It is obvious that there may be matters of the sharpest exigency for the national well-being that an act of Congress could not deal with" (since Congress is a limited agent of the sovereign) "but that a treaty . . . could" (since treaties are acts of the sovereign). The refutation of this dissipation of sovereignty, which Holmes accomplishes on prudential grounds in sentence 6, lays the groundwork for the argument that the organs of government may sometimes act for the nation, in contrast to their more limited constitutional role in other contexts where they may only act as the nation has previously, and expressly, directed.

Sentence 7 is not stated in the form of an argument *per se*, but rather as a reminder of the method Holmes is applying and from which we may infer the type of argument on which he will rest the holding. He tells us that he is not yet applying a rule to the particular facts of the case but rather is evaluating a proposed "test." This is the characteristic approach of the doctrinalist, whose opinions are efforts to fashion rules of general and neutral applicability. Accordingly, they are measured as possible precedents before, not after, they are used to construe the facts in the case before the court.

But is not every appellate opinion then an effort at doctrinal argument? And does that not collapse all the various forms into one? It is true that as we move from Supreme Court opinions to those of the lower courts the strength of *stare decisis* increases. But appellate opinions are not the only examples of constitutional argument; and even within an appellate opinion that relies on precedent and sees its purpose as crafting precedent, the various other modalities have important roles. And even as to the purely doctrinal opinion that relies on the precedent of similar cases, the various modalities are relevant because they determine what is *similar*. An opinion formulating a rule on the basis of a particular text will apply when that text appears again for construction; an opinion relying on historical argument as the basis for its holding will serve as precedent in a subsequent case when the intentions of the framers and ratifiers on the particular point that was decisive in the earlier case are again relevant; a prudential case is a relevant precedent not when the facts are the same, but when the two sets of facts present similar costs and benefits; a structural holding governs cases in which the structural relationships of the Constitution that were in play in the earlier rationale are again implicated. (For example, a case holding that a President may fire his subordinates at will on the structural grounds that the Constitution contemplates a relationship of Presidential control within the executive branch, will imply that the President does not have such freedom of action when confronting an official of the "independent" agencies.[21] The prior holding is not *precedent* for the simple proposition that a President is only able to fire subordinate employees, even though, as a fact, this is true as a result of the earlier case.)

Moreover, with respect to the crafting of a precedent, we can see in *Missouri* v. *Holland* that a doctrinal approach can measure its standards – neutrality and generality – against arguments generated by the other forms. Thus Holmes tries the proposed test against prudential and structural *hypotheticals* – no one is really suggesting, and the trial court did not find, that the threat to migrating game birds was in fact a threat to national security – to see whether the proposed rule really could apply generally to other statutes whose authority is based on treaties. But notice that Holmes never adopts the standards of those competing modalities as his own: thus his fastidious avoidance of the particular facts in the case until he has settled on a rule, facts that would be crucial to either prudential or structural approaches. Sentence 7 identifies the approach that ultimately will govern the opinion and thus while this sentence does not advance the argument, it is by no means without significance. In Holmes's hands, *Missouri* v. *Holland* will be a doctrinal opinion.

Sentence 8 returns to the play of modalities and considers textual argument. Holmes's approach exploits a distinction between modalities that has generally been overlooked by more recent commentators.[22] It is easy to confuse a construction of the text to determine intention (an historical approach no different from construing other documents that might be evidence of the rationale for a legally significant act in constitutional law) with the construction of the text for its own sake (a textual argument). Holmes reflects his awareness of the distinction when he notes that "we are dealing with words that *also* are a constituent act." He then sets the two forms against one another by observing that, in constitutional law, the very text has contributed to changed conditions and contexts that must be presumed to have been beyond the anticipation of the drafters.

Sentence 9 continues the attack on historical argument. In a move that will be familiar to commentators of our own day, Holmes accepts the essential premise of historical argument as a way of undercutting its application to the instant case. The ratifiers' intention (according to Holmes) was to create a nation-state. Since this was far from a reality at the inception, their intentions can scarcely have extended to the practical diplomatic requirements of the security of a nation-state once it became a reality. Indeed, Holmes almost implies that there was no nation-state until the Civil War destroyed the competing constitutional idea of a confederation. Thus the intentions of 1787 do not comprehend the issue raised by Congress's reliance on the treaty power of the nation-state.

Sentence 10 continues the attack on Missouri's historical argument, this time by means of a prudential exhortation to consider the case "in the light of our whole experience" and "not merely in that of what was said 100 years ago."[23] It should be observed, however, that Holmes does not dismiss historical approaches. Rather he modestly claims that other modalities must also be brought to bear on the question, "and not *merely*" that arising from the intentions of the ratifiers.

Paragraph 4 ends with three sentences drawn from one modality (textual). Sentence 11 is a textual argument, not unlike its successors from the pen of Hugo Black.[24] It and the two following sentences are typical of the textualist insistence that it is the present meaning of the constitution's words that governs the construction of the text. Accordingly, sentence 11 treats the narrow question of whether the treaty actually appears, on its face, to violate any of the explicit prohibitions of the Constitution. Because it does not – even Missouri has not made this claim – sentence 12 follows up this finding with a sarcastic reference to the "invisible" textual import of the Tenth Amendment. From a textual point of view, a vague prohibition is really no prohibition at all, a conviction that accounts, I believe, for the textualist strategy of "incorporation" by which the Fourteenth Amendment's luminous but vague phrases are given texts that can be applied in this mode.[25]

Finally sentence 13 reminds us that a textualist construction of the Tenth Amendment, because it aims at the present meaning of the words of the amendment, will necessarily be governed by the contemporary understanding of the relationships of federalism to which it refers. The text forbids the federal government to assume powers that are reserved. Unlike the usual constitutional situation, however, what is implicitly reserved to the states is not simply that which is not delegated to the federal government in Article I. Rather what is reserved must be inferred from our present conception of that which the states, and the People, expect of the nation-state.

Paragraph 5: Missouri's Argument Redefined

In light of the foregoing, what then *is* reserved to the states? Paragraph 5 approaches the question from a doctrinal perspective by citing cases that recognize an assertion of state power over game and archly observing that these holdings do not necessarily mean that state power is exclusive. Cases that implicitly concede the state's ownership of wild game are by no means authority for the conclusion that state ownership cannot coexist with federal regulatory power. Indeed these earlier cases are distinguished away on the ground that the courts that considered them were not called upon to decide a federal claim to regulate based ultimately upon the treaty power. In the final sentence of the paragraph, which the casebook author has unfortunately omitted, Holmes writes:

If we are to be accurate, we cannot put the case of the state upon higher ground than that the treaty deals with creatures that for the moment are within state borders, that it must be carried out by officers of the United States within the same territory, and that, but for the treaty, the state would be free to regulate this subject itself.

Paragraph 6: Exclusive Power of the State to Regulate Refuted

In the next paragraph Holmes attacks the rule for which Missouri had urged the cases just distinguished, viz, that the recognition of the state's regulatory authority on the basis of ownership is tantamount to affirming its exclusive power of regulation over that which is owned. In paragraph 6 he deploys a structural rationale against Missouri's claim of exclusive jurisdiction over the game as to which it asserts title. Conceding that Missouri may have lawfully regulated game up to now, Holmes replies that if the mere ability to regulate implied exclusivity, then most of the laws of the United States would fall since they all deal with matters which, in the absence of federal action, the states could assuredly regulate. Put in formal, structural terms, this might read:

1 Because the states are creatures of plenary power, they can act

in any sphere from which they have not been displaced by federal action.

2 Although the Constitution only empowers the federal government to act in certain areas, federal action in those areas will supersede previous state regulation in the same area.

3 Thus state regulation in the absence of federal action does not imply that federal action in the same area is beyond its permissible constitutional scope (since, in the absence of federal regulation, all subjects are open to the states).

Holmes then cites a number of decided cases – a string of doctrinal arguments whose citations, as is customary, the casebook editor has chosen to omit – for the proposition that treaties supersede the power of the states. Holmes concludes this paragraph with a vitally important sentence that the editor, unfortunately, has chosen to cut. It reads "Further illustration seems unnecessary, and it only remains to consider the application of established rules to the present case." This nondescript passage is just the sort of apparent surplusage so irksome to casebook editors. Having omitted the preceding citations, one could easily overlook that Holmes locates each of the arguments to which I have referred within the cited cases,[26] and then proceeds to announce that a rule has been decided upon. Seeing no need to emphasize the role of the modality of doctrinal argument – taking the citation of cases as mere support for an earlier assertion rather than as advancing an argument – the editor quite naturally cut the passage that underscored the importance of the citations. In fact the sentence is the dramatic moment of the opinion. Now we know that a rule has been crafted out of the process of evaluating the proposed, but rejected rule urged by Missouri.

With that climactic sentence Holmes proceeds to the final and decisive paragraph. He has now confirmed how he intends to fashion the holding: by applying established rules such that a *test* is crafted from the materials and habits, and the holdings, of the constitutional common law. Holmes has confirmed, that is, that *Missouri* v. *Holland* is to be a *doctrinal* opinion.

Paragraph 7: Rationale and Holding

There are eight sentences in paragraph 7. Six of these sentences present arguments why, in these particular circumstances, the treaty power must be presumed to have limits sufficiently spacious to include the protection of wild game. Only the seventh sentence indicates the test that Holmes has devised. This passage, hardly more than a line, is the most important in the opinion and it is followed by the eighth sentence, which simply reads, "We are of the opinion that the treaty and statute must be upheld."

Five of those six first sentences argue: that an important national interest (one we would nowadays call the preservation of an element of the "ecology" of the nation) is involved (1); that this element can be protected, in this case, only with international cooperation (2); because it is transitory and, being transitory it is only momentarily within the title of the state (3); the species is vulnerable to extinction so that, but for this cooperation, it might cease to exist (4); that accordingly it is not sufficient to rely on the states for protection of this element of the national ecology (6). Each of these is a prudential argument. But this is not a prudential opinion and thus Holmes does not stop with these assertions.

Embedded in this final paragraph, in sentence 5, Holmes makes the textual argument that, "We see nothing in the Constitution that compels the Government to sit by while a food supply is cut off and the protectors of our forests and our crops are destroyed." This is quite distinct from the prudential observations that surround it because it is a remark not about the world but about the text of the Constitution. We learn its importance from the final phrase of the final substantive sentence. Sentence 7 reads, "reliance [on the states] is vain, and were it otherwise, the question is whether the United States is forbidden to act."

Now why is *that* the question? Only now are we given the test that Holmes has developed: whether the treaty transgresses a specific constitutional prohibition. The rationale for this test is the following: if Congress relies upon its enumerated power, it is limited in the statutes it passes to those that are neither explicitly nor implicitly prohibited. The explicit prohibitions are scattered but occur mainly in Article I, section 9, Article IV, and in the Bill of Rights. The implicit prohibitions are simply those formed by the outline, the limit, of the enumerated powers. Thus Amendments 9 and 10 do not specify *explicit* prohibitions but remind us of the source of the *implied* limits in the scheme of the enumerated powers: what is not permitted is forbidden. But where, as here, Congress is not relying on the enumerated powers of Article I, but only on the power to carry treaties into effect, there are no implied prohibitions. It remains then only to see whether there are explicit prohibitions in the way. Here there are not. The prudential arguments that precede the statement of the test are highly relevant, but not, as is usually supposed, because they form the basis of the holding. That conclusion is utterly refuted by the remark "and were it otherwise" which entails the judgment that the prudential sentences are not decisive. By carefully noting that even if the factual assertions made in those five sentences were *not* the case and reliance on the states to protect the migrating birds were *not* in vain, the holding would be the same, Holmes precludes the conclusion that his prudential observations are the basis of the holding.

The role of the prudential statements that precede the statement of the test is nevertheless an important one: they establish the predicate for national action, which is crucial not because necessity legitimates the acts of government (for we are told that the holding would be the same even if the facts were "otherwise") but because apparent necessity engages the Constitutional power to act "under the Authority of the United States" rather than on the basis of the enumerated powers of Article I. That is why this is a doctrinal opinion (providing a test for when the Congress acts on the basis of "the Authority of the United States") and not a prudential one (telling us under what factual circumstances it is propitious to hold that the Congress has acted "under the Authority" etc.)

Missouri v. Holland is written with great economy by a master of the common law method. It would be absurd to claim that Holmes's rationale is unavailable to commentators who do not share a modal perspective. I say only that such a perspective makes the arguments so much more perspicuous. Knowing what to look for enables one to see what sort of opinion this is, and thus what type of precedent it is. And, in fact, *Missouri v. Holland* was long misconstrued, indeed to such an extent that an amendment was proposed to overrule it, prompting an embarrassing political crisis following the Second World War.

Missouri v. Holland was presumed to embody no more than a crude principle of necessity,[27] the sort of prudentialism it is easy to see in an unjustified prominence if one is not really aware of the nature of prudential argument and doctrinal argument and the distinction. Thus misunderstanding the opinion, many commentators concluded that Congress could now pass any statute, indeed even one violating the Bill of Rights, so long as it could be plausibly maintained as one in aid of a treaty.[28] In the 1950s, concern arose that elements in the federal government might use the United Nations Charter to override practices that were thought to be constitutionally protected (specifically, racial segregation and, perhaps from different quarters, freedom of the press).[29] Some cited Article 55 of the United Nations Charter, a treaty to which the United States is a signatory. It provides that the United Nations shall promote "universal respect for, and observance of, human rights and fundamental freedoms without distinction as to race, sex, language, or religion."[30]

It was feared that this passage, or resolutions by UN agencies, would empower Congress to act in areas at that time thought closed to federal legislation. Such anxieties produced Senator Bricker's celebrated amendment which rather absurdly provided: "A provision of a treaty which conflicts with this Constitution shall not be of any force or effect."[31]

Throughout 1954, a political battle raged in Congress over the amendment. It was finally defeated in 1957 after the United States Supreme Court handed down *Reid* v. *Covert*,[32] a case dealing principally with Congressional power to provide for military jurisdiction over civilian dependents of American servicemen overseas. The plurality opinion by Justice Black held that US Status of Forces Agreements could not validly authorize the trial by court martial of civilian dependents of American soldiers overseas since the Constitution guarantees them trial by jury. The opinion contained a passage that appeared aimed directly at the Bricker controversy. Replying to the suggestion that a treaty or executive agreement might provide the basis for Congressional action (the court martial was held pursuant to a federal statute) that would otherwise be constitutionally impermissible, Justice Black wrote:

The obvious and decisive answer to this, of course, is that no agreement with a foreign nation can confer power on the Congress, or on any other branch of Government, which is free from the restraints of the Constitution.[33]

This language had the effect of putting to rest concerns that treaties might provide the basis for domestic action curtailing constitutional rights. But how many noticed the price at which this was done? For Justice Black, our most noted textualist, as Holmes was our most gifted doctrinalist, accomplished this goal by narrowing the scope of Constitutional prohibitions to only the textually explicit. Justice Black's constitutional jurisprudence gave him strong grounds in a particular modality to do so. But the effect was not to limit Holmes's opinion, as was widely thought at the time, but instead to expand it to govern even Article I empowerments. If Black had had his way, the Ninth and Tenth Amendments and the rights they protect, would simply have vanished, because they were too textually vague to serve as the basis for textual arguments. Missouri would not have been protected from congressional regulation of its migratory game, even in the absence of a treaty, on this view; and individuals could not rely on the protection of their unenumerated rights whenever a treaty purported to override them, regardless of whether the exercise of "national authority" was at stake.

3

THE IRAN–CONTRA AFFAIR

What has become known, misleadingly, as the "Iran–Contra Affair" arose from a lawyer's scheme. At the bottom of events lay advice given to the President, advice that resembled that which corporate and tax counsel render to their multinational clients every day: in order to escape regulations that have the effect of making the client's business operations uncompetitive, the lawyer proposes a corporate entity whose characteristics, unlike those of the original business, take it outside the domain of the regulations.[1]

Imagine a corporate executive officer who believes that a United States statute or regulation[2] makes it impossible for her company to compete successfully in a foreign market where other companies whose corporate activities are governed by Dutch or British or French law, are not similarly restrained. What can be done, asks the CEO? If she asks her lawyer, she might well get a reply like this: Either abandon the market or set up a joint subsidiary, which you do not own or control on paper (but on which you can rely to do as instructed), in another country where it will not be subject to American law.[3]

In an analogous way various developments, including the adoption of American laws and regulations, were believed by the US Executive to have hamstrung its intelligence activities in the late 1970s and early 1980s, leading, as we shall see, to a proposal to set up a controlled but unacknowledged "subsidiary" government agency analogous to the corporate entity mentioned above. One can easily imagine a President asking for legal advice when contemplating the development of a secret, quasi-private covert action agency. I have claimed that one virtue of modal approaches is that they more easily enable non-judicial actors to do constitutional analysis. How would this have been done for – or by – the President? In this chapter we will look at this problem.

Covert action[4] must be distinguished from other clandestine activities such as intelligence collection and counter-espionage. Despite its rather general name, "covert action" is limited to attempts to influence the policies of other states. Usually this is done through financial and technical support of local elements with whom the United States is in some sympathy; but occasionally in the post-war period, arms and even paramilitary forces have been organized around a particular covert action operation. In part for this reason, covert actions, though comprising a small fraction of US intelligence operations, have been the focal point for much controversy.

In the 1970s the United States, in the aftermath of the revelations of the Church Committee that had convened to explore connections between the CIA and the Watergate Affair, had put into place various statutory and regulatory restraints on covert action activities – including a highly restrictive Executive Order promulgated by the Ford Administration – that many intelligence professionals felt hampered their ability to compete effectively abroad. Moreover, covert action as a policy implementing option had been severely cut back in the Carter Administration; and indeed one of the criticisms made by the incoming Reagan Administration was that its predecessor had been too wary of aggressive covert action proposals. Perhaps nowhere was this new attitude more dramatically manifested than in Central America where a communist insurgency in El Salvador was being supported by the new Marxist regime in Nicaragua. The very enthusiasm and energy with which the Reagan Administration set about challenging these forces provoked a reaction in the domestic political sphere of the United States, where there was a long tradition of respect for self-determination by other nation-states, and an equally long, and much criticized, history of intervention in regional affairs. Soon elements in the US Congress were questioning appropriations proposed for covert action operations in the Central American theatre; by late 1983 it was clear that such financing would be sharply cut back and the future support and management of a covert action to mobilize an anti-Sandinista insurgency,[5] the "Contras," was cast in doubt. The debate over Contra funding had turned one of the largest post-war covert actions into an overt, para-military intervention. Indeed, it seemed increasingly difficult to plan and execute covert actions generally without their exposure in the press. At one point, it was even rumored in the Administration that Senator Biden, a member of the Senate Intelligence Committee to which all covert actions were to be reported, had said that he regarded public exposure of ill-conceived plans as a legitimate means of thwarting unwise operations.[6]

This picture of covert action operations in the early 1980s – facing a funding cutoff in Central America, risking exposure there and elsewhere from Congressional committees who were, by law, required to be informed of these secret plans – was complicated further by the rise of anti-American terrorism and the apparent inability of US clandestine operations to penetrate and neutralize the groups responsible. Throughout 1984 the United States was the target of bombings, assassinations of its diplomats, hi-jackings of sea- and aircraft, and ominously, a wave of kidnappings originating in the stateless chaos of Lebanon. The traditional methods of counter-terrorism that depend upon firm local authority and careful police work seemed impossible in such circumstances.

It was in this context, then, that the development of a quasi-private, covert action capability was proposed. This scheme offered several important advantages to the Administration. First, the "private" agency it envisioned could manage the Contra insurgency, fulfilling the oversight role played by the CIA before its funding and participation were curtailed through a series of statutes incorporating versions of the "Boland Amendment."[7] Second, the plan would avoid the unwelcome scrutiny of Congress since it would not be a government agency subject to congressional funding. This, it was believed, would enhance the secrecy of its projects. Third, a private agency could act more daringly, avoiding the legal restraints of Executive Orders that it would be embarrassing to repeal, and in defiance of certain international norms against reprisal, because it would not be associated with the US government. Thus it might recapture the initiative that seemed to have been surrendered to terrorist groups. Finally, because of the agency's dissociation with the official government it would afford the President the opportunity to provide a plausible denial of US responsibility should the private agency's operations be exposed. Statutes adopted in the late 1970s had greatly increased the political costs of maintaining such official denials, since these laws required that the President actually execute a written verification of the necessity of each covert operation and there remained the possibility that such written "findings"[8] might be discovered by the press after a denial had been issued.

The scheme of using a privately funded agency has been attributed to the Director of Central Intelligence, Mr William Casey.[9] This agency was to provide a "self-sustaining, stand-alone, off-the-shelf covert action capability."[10] Translated from the hi-tech language of the modern manager, these phrases mean a self-financing entity that maintained the ability to mount operations when called upon and which was not formally associated with any other agency. With evident admiration, Lieutenant Colonel Oliver North described the plan (so obviously a lawyer's scheme) as "a neat idea."[11] This is the "infrastructure" that North ran and Major General Richard Secord operated on a day-to-day basis. Secord called it "The Enterprise."[12] Until its activities were exposed in November, 1986, its existence was a well-kept secret. Even now, one wonders how many realize that this scheme was the basis for the débâcle that came to be known as the "Iran–Contra Affair."

That Affair has now dissolved into a vague and confused after-image so that many people might ask "What was all the shouting about?" Indeed I believe that most people would be surprised by the following account of what really happened in the Affair and what its significance is for the Constitution. For the most important lessons of the Affair were largely missed by the public; these lessons were constitutional in nature; and they continue to pose a fundamental challenge to constitutional government in America. To all of these dimensions, the modalities of constitutional argument are relevant. Armed with them, the significance of the Affair would have been apparent; indeed, as some within the Administration urged – notably James Baker – if the scheme had been evaluated on a constitutional basis, the infrastructure that led to the scandal would never have been created.[13]

What Actually Happened

When the Senate Select Committee, appointed to investigate the Affair, began its work in early 1987 the public and the Congress already had a relatively clear picture of the facts in the Iran–Contra scandal. This picture was the result of the conscientious efforts of the Tower Commission.[14] The Commission's account went this way: the President, in a desperate effort to rescue American hostages held captive in Lebanon, had agreed to sell hitherto embargoed arms to the Iranian government; because these weapons were procured at wholesale cost to the US government and sold at a black market price to the Iranians, a substantial profit occurred; instead of being returned to the US Treasury, which had purchased the arms in the first place, the funds generated by these sales were then "diverted" to the Contras. The question of the hour was: did the President know about this diversion?[15]

Documentary evidence produced for the Senate Select Committee, much of it not available to the Tower Commission, reflected, however, a far different picture than that of the Tower Commission's Report. The Affair did not in fact begin in the summer of 1985 with an Israeli overture to the United States regarding Iran. Rather the origin of the Affair lay in late 1983 with an American overture regarding Central America.[16] The Administration decided in that year to seek money and assistance from foreign countries and private sources to replace US aid to the Contras. When the CIA was subsequently removed by law from its role as the manager of these funds and of the logistics and tactics of the Contra war, a secret quasi-private infrastructure was put in its place to direct the insurgency.[17]

Managing the Contras was the first "account" for this Enterprise. In time, however, it took on other accounts. In addition to managing, procuring arms, and organizing an American-based re-supply effort for the Contras with funds largely solicited by US officials from third countries,[18] the Enterprise attempted to ransom hostages in Lebanon,[19] sold illicit arms to Iran, and conducted covert operations in the Carribean, the Mediterranean, and in the Near East.[20] After commencing elsewhere in the bureaucracy, the management of the Iranian account came to this group through the efforts of Lt. Col. North. Had the Enterprise not been exposed in its handling of the Iranian account, its operatives believed that it would have taken on still other operations, in Angola and elsewhere.[21]

This secret infrastructure – the Enterprise – had an informal board of directors that included the Director of the Central Intelligence Agency, William Casey, the National Security Advisor, Robert McFarlane,[22] and his deputy, Admiral John Poindexter. This group directed the efforts of the infrastructure's chief executive officer, Lt. Col. North, who in turn recruited a chief operating officer, retired

Maj. Gen. Richard Secord. The Enterprise was financed by money from non-US government sources – the $10 million solicited by Secretary of State George Shultz from the Sultan of Brunei was intended for an Enterprise account, not, as is usually supposed, a Contra bank account – by profits from arms sales that included but were by no means limited to those with Iran, by trading in currency and even in timber, all totaling about $50 million.[23] The Enterprise planned to recruit a small militia in Lebanon.[24] It had access to key CIA personnel (although its efforts were largely hidden from the Agency), to classified documents, and to secret government communications equipment.[25]

The purpose for creating and sustaining such an entity was to provide the President with the capability to conduct covert operations that would be funded by extra-constitutional means and thus would not have to be reported to Congress. By this method, Director Casey sought a more responsive and flexible covert action instrument that would not be affected by legal and bureaucratic restrictions, indeed could not be affected by such restrictions so long as it remained secret. As Lt. Col. North and Maj. Gen. Secord testified, the life of the Enterprise was not confined to running the Iranian operations. Rather it was to be staffed and available for use for any covert operation that needed its special scope and freedom from restraints. Accordingly, its financing had to be assured beyond the life of any one operation.

Now what is the significance of this account of events rather than the Tower Board's?

There Was No Diversion

It is easy to see why Justice Department officials, who thought they were investigating the Iranian arms-for-hostages scandal, were electrified to come upon a memorandum that quite casually listed the Contras as recipients of profits from the illicit arms transactions. The public, no less sensationally, first learned of a "diversion" from the Attorney General, who hurriedly met with Director Casey after the Justice officials' startling report. And it is easy to see how the Tower Commission, which did an excellent job but was shut off from any documents not linked to the Iranian transaction, should also have focussed on the transfer of funds from Iran to the Contras. In retrospect we can see that this was only part of the picture.

The Enterprise did spend money on the Contras that originally came out of profits from the Iranian transactions. But even earlier, the Enterprise had spent money solicited *from* the Contras to use for ransom payments in Lebanon. Was this also a "diversion?" And we now know that money was to be spent from both these sources on still other covert action projects. Would these have been "diversions?" The point is that the arms profits sent to the Contras appear to have been *diverted* only if you think the Iranian ransoms were the sole project of the Enterprise.

Gen. Secord's questioners were skeptical when he conceded that less than a third of the Iranian arms profits had actually gotten to the Contras; his interrogators suspected that the General's avarice had intervened. In fact, the General was telling the truth: it was never intended that the entire proceeds of the arms sales should go to the Contras. That would have put the Enterprise out of business when it had other projects to pursue.

The mistaken focus on the diversion removed scrutiny from profound constitutional issues, doubtless to the relief of the President's supporters. It also reflected a constitutional mistake among the President's political enemies, namely, the view that only a felony violation of the US Criminal Code could serve as the basis for an impeachment. Relying on this view, they realized that the "diversion" was probably the sole basis that would support such a charge. If the President had contrived to misappropriate US funds that properly belonged to the Treasury – by authorizing that the profits from the sale of US war materiel be sent to the Contras – then proof of that fact would serve as the predicate for his removal from office. The House majority staff conducted an investigation that appeared to be based on such erroneous assumptions. Interestingly, and with perhaps greater insight, the President's closest counselors were also willing to stake their hopes on the outcome of a contest over the President's knowledge of the diversion. They believed that the President would not have paid much attention to what was, we can now see, little more than an accounting method. They believed the President when he said he had not known of the diversion, and so, for that matter, do I. By contrast, few believed Gen. Secord when he said there was no diversion.

The impression has been left by the hearings that the Enterprise was outside of government, that its activities were largely self-serving, even corrupt. But the dramatic fact about the Enterprise is that it was very much a part of the government. Among other events, this accounted for the sickening spectacle of Mr Albert Hakim's negotiations on behalf of the United States, in which he agreed to use official American pressure to release imprisoned terrorists as part of the hostage ransom.

A Constitutional Evaluation

It is disheartening that the most serious constitutional issues were scarcely addressed in the hearings. The Congress, for its part, often seemed more interested in inserting itself into executive foreign policy decisionmaking, where it has little place, than in its own profound Article I responsibilities. And the White House, for its part, did not seem to have any idea that there was a constitutional problem with its activities. Finally, I wonder how many people in the public at large even noted the basic constitutional issue at the core of the Affair?

That issue is whether the President may direct a governmental activity – here it is covert action – that relies on non-appropriated funds. Intuitively, without confining ourselves to the rigors of the various modalities of constitutional argument, we might think that such a situation is analogous to the following hypothetical problem, familiar to state governments. The governor of a state facing a severe budget crisis finds he must propose reduced funding for a museum. Perhaps half the museum's budget is cut. But then the governor organizes his friends to rally around the museum; a charity function is held and the balance of the necessary funds is raised. It is a triumph: the museum's functions go on and the hard-pressed tax-payers do not have to pay the bill. No doubt this solution has been re-enacted with success countless times in many states. Some readers may already have grasped what is wrong with this solution when applied to the federal government, but let us proceed through a systematic analysis.

Article I provides for the lawmaking power of the United States, including the power to appropriate money for government operations. Moreover it also provides that

No money shall be drawn from the treasury, but in consequence of appropriations made by law; and a regular statement and account of the receipts and expenditures of all public money shall be published from time to time.[26]

All this relates, however, to the expenditure of public money for government operations. What about private money?

(a) Historical Argument

Article I provides the link between government operations and the democratic mandate by requiring that all funding take place by statutes, that is, by the actions of persons who can be turned out by the voters every biennium. If government operations could be funded without statutory action, then the system of representative government would be circumvented. Is that necessarily unconstitutional with regard to government operations? After all there is a substantial role played outside the institution of representative government by private charities, schools, and non-governmental operations.

If we reflect for a moment, we can see the significance of the distinction between government and non-government operations in the federal context. The framers do not appear to have believed that Americans were perfectible; nor did they believe that a democracy is composed of persons committed above everything else to being good citizens. They knew that most Americans were, and would remain, principally interested in their homes, their families, their churches and other religious institutions, their farms and businesses. Therefore the Constitution provides a crucial link between the citizens of the democracy and the actions of the government in a way that is calculated to engage the attention of a busy and preoccupied people. That link is the oversight of how their money is being spent; this, and not native virtue, was supposed to make the American people pay attention to what was being done in their name. Operations done on behalf of entities other than the federal government do not depend on this relationship, nor it on them.

To circumvent Article I by relying on non-appropriated funds, no matter how noble the purpose and no matter how beneficent the source, is to strike at the heart of this idea. This error is compounded by the solicitation of operating funds from foreign governments with whom the federal government alone has institutional – economic, security, and diplomatic – relations. In some cases, where the "donating" country is the recipient of federal assistance, the solicitations almost seem to amount to little more than kickbacks, avoiding the legislative process regarding intelligence appropriations by padding the assistance program budget.

The framers were familiar with the use of private secret agents and, for that matter, with covert action. The Continental Congress fired Tom Paine as its secretary when he leaked the news of French covert support for the American revolution; having dismissed him the Congress and the French issued statements denying such support. The same Congress dispatched a covert team to Canada, along with a priest and a printing machine, to incite an insurrection. But there is no evidence of Congress's intention that such agents could carry out government policy and mount US operations and yet be paid and supervised outside of the US government.

The Federalist Papers do not treat this exotic subject directly, but there is a relevant discussion to be found there. In Federalist no. 26, the author observed:

It has been said that the provision, which limits the appropriation of money for the support of an army to the period of two years, would be unavailing; because the executive, when once possessed of a force large enough to awe the people into submission, would find resources in that very force sufficient to enable him to dispense with supplies from the acts of the legislature.[27]

Hamilton goes on to discount this fear, reflecting the profound importance of biennial elections for maintaining control through appropriations. This would seem to underscore the centrality of the appropriations process, even in – perhaps especially in – the arena of national security.

(b) Structural Argument

This point is absolutely basic in the unique American system: in that system, the people and not the state are sovereign. Therefore the legitimacy of acts of state must ultimately come from the messy and tedious process of elections. When elections are fought, as they are all across the United States every two years, the issues divide candidates. One candidate is for Contra aid, his opponent is against. One candidate is for Gramm–Rudman, her opponent is against it, and so on. The outcome of these elections sends to Washington persons who have engaged in a dialogue with their fellow citizens. The officials thus elected are not bound by their campaign promises but they know they will have to defend their actions at the next election.

Imagine, however, that the discussions of an important issue, pro and con, were simply a sham. Imagine that some position unknown to the candidates and to the public was the real policy being pursued by the government. The entire system is thus subverted. Elections and public discourse would be simply irrelevant, although only a few would know this.

During the Iran–Contra hearings, this clear offense of secret policies was submerged in the murkier question of secret *operations*. Many indefensible things, such as the destruction of documents as a means of deceiving federal investigators, were defended on the grounds that they were necessary to secret operations. The defense that secrecy from the public was crucial to protect the hostage ransom, when in fact it merely facilitated an undeserved claim of diplomatic virtuosity, was maintained at the President's press conferences. And some voices, on the other side, were raised to deplore the very idea of secret operations in a democracy.

These claims, on either side of the issue, confuse two different things, operations and the policies they serve. Every government has secret operations and every branch within government is entitled to the integrity of its own deliberations. What the American system does not tolerate is secret policies. When Lt. Col. North claimed that documents were destroyed to protect sensitive sources, or Admiral Poindexter testified that the President's covert action "finding" had been withheld from Congress so as not to jeopardize the success of the hostage operation, they were implicitly defending secret operations; but when one comes to believe, as I have, that these persons never intended to inform the public or Congress at any time in the future of the true nature of the ransom, it becomes clear that they were really executing secret policies. And that, not the deception of the Iranians or the Russians or the Sandinistas, was the true object of their secrecy.

There is a second, important point to be made from a structural

point of view. The contingent system of appropriation and expenditure is a principal example of the relationship of enforced cooperation
that the Constitution ordains among the structures of government.
Just as the executive may sign a treaty, yet it must be ratified by
the Senate to become law, or the president may nominate a judge
who must nevertheless be confirmed in his appointment by the
Senate, so funding for government operations follows this contingent
pattern. The action of one branch of government is not sufficient in
itself to make law. The President may submit a budget; both houses
of Congress must approve it; and any congressional appropriation
must then be approved by the President or sent back to Congress
with the requirement that dispensing with the President's endorsement will necessitate a supra-majority before the bill can become
law. Such a system is emphatically not a "separation of powers" (as it
is sometimes misleadingly called),[28] nor does it follow Montesquieu's
model of functionally separated branches of government (as is sometimes mistakenly claimed).[29] Rather it partially constrains each
branch, even in what are usually taken to be the basic responsibilities
of that branch. These constraints require cooperation from the other
branches before the action of any single branch can become law and
be enforced as such. That cooperation makes the difference between
power and law. An off-budget funding mechanism might allow the
avoidance of compromise and consent with Congress. Perhaps that
was its purpose. It is scarcely compatible with the constitutional
structure.

(c) Textual Argument

Textually, the Constitution explicitly provides for the engagement
of quasi-private entities to conduct paramilitary operations; this is
the meaning of Article I, section 8, paragraph 11's language that
"the Congress shall have Power to grant letters of marque and
reprisal."[30] On the larger issue of off-budget funding, the text is also
clear: "the Congress shall have power to pay the debts and provide
for the common defense" (Article I, section 8, paragraph 1)[31] and
"No money shall be drawn from the Treasury, but in consequence
of Appropriations made by law" (Article I, section 9, paragraph
7).[32] Assuming that the President has an inherent authority to pursue
covert action operations by parties under his command as an incident

of the executive power over foreign relations, the text would appear to require that the costs of such operations be borne by appropriated funds (or, alternatively, that the Congress be solicited to grant authority to a private entity).

(d) Prudential Argument

(1)   Some critics of US diplomacy deplore on practical grounds the fact that the American system does not tolerate secret policies. They would like the United States to have the freedom of action and the scope for initiative that other great powers have. Having studied and taught the history of strategy for several years,[33] I am not insensible to the benefits of secret policies. The American system, however, will not tolerate them. A secret Molotov–Ribbentrop Pact is an impossibility for the United States because its exposure collapses public support for the government that has concealed it and has sought support for policies it was not in fact pursuing. This diplomatic resource is forgone in exchange for gains in public confidence, an indispensable requirement in the American democracy. I think American history shows this was a wise trade.

When a radical orator claims that the CIA is responsible for the AIDS virus in Africa or that Chernobyl was an American plot, we laugh. That laughter is both Americans' pride and security. A US government that pursues secret policies – like the ransoming of hostages in the very face of a debate in which it proclaimed a policy of refusing to negotiate with terrorists – undermines this confidence. The political debate is reduced to an irrelevant sideshow that can neither legitimate nor protect the government. For men who have contempt for the American political process, this may not seem like much of a sacrifice: but I suggest that is because they have never lived in a society where the public instinctively distrusts the government and the military, and where the statements of the government are simply ignored. Our constitution could not function in such a society.

(2)   Nevertheless, there may be much to be said for the Enterprise on practical grounds. Such an agency can act boldly, and with expedition. It allows the President to pursue policies he has openly disavowed, a course that all national leaders must sometimes follow when their strategies have outrun public opinion and opportunity

cannot wait. Moreover, because it re-introduces the notion of "plausible denial"[34] it is useful to protect the Presidency. It does, however, have this shortcoming: if the other organs of government are isolated from the Enterprise, then it is politically on its own, and should its projects fail, the cost to its sponsors will not be mitigated by the shared responsibilities of potential critics. Perhaps this was what President Kennedy had in mind when he remarked, after the Bay of Pigs débâcle, that "Success has many fathers; failure is an orphan."[35] Moreover, it is hard to gauge the precise costs in the long run of raising funds abroad to finance such entities. Not only is there the inevitable *quid pro quo*; precisely because the Enterprise, and not just its operations, is secret and politically vulnerable if exposed, foreign parties are possessed of an embarrassing fact with whose disclosure they can threaten the United States.

(3) "Plausible denial," which the Affair made, for a while, a common phrase, is a very old diplomatic tactic. It was the US Administration's application of the idea within the American context that was an innovation, because in so doing the Administration ignored the fundamental constitutional fact that the United States, unlike most other countries and even some other democracies, does not identify the executive with the constitutional sovereign.

When Philip II of Spain was courting Elizabeth I of England, he sent her a number of inquiries about the English privateering that was harassing the sea lanes to Spanish possessions in the New World.[36] Elizabeth denied that buccaneers like Sir Francis Drake were in league with the English Crown. The true fact is, of course, that Elizabeth knew about their activities and encouraged them; she knighted Drake on the deck of his warship. A further fact is that Philip knew that she knew. And we now know that English diplomats in Madrid informed her of this, so that she knew that he knew that she knew. And yet she continued to deny involvement and the formal political relationships between the two sovereigns continued for some time. The possible union of the Spanish and English crowns was a crucial triangulation of the relationships among England, Spain, and France, the "China card" of its day.[37]

"Plausible denial" allows states to continue their political relationships, and to cooperate in areas where they have mutual interests, while continuing to assert their security needs in areas where their interests conflict. Covert actions – because they typically violate both international law and the law of the state where they are carried out – require denial. Usually these are not paramilitary assaults like the Contra insurgency (or English buccaneering); typically they involve supporting a local newspaper in a neutral country, providing a radio transmitter to opposition elements in a hostile country, helping democratic unions to organize. Today, they often involve training and cooperation in narcotics traffic interdiction, hostage location, and counter-terrorism. These projects are not things most of us would disapprove of; nevertheless, the state engaged in the practice, in part to avoid discrediting the party it is helping, might want to deny involvement. Not to deny it would often compromise the elements the action seeks to help while forcing a confrontation with the state where the actions are carried out (often a state that has quietly solicited US action in the first place). When the American Continental Congress received covert aid from France and Spain, both these states denied this fact to England. There is nothing new about plausible denial among states.

What the Administration apparently did not accept is that the US Constitution does not make the head of state, the President, the national sovereign. For there can be no plausible denial *within* the US government, only *between* the US and foreign governments. Despite Lt. Col. North's testimony, "plausible denial" emphatically does not apply in order to permit the executive branch to deceive other branches.

The Intelligence Oversight Act recognizes the President's constitutional responsibility to protect the security of intelligence activities. It is a travesty of that statute, however, to contend that the President, by simply not signing the documents required to initiate covert action, or signing them and then having them destroyed, could evade knowledge he in fact had and thus maintain a plausible lie before the other branches.

(e) Doctrine

Doctrinally, there is not much caselaw on these subjects. This fact, however, is one of the points in favor of a modal approach, for it permits the President to consider the constitutional consequences of his acts even when court judgments are not available. (There is, to be sure, some caselaw reiterating the understanding that private gifts to the fisc can only be spent with, indeed cannot be accepted without, statutory approval.)[38]

The most important doctrinal approach, however, is not one simply applying a test from precedent, but, as we saw with *Missouri* v. *Holland*, crafting a test from precedential materials. Here the test would seem to be: is the disputed activity – the operations of the Enterprise – comparable to that of *private* charity (like a museum or a school) or to an exclusively *public* activity (like the police). To answer this, presumably, we might begin by looking at the relationship between government and the activities of the Enterprise: what precisely did its agents do? Would they claim the imprimatur of the US government? Would the officers of the Enterprise be expected to be obedient to their government contact? Would they have access to government technology and information that is denied to private citizens by law?

The President might also ask how off-budget funding would be accomplished: if it is from foreign sources, is there an implied obligation? Would the funding party expect increased foreign assistance to compensate for the money contributed to support the Enterprise, or favorable consideration to requests before the government (and thus expect a favor that only the US *government* could give). Does the Enterprise plan to be self-sustaining through black market profits that only the US government can arrange, since the profit margins depend on procurement prices at which only US government agencies can purchase? These questions would determine whether the funding being contemplated for a government operation is illicit, no matter what the legal facade.

As a footnote, *Missouri* v. *Holland* does not apply. That case does show that, in some circumstances, Article I is not the only basis for government operations. The scope of acts relying on the "Authority of the US" (as an alternative to Article I) confirmed by that case, however, is confined to treaties. Presidents may feel they embody the state; their responsibilities to protect the national security no doubt encourage this identification. But, of course, they do not. When they have acted beyond the authority granted by the sovereign, as perhaps Franklin Roosevelt did in aiding Britain in defiance of the Neutrality Act[39] or as it is sometimes claimed (wrongly) that Thomas Jefferson did in purchasing Louisiana without a Constitutional amendment,[40] they have acted *ultra vires*. As Jefferson put it:

The Executive in seizing the fugitive occurrence which so much advances the good of their country, have done an act beyond the Constitution. The Legislature in casting behind them metaphysical subtleties, and risking themselves like faithful servants, must ratify and pay for it, and throw themselves on their country for doing for them unauthorized, what we know they would have done for themselves had they been in a position to do it. It is the case of a guardian, investing the money of his ward in purchasing an adjacent territory; and saying to him when of age, I did this for your good; you may disavow me, and I must get out of the scrape as I can: I thought it my duty to risk myself for you. But we shall not be disavowed by the nation, and their act of indemnity will confirm and not weaken the Constitution, by more strongly marking out its lines.[41]

Like the brave stockbrokers who sell their clients' holdings during a market crash even without sell orders, these men bet that their choices in an emergency would ultimately be ratified. They were right. Does that mean that constitutional analysis is beside the point, since history will judge (and not the courts or the law professors)? Not at all, for to disregard a rule intentionally requires that one be aware of the rule; and this cannot but help to restrict acts beyond the law to truly dire or momentous circumstances. The verdict of history, like other truths, may be the daughter of time. FDR or Jefferson might have been impeached; it was Aaron Burr who went to prison.

(f) Ethical Argument

Roughly speaking, there are two ways Americans look at law. Law can be treated either as an obstacle, to be complied with or evaded as necessary, or as a guide to action. Neither way is superior in every context. To the businessman, who is anxious to get from point "a" to point "b," and who has a very clear idea of where "b" is located, the law is simply a set of rules that imposes certain costs on doing business. To the bureaucrat, on the other hand, law is a map, a set of directions in a contentious democracy where there are many different views of where "b" lies, or even what it is.

The officials of the Administration who testified before the Iran–Contra committees – with some notable exceptions – repeatedly emphasized that they regarded the statutes and executive orders that purportedly governed their actions in much the way a member of the private sector might regard an inconvenient part of the local building and zoning code. These were patriotic and highly intelligent men and women, committed to serving their country. But at some point they replaced their country's vision of itself, as expressed in law, with their own vision for it. In a sense, the quasi-private nature of the Enterprise was consistent with this view. Although it was created in aid of certain policies pursued by the executive, it is perfectly clear that it would not have been available to a new President with whose policies it disagreed. The Enterprise did not reflect a commitment to serve the nation's policies whatever they might be. This is a disturbing and unwelcome departure from the tradition of non-political military and intelligence services.

Perhaps this confusion between what is appropriate for the private sector and what is appropriate for government should not surprise us. It brought low a number of former senior officials of the Reagan Administration, each of whom assures us, sincerely I believe, that he continues to think he has done nothing wrong. It was perhaps inevitable that this confusion would find its way into the national security area. But let us make no mistake: this is an important confusion of fundamentals, and one that is, at bottom, based on an ignorance of the nature of the American system. Ironically, it is the socialist states that have systems of state capitalism: the business of their government is business, and vice versa. The American system proceeds according to a different arrangement.

Conclusion

These, in sum, are the considerations that a constitutionally conscientious President ought to review when deciding on whether to establish something like the Enterprise. Precisely because no court will do this the President must do so. His oath to uphold the Constitution imposes this duty. The availability of these modalities makes it possible.

When the system of third-country funding for covert action was first proposed to the National Security Planning Group on June 25, 1984,[42] the Secretary of State reported to the meeting that the White House Chief of Staff, a very able lawyer who was absent, believed that such funding constituted "an impeachable offense." Casey, the CIA Director and an extremely shrewd and experienced lawyer himself, ridiculed this conclusion and the plan went forward.

The result was a government-run operation, with decisionmaking at the highest levels of the Administration, but funded in a way that would avoid constitutional scrutiny. And, it seems, after that meeting no constitutional analysis was ever brought to bear.

But why were the constitutional dimensions of this supremely constitutional issue missed despite weeks of televised hearings? Partly this was the result of the mass of information being declassified and the unavoidable fact that many of these documents were heavily redacted. The single most important document of the Affair, a rare surviving "non-log" memo (designating that it never went into the filing system and therefore that its destruction could not be traced) reflecting a complaint from the informal board of directors of the Enterprise to Lt. Col. North and his reply, was difficult to appreciate in its redacted form, and was scarcely noticed by the press.

Partly the lawyers were to blame. By treating the hearings as if they were a trial, by looking for individual venality which was largely absent, and subordinating constitutional subjects, the lawyers reflected their practices. It was not always an edifying process. The House Counsel, it seems now generally agreed, was not equal to the tasks of examining Gen. Secord or Lt. Col. North. The Senate Counsel, a figure of real courage, was hamstrung by the division of witnesses with the House and a prudent but mistaken bargain with Lt. Col. North's lawyer to forgo a pre-hearing examination.

Partly it was the media. Relying too heavily on less complex scenarios than the facts warranted, the media naturally turned to the fascinating personalities involved. Once the diversion testimony had been given, and the last of the persons made notorious by the Affair had testified, the press's interest began to fade.

Partly it was the Congressmen. A busy Senator or Congressman does not make a good subject for the lengthy factual immersion that this case demanded. The model of a joint hearing between House and Senate committees was, as all now realize, a fiasco.

But finally, it is we the people who are responsible for this aspect of the Affair. Throughout that summer, we listened but we did not really hear. The basic constitutional structures we have labored for two centuries to preserve are so little a part of our understanding that we could watch them compromised without even noticing.

4

THE NOMINATION OF ROBERT BORK

On July 7, 1987 the Judiciary Committee of the United States Senate received the President's nomination of Judge Robert Bork to be an Associate Justice of the Supreme Court. Hearings on the nomination began on September 15, and continued until the end of the month, during which the nominee himself testified for thirty hours.[1] It is an important and by no means settled question in constitutional law what the scope of confirmation hearings should properly be. This is a constitutional question, that is, a legal question to be resolved by the methods appropriate to construing the United States Constitution, since it arises from the provision in Article II, section 2, clause 12 that "The President . . . shall nominate, and by and with the Advice and Consent of the Senate shall appoint . . . Judges of the Supreme Court . . ."[2]

Roughly the question is usually put thus. May the Senate inquire into the *political* views of the nominee (and, *a fortiori*, use this as a basis for voting on the question of confirmation) or is the judgment on the basis of which the Senate may give its consent to the appointment confined to an assessment of the nominee's abilities, probity, and, insofar as he can properly give them, his views on judicial matters? As to this last, there has developed among persons nominated for the bench a recent tradition – recent perhaps only because the practice of questioning nominees is itself quite recent[3] – of refusing to comment on matters that might come before the Court on which the nominee would sit if confirmed.[4]

The leading essay on this question, reprinted in the Judiciary Committee Report of the Bork Hearings, is Charles Black's classic

"A Note on Senatorial Consideration of Supreme Court Nominees" – "classic" not only because it has been so frequently relied upon by the Senate, but because its lucid exposition systematically proceeds through the forms of argument. Like *Missouri* v. *Holland*, there is not a sentence or phrase that is outside the classic forms.

Black begins his essay with the prudential observation that a judge's judicial work is influenced by his economic and political understanding and his sense of where justice lies in respect of the great questions of his time. If, as a practical matter, it is generally conceded that these elements are factors that in part determine the quality of a judge, the contention that they may not be considered by the Senate amounts, as a practical matter, to the view "that some things which make a good or bad judge"[5] may not be considered.

Moreover, it is generally also conceded that these are factors properly considered by the President. As a textual matter, does not the mandate to "Advise and Consent" on a subject imply a consideration of the evaluation proposed by the party seeking advice and consent? "In the normal case, he who lies under an obligation of making up his mind whether to advise and consent considers the same things that go into the decision whether to take that step."[6] By soliciting the reader's concurrence, Black makes clear that what he means by the "normal case" in construing the text, is what the words mean to a contemporary, average "man-on-the-street:" he asks, "He who *advises* gives or withholds his advice on the basis of all the relevant considerations bearing on the decision. Am I wrong about this usage?"[7]

Next Black takes up structural argument: "Is there something . . . in the whole structure . . . something unwritten, that makes it the duty of a Senator to vote for a man whose views on the great questions the Senator believes to make him dangerous as a judge?" [8] Black's reply continues in this mode. First, he considers the case of Presidential appointments to the *executive* branch. Here, as with appointments to the judiciary, there is a requirement that the Senate consent to the nomination. Black's structural analysis allows him to infer a rule supporting the customary practice of narrow and relaxed scrutiny for such nominations. His argument can be parsed this way:

1 The Constitution places certain offices within the executive branch in order to carry out the decisions of the President.
2 The relationship between the President and the persons who fill

such offices is therefore that of Chief Executive and subordinates.

3 Withholding confirmation of nominees to those offices on grounds of disagreement with their policy preferences (which must be assumed to be acceptable to the President who nominated them) interferes with this relationship: the repudiation of their Chief is made the price of confirmation.

4 It would alter the structure of constitutional government if the Senate, which belongs to another branch of government, were permitted to interfere in the relationship of subordination within the executive branch.

By contrast, the judiciary is emphatically not a subordinate agent of the Presidency and the very reasons that prevent the Senate from using the power of confirmation to insinuate itself into the executive, count against permitting the President to use his nominating function to achieve control over the judiciary.[9]

This analysis is supplemented by a second structural argument regarding the democratic legitimacy conferred by the elected branches on the appointed judiciary. Obviously that mandate is not conferred by a body that can "consent" only, nor is it conferred to a lesser degree if the scope of consideration on which that consent is based, is restricted.

Next Black considers historical arguments. He notes that there was considerable support in the Constitutional Convention for the appointment of judges by the Senate alone and reasons that, since this support was substantial, the subsequent unanimous adoption of the compromise that forms Article III (which introduces a role for the President) points to a substantial role for the Senate. Those members who would have given the exclusive responsibility for selecting judges to the Senate ought to be presumed to have compromised rather than reversed their original views. Black properly puts greater weight on Federalist nos 76 and 77, from which he quotes extensively.

Finally, Black introduces the precedents of senatorial confirmation. Of course these are not written opinions, which instance *judicial* precedent; instead these "precedents" are composed of the historical incidents of earlier nominations and the tradition, the "doctrine" as it were, that has emerged from them. Specifically, various examples of the senatorial rejection of nominees on political grounds are given.

I commend Black's short essay to anyone who wants to see the modalities of argument in action on a non-judicial matter – or who simply wishes to see a master at work. There are few in any period, of course, but if one looks across the scene of constitutional lawyers and judges of the present day, only Black can be ranked with the highest class. Although each of those great figures in the law has a distinctive *style* – by which I mean the characteristic preference for a form of argument – what distinguishes them is their reliance on the entire family of classic forms while creating new and imaginative arguments. Without form, we have mere pyrotechnics (one sees this among law professors, especially); without creativity, we have arid formalism (which one is more likely to encounter from the bench). Neither persuades because neither really fits our expectations of constitutional argument that it be organic and therefore obey the rules of its ecology even as it interacts with and modifies its environment.

The Senate's inquiry into President Reagan's nomination of Robert Bork never forthrightly addressed the issue of the proper scope of the inquiry that precedes advice and consent. To the end of a long and bitter debate, some Senators were claiming that the nominee was being rejected on "political" grounds while others appeared to manufacture bizarre interpretations of Bork's judicial work in an effort to provide "non-political" grounds to justify their condemnation of the nominee. None of this was necessary if the Senate – and the public, and the media that instruct them both – were competent to resolve such questions on a constitutional basis. In fact, the answers were rather simple, and the participants knew these answers, even if they did not always know that they knew them. Moreover, having determined the scope of review, the hearings provided ample evidence – if properly analyzed – to determine the outcome of that review. All that was required, as I will endeavor to show, was an attentiveness to the forms of constitutional argument. Instead, the public was given a rather monstrous caricature of an able public servant, a man who – even if, as I shall argue, one who did not really know himself in constitutional terms – would scarcely be recognized in the ugly disfigurement to which he was subjected.

The important point is that, under the Constitution, Congress has the legal responsibility to interpret the Constitution along legal lines.

Misunderstanding of the nature of this congressional responsibility is common, even among the Representatives. During debates in the First Congress over the President's power to remove unilaterally officers appointed with the advice and consent of the Senate, James Madison was shocked by the suggestion that congressional interpretation of the Constitution was somehow improper:

It has been said by one gentleman, that it would be officious in this branch of the Legislature to expound the constitution, so far as it relates to the division of power between the President and Senate; it is incontrovertibly of as much importance to this branch of the Government as to any other, that the Constitution should be preserved entire. It is our duty, so far as it depends upon us, to take care that the powers of the constitution be preserved entire to every department of Government; the breach of the constitution in one point, will facilitate the breach in another; a breach in this point may destroy the equilibrium by which the House retains its consequence and share of power; therefore we are not chargeable with an officious interference.[10]

Early on in the hearings, the nominee was asked by a friendly Senator:

I am wondering if I can hear your view on what Article II, section 3 means? [This is the provision in the Constitution that calls for the advice and consent of the Senate to Presidential appointments to the federal courts.]

The nominee replied:

I think to begin with the obvious meaning is that you can judge a candidate's intelligence, temperament, integrity, and so forth, and relevant background. I think it is also clear that you can judge a candidate's judicial philosophy.[11]

The Senator pressed, offering the nominee an opportunity to argue that the field of inquiry should be narrowed to exclude political considerations:

Is it significant that the framers inserted a two-thirds approval requirement for advice and consent on treaties proposed by the President but made no such vote requirement for Executive appointments? . . . [and then, as if Bork had not quite grasped the implication of the question] How deferential do you believe the framers intended the Senate to be toward executive appointments?[12]

But Bork declined the opportunity:

I wish I could say that I thought it was extremely deferential, but I have no idea how deferential they meant it to be.[13]

Indeed, the nominee gave the constitutional answer that I judge to be correct even though he must have known that it might provide the basis for his rejection:

I think given the nature of the structure of the nominating process and the confirmation process and the structure of the bodies involved, the Senate should assure itself that the candidate's judicial philosophy is a respectable one and one that is allowable on the bench in the United States.[14]

"Judicial philosophy," in its broadest sense, is what the Senate had to consider. But how might this be determined? What questions would elicit it, and how might one evaluate the answers?

Judge Bork was a man who believed, and of whom it was believed, that he possessed a rather clear idea of his judicial philosophy regarding the Constitution. In modal terms, he was a "strict constructionist" – that is, one who relies solely on the historical, textual, and structural methods of construing the Constitution. Yet he quickly let the litany of "history, text, and structure" drop when the hearings began and portrayed himself instead as one committed to a single modality of argument, the historical approach. Thus in his Opening Statement, he said:

I want to make a few remarks at the outset on the subject of central interest. That is, my understanding of how a judge should go about his or her work. That may also be described as my philosophy of the role of a judge in a constitutional democracy. The judge's authority derives entirely from the fact that he is applying the law and not his personal values. . . . How should a judge go about finding the law? The only legitimate way, in my opinion, is by attempting to discern what those who made the law intended. The intentions of the lawmakers [of the Constitution . . .] are those [of the persons] who ratified our Constitution and its various amendments.[15]

The judge's responsibility is to discern how the framers' values, defined in the context of the world they knew, apply in the world we know.

If a judge abandons intention as his guide, there is no law available to him and he . . . goes beyond his legitimate power.[16]

He concluded by saying, "I am quite willing to discuss with you my judicial philosophy and the approach I take to deciding cases."[17]

For Bork, as for us, his *approach* to judgment was a matter of using the available modalities. At first, committee members refused to see this point. The Senators who were disposed against the nomination repeatedly tried to get the nominee to say that he would overrule popular decisions whose opinions he was on record as criticizing. Doggedly, Bork refused to do this, saying only that he would not endorse the particular mode of argument used in the case. For example, note this exchange between the committee's chairman, Senator Biden, and the nominee:

Senator Let's talk about the *Griswold* case . . . The Court said [in that case] that the law [which prohibited the use of contraceptive devices] violated a married couple's constitutional right to privacy. You criticized this opinion in numerous articles and speeches, beginning in 1971 and as recently as July 26th of this year . . .
Bork I will straighten it out. I was objecting to the *way* Justice Douglas, in that opinion, derived this right. It may be possible to derive an objection to an anti-contraceptive statute in some other way. I do not know. But starting from the assumption . . . that there is nothing in the Constitution, in *any legitimate method of constitutional reasoning* about either subject, all I am saying is that the judge has no way to prefer one [outcome] to the other . . .[18]

and later:

Senator Well, that is my point: so [the right to use contraception] is not a constitutional right. I am not trying to be picky here . . . I do not want to get into a debate with a professor, but it seems to me that what you are saying is what I said . . . no such right exists.
Bork No, Senator, that is what I tried to clarify. I argued that the way in which this . . . right of privacy that Justice Douglas elaborated, that the *way* he did it did not prove its existence.[19]

and later still, wearily:

Bork All I have done was point out that the right of privacy, as defined or undefined by Justice Douglas, was a free-floating right that was not derived in a principled fashion from constitutional materials. That is all I have done.[20]

But the Chairman did not see the point. He persisted:

Senator Judge, I agree with the rationale offered in the case. Let me just read it to you . . . I happen to agree with it. It said, in part, "would we allow the police to search the sacred precincts of marital bedrooms for telltale signs of contraceptives? The very idea is repulsive to the notions of privacy surrounding the marriage relationship. We deal with the right of privacy older than the Bill of Rights. Marriage is a coming together for better or worse, hopefully enduring, and intimate to the degree of being sacred. The association promotes a way of life, no causes. A harmony of living, not political face. A bilateral loyalty, not a commercial or social project."
Bork I could agree with . . . every word you read but that is not . . . the rationale of the case. That is the rhetoric at the end of the case. What I objected to was the way in which this right of privacy was created.[21]
Senator As I hear you, you do not believe that there is a general right of privacy that is in the Constitution.
Bork Not one derived in *that* fashion.[22]

This early questioning, which seems so obtuse,[23] did nevertheless have a positive effect. Both the nominee's partisans and his opponents, eventually took his "judicial philosophy" to be the *way* in which he would decide cases, not the outcome of that process. The nominee and Senators further agreed that the basis on which he would decide constitutional cases was historical argument.

This clearly emerges both from the testimony and from the highly selective Summary compiled and published before the entire report was released. As we will see, this characterization was to some extent misleading, but both the nominee and his attackers collaborated in such a portrayal. Thus this exchange:

Senator Could you give me again, then, your general approach to the problem of applying the . . . Constitution to problems that the founders could not have foreseen?
Bork I think, Senator, one way of putting that is that you look at the founders and the ratifiers, and you look at the text of the Constitution, their words, what it was that was troubling them at the time, why they

did this, and you look at the Federalist Papers and the Anti-Federalist Papers and so forth and so on, to get what the public understanding of the time was, of what the evil was they wished to avert, what the freedom was they wished to protect. And once you have that, that is your major premise; and then the judge has to supply the minor premise to make sure to ask whether that value, that freedom, is being threatened by some new development in the law or in society or in technology today. And then he makes the old freedom effective today in the new circumstances.[24]

This is the historical approach – notice the distinction between this form and textual argument, and the important reliance placed on the ratifiers, the "public understanding" – expressed in a clear and straightforward statement. The logic of this approach, like that of the other forms of argument, asserts a claim to legitimacy; indeed when transformed into an ideology, this form asserts its sole claim to legitimacy ("the only thing a judge has to prove to the public is that what he does in this case, and why this person loses, and why the rule is as it is, is a legitimate rule and a legitimate result.")[25] Historical argument has a rule for cases in which the intentions of the ratifiers are unclear, as is often – though in my view quite erroneously[26] – thought to be the case with the Ninth Amendment. But this is a solution to a problem that the approach itself creates. In the following exchanges we learn nothing about the Ninth Amendment; rather the nominee clearly establishes his allegiance to a single form of argument by professing no resources outside that form to enable him to construe the amendment in question:

Senator Thurmond What do you believe the Ninth Amendment means?
Bork That is an extremely difficult question, Senator, because nobody has ever to my knowledge understood precisely what the Ninth Amendment did mean and what it was intended to do.[27]

and the next day:

Senator DeConcini You said . . . relating to . . . the Ninth Amendment, its application . . . that nobody really knows what that amendment means. Is that correct?
Bork I do not know. I know of only one historical piece . . . If anybody shows me historical evidence about what they meant, I would be delighted to [apply] it. I just do not know.[28]

By contrast, in a textual mode *every* text has meaning since its proper construction is available by consulting contemporary audiences. Historical argument, however, can cope – as the textualist sometimes cannot – with changing socio-political facts. Consider whether the Congress can make regulations for the Air Force (the text provides only for regulations of the Army and Navy). The partisan of intention (historical argument) would reply that the very clause that ensnares a textual approach (by providing *only* for an Army and a Navy) frees us for the conclusion that the framers and ratifiers intended to provide for armed forces, whatever their precise organization or weaponry. If we may resort to the purposes of the text, we cease to be narrowly bound by the text's specific provisions since these are only examples of what the ratifiers had in mind. Indeed there are well-established doctrines within this approach to handle cases that could not have been foreseen by the framers. Earlier, we considered whether wiretapping, unknown at the time of the ratification of the Fourth Amendment, requires the state to comply with the search and seizure provisions of that amendment. Judge Bork testified that one only had to reflect on the *purpose* of the Amendment to conclude that wiretapping clearly came within its ambit.[29] This is a standard move within this approach.

In a similar vein, consider this colloquy: Bork has just been asked to justify the holding in *Brown* v. *Board of Education*, which struck down segregation in education on the basis of an amendment whose ratifiers did not appear to be greatly hostile to segregated institutions.

Senator Thurmond   [once an ardent segregationist, but now the representative of a significantly black constituency] Judge Bork, does this conflict with your views on how the constitutional law should read?
Bork   No, I do not think it does, Senator . . . [L]et me proceed on the assumption that [segregation] was intended by those who framed the 14th amendment. The rule they wrote was no individual shall be denied the equal protection of the law. They may have written that rule on the assumption – a background assumption– that you could get equal protection or equality with separation or segregation. If they did, then by 1954 it had become abundantly clear that the background assumption was false. You cannot get equality with segregation. At that point the Court is faced with a choice: Does it enforce the rule – equal protection – or enforce the background assumption that the framers and ratifiers made? I think it is clear that you have to enforce the rule, the background assumption being false . . . and it leads to *Brown* v. *Board of Education*.[30]

This, as I say, is a standard part of the middle game of historical approaches. Because such approaches ask us to focus on the intentions of the ratifiers, we must decide to what extent changed circumstances may require outcomes that were not originally contemplated.

Another characteristic of the judicial philosophy of original intent that also follows from the general approach is its disavowal of precedent. For the same reason that we would overrule *Plessy* v. *Ferguson*[31] (that upheld racial segregation despite the equal protection clause) once we discovered that social conditions rendered that holding inconsistent with the intentions of the ratifiers of the Fourteenth Amendment, so we are compelled to overrule other precedents when we discover that they have lost or are otherwise without historical endorsement. Judge Bork had put this succinctly in the following passage:

> [T]he role of precedent in constitutional law is less important than it is in a proper common law or statutory model . . . So if a constitutional judge comes to a firm conviction that the courts have misunderstood the intentions of the founders, he is freer than when acting in his capacity as an interpreter of the common law or of a statute to overturn a precedent . . . [A]n originalist judge would have no problem whatever in overruling a non-originalist precedent, because that precedent by the very basis of his judicial philosophy, has no legitimacy.[32]

This proved to be a crucial issue in the hearings. Whatever their command of the constitutional modalities, the Senators realized the political significance of such a statement. It meant that decisions like *Roe* v. *Wade* (the abortion case), *Reynolds* v. *Sims* (the re-districting opinion that mandated one-man-one-vote), *Shelley* v. *Kraemer* (outlawing racially restrictive real estate covenants), even *Brown* itself – all of which the nominee had criticized at one time or another – could be overturned even if the nominee was careful not to say he would do so. Bork's implicit demand that such holdings be re-examined for legitimate support was enough to cause an avalanche of public disapproval. His opponents concentrated on this point and Judge Bork did not disappoint them.

Senator Kennedy Judge Bork, in the *Reynolds* v. *Sims* case back in 1964, the Supreme Court held that the Constitution requires [a] one man, one vote standard so that each legislative district contains roughly equal population. Is it not true that in 1968 you wrote in Fortune Magazine, and I quote: "On no reputable theory of constitutional adjudication was there an excuse for the doctrine it imposed?"

Bork   I think, Senator, I not only wrote that, I still think I was right.[33]

Later Senator Kennedy played the tape of an address by Bork to the Federalist Society in 1985 in which this exchange had occurred:

Question   Now, the relationship between the judge, the text and precedent, what do you do about precedent?
Mr Bork   I don't think that in the field of constitutional law, precedent is all that important . . . [I]f you become convinced that a prior court has misread the Constitution, I think it's your duty to go back and correct it. Moreover, you will from time to time get willful courts who take an area of law and create precedents that have nothing to do with the name of the Constitution. And if a new court comes in and says, "Well, I respect precedent," what you have is a ratchet effect, with the Constitution getting further and further and further away from its original meaning because some judges feel free to make up new constitutional law and other judges in the name of judicial restraint follow precedent. I don't think precedent is all that important. I think the importance is what the framers were driving at, and to go back to that.[34]

Correcting for the relaxed atmosphere of an after-dinner talk, this is a rather standard view of historical argument as ideology, that is, not as merely a technique for deciding cases, but *the* technique that alone is justifiable. Embedded in this answer are criticisms of the legitimacy of other approaches.

This apparent attitude toward precedent was to prove decisive. Organized opposition to the nomination materialized among Senator Heflin's black Alabama constituents who had been silent during the Rehnquist nomination; among Senator Specter's female constituents, who did not mobilize when Justice Scalia – reportedly a more rigid anti-abortionist than Bork – was examined. Losing the swing votes on the Committee tended to firm up opposition among those the White House did not hope to win over but hoped would take a low profile in the debate. Eventually the battle to confirm Bork became a rout. The Summary Report to the Senate floor condensed Bork's statement to simply:

I don't think precedent is all that important. I think the importance is what the framers were driving at, and to go back to that.[35]

So, in the end, the Senate rejected the nominee because it rejected the judicial philosophy of constitutional intentionalism with which

Judge Bork had associated himself. But was this really Bork's view? Consider this somewhat more complex exchange over *Roe* v. *Wade*:

Bork That's what I object to about the case. It does not have legal reasoning in it that roots the right to an abortion in constitutional materials.
Senator Hatch . . . I presume that your concerns about the reasoning of the . . . case do not necessarily mean that you would automatically reverse that case as a Justice of the Supreme Court?
Bork No [meaning, in context, that he would not necessarily reverse]. If that case, or something like it, came up and if the case called for [a complete reconsideration of the precedent] which it may not, I would first ask the lawyer . . . "Can you derive a right of privacy, [even if] not to be found in one of the specific amendments, in some principled fashion from the Constitution so I know not only where you got it but what it covers?" There are rights that are not specifically mentioned in the Constitution, like the right to travel. . . . [I]t's conceivable he could do that, I don't know. If he could not do that I would say, "Well, if you can't derive a general right of privacy, can you derive a right to an abortion, or at least to a limitation upon anti-abortion statutes legitimately from the Constitution?" If after argument that didn't sound like it was going to be a viable theory, I would say to him, "I would like you to argue whether this is the kind of case that should not be overruled." Because, obviously, there are cases we look back on and say they were erroneous or they were not compatible with original intent, but we don't overrule them for a variety of reasons.[36]

Although the excerpts in the Senate Committee Summary – which does not contain the passage just quoted – are revealing of what the Committee took to be Judge Bork's judicial philosophy, I believe a better reading of his entire testimony reveals a rather different figure, jurisprudentially, than the intransigent originalist Bork often depicted himself as (particularly, it seems, after dinner). As I have categorized the modalities, I think it can be clearly shown that Bork, like his friend and mentor Alexander Bickel, is essentially a prudentialist and that, also like Bickel, he shrinks somewhat from the recognition of this fact.

Let us return to that speech before the Federalist Society, used with such effect by Senator Kennedy, and quoted in the conclusion of the Committee's deliberations as support for their negative recommendation to the full Senate. When asked about it, Bork replied:

If you look at the next paragraph of that talk, which was the written out part and not the extemporized part, it contradicts that statement. The very next paragraph states that the enormous expansion of the commerce power . . . is settled and it is simply too late to go back and reconsider that, even though it appears to be much broader than the framers or ratifiers intended . . .[T]his Nation has grown in ways that do not comport with the intentions of the people who wrote the Constitution – the commerce clause is one example – and it is simply too late to go back and tear that up. I [also] cite to you the *Legal Tender Cases*. These are extreme examples admittedly. Scholarship suggests that the framers intended to prohibit paper money. Any judge who today thought he would go back to the original intent really ought to be accompanied by a guardian rather than be sitting on the bench.[37]

Why is that? What difference does it make that the Supreme Court has been in error for a long time, rather than for a short time? Bork testified:

I suppose the passage of time by itself is not important. The only reason it is important is that if expectations and institutions and laws and so forth have grown up around the decision in that passage of time. That certainly weighs in favor of not overruling the decision. In a very short period of time, obviously, things are unlikely to have occurred.[38]

This, at first blush, would only seem to get the nominee in deeper waters, at least as regards *Brown*. For he was forced to concede that, "*Plessey* v. *Ferguson*, which allowed segregation, was 58 years old when it was overruled, and a lot of customs and institutions had grown up around segregation,"[39] and his effort to extricate himself by saying, "I guess *Plessy* was a sharply divided court . . . I would think a sharp division in the Court would lessen the weight of the precedent,"[40] was in fact erroneous.[41] But the important thing to notice is that none of these factors has anything to do with originalism.

Whether a precedent was decided by a unanimous or divided court, whether or not it has been on the books for a century or a few months, whether institutions and practices (like segregation) have grown up in reliance on it – none of these facts has anything to do with fulfilling the intentions of the ratifiers of the Constitution. When asked for his "philosophy" of precedent, Bork answered: "It is a complex question . . . and I do not know that I have a philosophy.

I know that I do not. I know the *factors* I would consider, some of them."[42]

This refusal to be doctrinaire is the beginning of wisdom, a prudentialist would argue. Indeed Bickel made precisely this argument: "The accomplished fact, affairs and interests that have formed around it, and perhaps popular acceptance of it – these are elements . . .that may properly enter into a decision . . ."[43]

This is a lucid statement of the prudential point of view in constitutional law: I have quoted it earlier in the description of this modality in Book I. Once one is sensitive to its peculiar resonance, one can hear it again and again in Judge Bork's testimony:

Bork I will be glad to discuss my general approach to *stare decisis* and the kinds of factors I would consider . . . It has to be in the first place clear that the prior decision was erroneous. I mean, not just shaky but really wrong in terms of constitutional theory . . . But that is not sufficient to overrule. I have discussed these factors before . . . For example, the development of private expectations on the part of the citizenry . . . The growth of institutions, governmental institutions, private institutions around a ruling . . . The need for continuity and stability in the law . . . The need for predictability in legal doctrine. I think the preservation of confidence in the Court by not saying that this crowd just does whatever they feel like as the personnel changes . . . [citing Brandeis, Bork says it] is a very fact-based consideration, a very particularistic consideration about whether this is the kind of case that goes one way or the other.[44]

This was never really appreciated by some Senators, an ironic fact in light of the usual assumption that prudentialism is the only modality of constitutional interpretation to which Congress has consistent recourse. Senator DeConcini appeared mystified when, in response to questions about *Finzer* v. *Barry* (the constitutionality of a statute limiting demonstrations outside foreign embassies), Judge Bork cited a letter by President Fillmore written in 1851, an article on the law of nations in 1863, and an incident in Philadelphia in 1902 in which a foreign flag was burned – all data originating from well after the adoption of the First Amendment.

Senator DeConcini How would you respond to the statement, when you [say you] are a strict constructionist, [that you] believe in the original intent . . . how do you rationalize this long historical basis for your decision that seems to go far away from the original intent?

To this Judge Bork quite plausibily replied that he was attempting to show that the provisions he was upholding had been ratified by long practice.[45] The nominee then cited to the Committee a prudential passage in *McCulloch*[46] – perhaps better known to Constitutional law scholars than to the Committee or even to a busy federal appeals judge – in which Chief Justice Marshall, called upon to determine the constitutionality of the Bank of the United States, had written that, even if the Bank were unconstitutional he would hesitate to strike down an institution around which important interests had grown up and on which they relied. Again and again Bork testified, "[T]o say that the reasoning of any case seems not adequate is not to say you want to overrule it."[47] Although he conceded having criticized the rationale in *Bolling* v. *Sharpe*, which "invented," if you like, an equal protection component in due process to resolve the anomaly of striking down segregation in the states while permitting it to continue in the District of Columbia, he denied any suggestion of overruling it: "Oh, that is absolutely preposterous . . . You know, all kinds of expectations and institutions have grown up around [the decision]."[48]

But this was difficult for the Senators to accept since they had, with his complicity it must be said, typecast him in another mode.

Senator Specter   But, Judge Bork, if you accept that, you're totally away from original intent.
Bork   What I am trying to say is that there is a settled line of Supreme Court precedent running back at least 90 years.
Senator Specter   No doubt about that. And the Court, in doing that, has departed totally from the original intent of the framers and ratifiers.[49] . . . I'm not objecting to that interpretation. But what I'm trying to do is square that with your very forceful statement that you are going to carry out original intent.[50]

This had the effect of confusing the judge's supporters who now had to answer charges that the nominee was tailoring his opinions to win appointment.

Senator Thurmond   [Y]ou have criticized certain . . . decisions, [but] you have also indicated that some of these decisions are accepted law, and should not be disturbed by the Supreme Court. This has been taken by some as change in your views, in order to enhance the probability of your confirmation. I do not believe this is the case. However, would you comment on this criticism?

Bork From the beginning of these hearings, Senator, I have said that . . . the ultimate touchstone for a judge . . .in constitutional law . . . is the original understanding; that means what the ratifiers understood when they ratified the Constitution. But I have also said that the law has developed, and the nation has developed, and decisions have been made around which too much has been built, and around which too many expectations have clustered, for them to be overruled . . .The commerce clause cases cannot be overruled. You cannot cut the commerce clause back . . . The equal protection cases cannot be overruled . . . I have mentioned some first amendment cases that cannot be overruled. I have mentioned a lot of cases that I think are now part of our law, and whatever theoretical challenges might be levelled at them, it is simply too late . . . for a judge to overrule them . . .Incorporation doctrine [by which the Bill of Rights is applied to the States, the source for the principal due process decisions of the Warren Court] I mentioned . . . is also something that is now thoroughly established.[51]

In this reply we can see that Judge Bork believes that his theory of precedent – a prudential one – is supplementary to his axiom of interpretation – a historical, originalist approach. He is mistaken, however, because determining which questions will be settled by reference to history necessarily governs the results of an historical inquiry, whatever they may be. This is concealed – perhaps the judge, in his desire for firm ground, has even concealed it from himself – by the sequence in which he describes his decisionmaking. He repeatedly says that the historical inquiry comes first, then the prudential assessment. ("What would I look at? Well, I think I would look and be absolutely sure that the prior decision was incorrectly decided. That is necessary. And if it is wrongly decided – and you have to give respect to your predecessors' judgment on these matters – the presumption against overruling remains, because it may be that there are private expectations built up on the basis of the prior decision. It may be that governmental and private institutions have grown up around that prior decision. There is a need for stability and continuity in the law. There is a need for predictability in legal doctrine. And it is important that the law not be considered as shifting every time the personnel of the Supreme Court changes.")[52] But whatever the reconstruction of one's thoughts, as a matter of legal argument it ought to be absolutely clear that the remark just quoted is a summary of prudential considerations and that, by governing the scope of the historical inquiry – and not the other way around – it is the prudential decision that is determining the modality of the decision. If a realistic assessment of practical, political affairs – including even the public perception of the court's politicization – leads one to conclude that, whatever the historical inquiry reveals, the state of the caselaw will remain undisturbed, then, as a matter of argument, it is as if the historical inquiry were never made. Legal argument drives legal opinions. Whatever the sequence, if prudential factors are decisive then the initial historical inquiry has become mere antiquarianism.

It is moving and yet ironic that Alexander Bickel faced a deeply similar intellectual and moral dilemma, because the figure of Bickel haunts the pages of Bork's testimony. The nominee refers to his dead friend fourteen times, as compared with eleven references to Holmes, and ten to Marshall and ten to Story or Brandeis. For Bickel, prudential argument was a device to protect and enable principled, doctrinal decisions. A refugee from Naziism, he was acutely sensitive to the fragility of democratic institutions that other Americans were inclined to take for granted. Bickel thought that by prudently avoiding some controversies and by handling others in subtle, indirect ways, the Court could preserve its independence and stature for those important cases that should be decided on their merits alone. Determining which cases deserved this treatment was first a matter of prudence: an anti-miscegenation statute, which Bickel surely found as repulsive as the lawyers against the state in the wonderfully styled *Loving* v. *Virginia*, ought none the less to be put off for decision, for example, rather than be taken up in the same term as school desegregation, thus intensifying political reaction. Numerous other examples are given in his ingenious and elegant essay "The Passive Virtues",[53] which details the strategems, and illustrates the finesse, required to handle the constant threats to the Court's political position, threats that come as invitations to decide. Worldly and shrewd, he sought to protect the institution of judicial review for its ethereal labors of doctrinalism. No one admired the Anglo-American tradition of deciding appeals according to precedent more than Bickel; that is why he tried to protect its institutions. So Bickel was stung when, with the publication of the essay, in his second book, it was sharply criticized by Gerald Gunther, a distinguished exponent of the doctrinal approach in constitutional law. Bickel, Gunther wrote in a telling and brilliant phrase, demanded "100% principle, 20% of the time." Gunther correctly saw that Bickel's approach "would endorse conjecture about the complexities of political reactions as a primary ingredient of court deliberations," and he rejected it as intolerable. "Doctrinal integrity must be more than a sometime goal [if] devotion to principled adjudication is [to be] taken seriously."[54]

Of Bork it might be said "he insists on 100% original understanding, 20% of the time."[55] Referring to his search for a general constitutional principle that would rationalize legitimate government coercion, Bork testified:

I think that was wrong because I do not think any general principle is available. I now take what I would call – at least what Bickel described as – the Edmund Burke approach, which is you look at each measure – this is a political matter, not a judicial matter – you look at each measure and ask whether it will do more good than harm.[56]

Bork's prudentialism is not identical with Bickel's, to be sure. Bickel sought to protect the Anglo-American tradition of doctrinalism by "supplementing" it with prudence. It is doctrinalism, however – the application of the common law method of analogical reasoning – that has brought about the very precedents that disgust Bork ("the Constitution getting further and further and further away from its original meaning").[57] Doctrine, *per se*, and the doctrinal method have no call on his allegiance. This is made clear in the following exchange:

Senator Heflin But subject to the kind of prudential restraint where people have relied on precedents, a body of legal doctrine, your views would be that a Justice is entitled as part of his responsibility to re-examine constitutional questions *de novo*.
Bork I would think that is true of a judge . . . After all, there are a lot of considerations that go into it. But at the bottom, a judge's basic obligation or basic duty is to the Constitution, not simply the precedent [citing, interestingly, Brandeis and Douglas, two influential prudentialist judges].[58]

In American constitutional jurisprudence, prudential argument initially turned attention on the relative institutional capacities of courts. On that basis Brandeis endowed the policy of judicial self-restraint in *Ashwander*,[59] a policy that Frankfurter pursued when he took up Brandeis's seat on the Court.[60] An assessment of the particular capabilities of the judiciary is also the usual prudential basis for legitimating practice of judicial review. That argument, Bork once wrote,

is one of relative institutional capacities; courts are simply better than legislatures in dealing with principles of long-run importance as opposed to immediate problems. Alexander Bickel said: ["C]ourts have certain capacities for dealing with matters of principle that legislatures and executives do not possess. Judges have, or should have, the leisure, the training, and the insulation to follow the ways of the scholar in pursuing the ends of government." Professors, apparently, have very romantic notions about judges' lives. But were we to assume that courts have superior capacities for dealing with matters of principle, it does not follow that courts have the right to impose more principle upon us than our elected representatives give us . . . Courts have no mandate to impose a different mix merely because they would arrive at a tradeoff that weighed principle more heavily.[61]

It is plain from this passage that Bork is not intoxicated, as was his friend, with the "thrilling tradition of Anglo-American law" – a phrase of Henry Hart's that Bickel was fond of quoting. For his part, we can only speculate what mordant sarcasm Bickel would have reserved for the "philosophy" of originalism. In its way, it is no different from the libertarianism he confronted in his younger, Midwestern friend fresh from Chicago, for it too represents a yearning to escape from mere politics to a decisive world of rules. For the libertarian, difficult social decisions are resolved, as for the micro-economist, by allocating them to the market (including the political market, the legislative process). For the originalist, they are allocated to the framers and ratifiers. In either case, the decisions of these groups are endowed with an axiomatic correctness that does not open up the confusing and relativistic issues of the merits.

Bickel taught Bork that politics could not be ignored in constitutional interpretation. It must have been an interesting seminar, that first year: the dapper, urban Jew exiled from Mittel Europa, with English shirts and a clipped New Yorker's accent, cynical and sentimental, one quick step ahead of the awkward, earnest, perpetually disheveled ex-Marine who had left a thriving law practice to pursue the life of the mind. One can scarcely imagine Bickel, who coveted appointment to the Court, replying that he wished to sit on that bench because it promised an "intellectual feast." He was too worldly, too vain perhaps, to say anything so ingenuous. If Bickel taught Bork, as Bork testified, to accept the political dimension of law, he did not apparently persuade him that there was no avoiding this fact by resort to the bright-line rules of a jurisprudential ideology. It is hard to imagine, whatever mutual affection may have obtained between these two men, that Bickel could ever endorse the remorseless attack on our civil institutions that Bork has waged in the name of an approach – originalism – that Bickel regarded as absurdly naive.[62]

It has been shown that Judge Bork is no doctrinalist. It is even easier to demonstrate that he rejects ethical argument as a legitimate approach. Consider the case of *Franz* v. *United States*, which dogged the nominee throughout the hearings. A majority for the District of Columbia Circuit Court, on which the judge then sat, had found that the privacy decisions of the Supreme Court implied some constitutional protection for the right of a divorced, non-custodial father to maintain visitation rights with his child. An ethical argument would derive such a right from the principle that government (state or federal) has no mission to coerce the permanent separation of family members. The case would turn on whether Franz, in fact, faced such a coerced separation. I think it is fair to say that ethical arguments, such as these, are the sort of thing that revolts Judge Bork.

The unenumerated rights of ethical approaches are generated by inferences from the limits of the enumerated powers. When a particular means is inappropriate to any federal power, its demarcation beyond such power also marks it off as a norm of federal human rights. One reason we cannot coerce persons into donating body organs, while we can induce them to do so with payments, is that the former (but not the latter) means is not necessary and proper to any enumerated end. For the same reason we can draft persons for the Army, but we cannot draft them for the Peace Corps or VISTA (the poverty program). One has an inferred right not to be drafted into non-military service because the Constitution limits the coercive power of regulation to provision for the armed services; one has an inferred right to refuse to donate organs at death on analogous grounds, i.e., that the federal government is limited to spending to provide for the general welfare when it casts about for a power to secure donated organs. This sort of rationale generates rights against the states by assuming that federal human rights norms were imposed upon the states by the Civil War amendments (which thus qualify the otherwise plenary nature of state power). For most cases, we can say that the means forbidden the federal government are also forbidden the states.

By contrast, Bork would employ a minimum rationality test (usually confined to assessments of economic regulation) to resolve the problems raised by the uneradicable, but vexingly unenumerated, human rights of the Constitution. A rationality test asks only whether a permissible legislative purpose can be hypothesized for a particular law: is the law, that is, plausibly related (as a *means* is related to an *end*) to a non-prohibited goal of government? This treatment of the problem of enforcing unspecified rights is incompatible with an ethical approach to the same problem, at least as regards state law. Whereas an ethical argument depends on the limits of permissible powers (from which it proceeds to infer rights), the traditional rationality test accepts no limits on state power except the enumerated prohibitions. Let me give an example.

Williamson v. *Lee Optical* is the foundation case for minimum rationality review. In *Williamson*, an Oklahoma statute was challenged that exclusively licensed ophthalmologists and optometrists to fit eyeglasses. The Oklahoma legislature would have been hard pressed to prove that such restrictions, while of enormous benefit to ophthalmologists and optometrists, conferred any health benefit along with the substantial cost they placed on the consumer. The doctrine of *Williamson*, however, does not impose such an inquiry on the state. Under *Williamson* it is enough to show that the legislature could have rationally believed there would be some benefit resulting from the regulation and that that benefit is not forbidden by a specific constitutional prohibition. In the absence of such a prohibition– and that absence is all that is meant by *unenumerated* rights – there is no limit on the power of the state and thus this approach forfeits any restraining power. For what statute is not related to some benign purpose, however attenuatedly? The ethical approach, on the other hand, achieves its restraining force by inferring limits on state power beyond those imposed by the explicit prohibitions of the Constitution. Without such limits a rationality test cannot give us unenumerated rights; or, to put it differently, once we accept the plenary nature of state power (which is the basis for *Williamson*'s rule for economic regulation cases), an ethical approach is emasculated. Judge Bork's hostility to such approaches is well known.

What does not appear so obvious, indeed what would perhaps surprise Judge Bork himself, is that he is no "strict constructionist" either – if by that one means confining oneself to historical, textual, and structural modalities. Consider these exchanges with Senator DeConcini, a textualist, a non-lawyer (as is often the case with partisans of this mode), and one for whom the words of the Constitution have a contemporary, not a recondite, meaning.[63]

Senator You said . . . that nobody really knows what [the Ninth] Amendment means. Is that correct?
Bork I do not know. I know of only one historical piece . . .
Senator [The words say] "Enumeration in the Constitution of certain rights shall not be construed to deny or disparage others retained by the People."
Bork Senator, if anybody shows me historical evidence about what they meant, I would be delighted to [apply] it. I just do not know . . . I do not think you can use the Ninth Amendment unless you know something of what it means. For example, if you had an amendment that says "Congress shall make no" and then there is an ink blot and you cannot read the rest of it and that is the only copy you have, I do not think the Court can make up what might be under the ink blot . . .[64]

These are hardly the words of a textualist. One does not revere the printed text and what it means to contemporary persons if a lack of historical evidence renders its words "an inkblot." Nor is Judge Bork truly a structuralist, either, as is reflected in his view that the relationships mandated by the Constitution should be interpreted "to allow room for the evolution of the power of various offices and branches, [and] that the Constitution's specification of these powers was made somewhat vague. The framers contemplated organic development, not a structure made rigid at the outset by rapid, judicial definition of the entire subject as if from a blueprint."[65] One need only contrast this with the views of a structuralist such as Chief Justice Rehnquist to see that arguing from such a perspective one *does* reason as if from a blueprint.[66] Bork's description is that of a prudentialist interpreting the structure in what, he hopes, will be an efficacious way.

Judiciary Committee appears to have rejected Robert Bork's nomination on the basis of an erroneous assessment of his judicial philosophy. He was not, in fact, a rigid originalist who wished to purify the caselaw of the Constitution by purging those decisions that cannot be justified by an appeal to the original understanding of the provisions on which these decisions are allegedly based. Some of the charges made against him will sound, some day, like pretty wild demagogery to those who heard them and knew no better. Nor was Judge Bork an ambitious coward, eager to conform his views to what he believed his interrogators, and an anxious public, wanted to hear. As I have endeavored to show, Bork was a highly principled, courageous nominee even if some of his principles were not precisely as they were taken to be.

Does this mean that the Senate was wrong to accept the Committee's recommendation and reject the nomination? Not necessarily. Bork's testimony was followed by that of numerous public figures, supporting or opposing the appointment. Perhaps the most telling was that of Barbara Jordan, the charismatic Congresswoman from the Watergate hearings who has become, for much of the American public, a keeper of the nation's constitutional conscience. None of the politicians present during her testimony were eager to engage her in discussion. Each was wary of the awful potential that an encounter with this formidable figure posed, and so her testimony is quite brief. Each Senator went to elaborate lengths to express appreciation for her testimony; one even went so far as to apologize for having tried to joke with her. When she concluded her statements, however, the constitutional case against the nomination had been made.

Miss Jordan began by distancing herself from the "knee-jerk reaction of followership to the people and organizations whose views I respect."

My opposition is a result of thinking about this matter with some care, of reading the White House position paper in support of Robert Bork, of reading the Judiciary Committee . . . response to that position paper, discussing the matter with friends and people I respect, reading some of Judge Bork's writings. But more than any of that, my opposition to this nomination is really a result of living 51 years as a black American born in the South and determined to be heard by the majority community. That really is the primary basis for my opposition to this nomination.[67]

Professor Jordan, as she has become since retiring from Congress, then recounted her struggle to be elected to public office in Texas.

Her first race, for the Texas House of Representatives, was lost.
Two years later she ran again, and lost:

Why could I not win? I will tell you why. The Texas legislature was so
malapportioned that just a handful of people were electing a majority of
the legislature. I was dispirited. I was trying to play by the rules, and the
rules were not fair. But something happened. A decision was handed down:
Baker v. *Carr*. That decision said this: The complainant's allegations of a
denial of equal protection present a justifiable constitutional cause of action.
The right asserted is within the judicial protection of the 14th amendment.
Following *Baker* v. *Carr*, a series of cases were decided. The Texas legislature was required, mandated by the Supreme Court to reapportion itself.
It reapportioned. So in 1966, I ran again.[68]

She was elected to a newly created state senatorial district. From
this narrative, which every politician in the Senate could palpably
appreciate, Jordan moved to her charge against Bork. It was not
simply that he opposed the reapportionment, or the poll tax
decisions.[69] Rather it was that he had campaigned for a seat on the
Court in a series of speeches and magazine articles going back fifteen
years, by attacking the legitimacy of the Court's work. It was one
thing to disagree on the way the rationale for a decision played
out; it was something else again to challenge the very method of
rationalizing itself. That was the linchpin of Bork's jurisprudence:
that the federal courts had usurped power through the means of
illegitimate ways of reasoning about the Constitution. And that was
the point of attack by Jordan: by linking partisan disagreement with
an assault on the legitimacy of the Constitutional instruments of
interpretation, Bork had impugned the Constitution as a protector,
as a refuge, since he had devalued the shelter it could provide. He
had cast doubt not on the vitality of *Baker* v. *Carr* as a precedent;
he was willing to let it lie; but he had cast a shadow across this case
and so many others from the Civil Rights period of American
constitutional history. He stigmatized them as not truly legitimate.
This undercut all that had been achieved not because it would
overturn the decisions won, but because it robbed the winners of
the proper laurels of their victories. It turned their successes into
condescending concessions.

When, in 1974, Barbara Jordan had electrified the nation by
announcing, at the outset of Judiciary Committee Hearings on the
Watergate scandal, that she came before the American public "as

one whose faith in the Constitution is whole and complete,"[70] she professed an allegiance to constitutional decisions that had brought her to Congress, the first black member from the South since Reconstruction. For fifteen years Robert Bork had been attacking the legitimacy of the means of judicial reasoning that undergirded the Warren Court decisions. To this campaign, in part, he owed his public reputation, his nomination, and ultimately his defeat. I trust that an appreciation of the legitimating role of the forms of constitutional argument, which I endeavored to show in Book I, now makes manifest how an attack on those modalities is an attack on the legitimacy of the decisions they support.

What Bickel and Bork both conscientiously sought was a justification for constitutional decisions, not merely a justifiable practice. But realism would not permit either man to conclude that the ideal of doctrinalism, in Bickel's case, or of originalism in Bork's, was sufficient to stand alone. Each looked reality straight on – their ambition demanded as much – and strove to protect their cherished methods by fully deploying the political sensibilities their lives in the law had given them. Neither was doctrinaire, even if Bork could appear that way, even if perhaps he wished to be that way, because each wanted justice and no one of any real insight can long work with American constitutional materials and believe that a single favored interpretive approach assures justice. Justice – and its relationship to the forms of constitutional argument – is the subject of Book III.

BOOK III

LEGITIMACY AND JUSTIFICATION

Introduction

Book II introduced the modalities of constitutional argument – the *ways* in which constitutional arguments are determined to be valid – and made the claim that various anomalies in American constitutional law arose from the confusion regarding the status of such modalities and the legal propositions whose truth value they determine. For a familiar example of such a confusion in everyday discourse, consider the following exchange between two persons about the "guilt" of a captured "criminal."

A: Did you read in the newspaper about that awful murder . . . at the convenience store . . .?

B: No; but they happen all the time nowadays. Did they catch the man?

A: Why do you assume it was a man? Anyway, yes they caught someone just after the killing; I think the attendant had pressed an alarm and the police showed up just as the cash register was being emptied.

B: Drugs, I suppose. I just hope they don't let the son-of-a-bitch get off.

A: Well, only if "the son-of-a-bitch" is guilty.

B: I thought you said they caught him red-handed? How guilty can he be?

A: You can't just assume everyone who's arrested is guilty. Guilt is a matter of proof, within strict rules; only a jury can say whether a person is *guilty*.

B: That's ridiculous. You mean if he gets off on some technicality, he's "innocent?" After killing someone?

A: Well you don't know that person killed someone; you didn't even read the newspaper account.

B: Alright. But assume he killed someone; are you saying he's not guilty of such a horrible thing unless he's actually convicted?

A: A person's innocent until proven guilty. You know that.

B: I know nothing of the kind. When did I forfeit my moral sense to a bunch of people I've never even met, picked by a couple of lawyers. Why that jury won't know as much as you do about the killing once the trial is over and the evidence is manipulated . . .

A: According to the rules . . .

B: According to the rules. Of course this man's guilty. Morally guilty. And the law can't change that. Suppose they hadn't caught him, suppose he'd gotten away. Are you saying he wouldn't have been guilty? That he would have been *innocent*?

A: Well, not guilty, anyway.

B: That's absurd. Suppose he's convicted. Is he guilty then?

A: Yes, if the conviction is upheld.

B: Upheld? So he can be tried, and convicted, and sentenced, but if some appeals judge throws out the conviction on some technical point of law, regardless of the facts, whether the guy did it or not, he's innocent again?

A: Not again. The person was never guilty. Anyway, that's the point: the appeals court is confined to the law because guilt is a matter of law. Anyway, it wasn't a man.

B: What?

A: It was a woman. And the paper said she made a full confession.

In this exchange, each speaker is claiming a kind of exclusivity for his (or her) use of the term "guilt."[1] Of course guilt will be determined according to the forms of a particular official system of criminal justice (for A); and by the forms of moral discourse (for B). What seems to make B so angry is that A refuses to concede there is any relation between the two, while B clearly implies that the duty of the "system" is to reach results that come as close as possible to those of moral discourse. And that is why this exchange cannot be resolved by an unctuous mediator ("C") who says, soothingly, "You're both right. You're just using the term in two different senses. 'A' is talking about the legal sense of the term; and 'B' is using the moral sense."

This won't really help. True, A is being stubborn and a little captious to claim the exclusive use of the word. But there is a point to be made about such possessiveness, such territoriality: once A admits there is an *essential* connection between the two uses, then one use becomes a function of the other. This is precisely the point she wishes to deny: otherwise she will end up trying to defend the dubious proposition that it is "*better* that 1,000 guilty men go free than that one innocent man be convicted" as the rationale for legal rather than moral standards of proof. (Moreover, some constitutional protections for defendants, like the exclusionary rule, and even the Fifth Amendment's bar against self-incrimination, principally function in the case of the "guilty" person.) Why not then accept the proffered hand of C: are these not simply two different "senses" of the term? That suggests, however, that law has nothing to do with morality, a claim that, however satisfying to the cynic, is difficult to square with the agonies of decisionmaking. Furthermore, there are simply too many cases where the "law" alone is not sufficiently determinative, no matter how much we may have steeled ourselves to the distaste of applying it without regard to non-legal considerations.

The problems of constitutional law share some characteristics of the dialogue. Like B most commentators want to ground their propositions of constitutional interpretation in some fact about the world – its history, its politics, its morals, etc. Like A they are sometimes led into making absurd claims about the exclusivity and thus the priority of essentially conventional systems, claims that make "justice" no more than the inadvertent, if unavoidable, byproduct of operating the system. Like C they try to elide the problem of interpretation by suggesting that the same proposition may have different uses – which is true – while implying that these uses are validated by the different communities they serve – which is half-true – a "resolution" that satisfies no one who really cares about either the justice of constitutional interpretation or its autonomy.

In Book I, examples were given of these sorts of confusions about constitutional interpretation. With respect to the most notorious of the anomalies to which these confusions give rise – the Countermajoritarian Objection to the legitimacy of judicial review – I had made the same claim more than ten years ago in my Dougherty Lectures and in the book from which they were drawn, *Constitutional Fate*.[2]

In Book II, I endeavored to show precisely how the sort of approach I am urging actually operates and some of the insights it offers. By analyzing a Supreme Court decision, a Presidential decision, and a Congressional decision, I also meant to imply that modal approaches offer a kind of analysis that is accessible to non-judicial constitutional deciders, and useful in fulfilling the duties of constitutional analysis that these deciders share with the judiciary.

In both Books I and II of the present work, I presented an

approach that was not simply taxonomical, but was topological. That is, I not only sought to classify the forms of argument, but also to characterize them in a way that showed the constraints they impose. Foremost among these constraints is the separation between legitimacy and justification. For while the forms of argument maintain legitimacy, and thereby justify judicial review within the American system of constitutional interpretation, they do not give us a means by which we can justify that system as a whole or its results. So long as a particular modality or modalities are adhered to – so long as the arguments are consistent with their premises, and they are not contradictory – the decision is legitimate. More than that – whether it is *right* – this approach did not enable me to say.

Therefore in Book III, I aim to treat this subject: how do we justify particular decisions in light of the severance of the modalities from any trans-modal, moral values? For if we have sought this approach to resolve certain problems in constitutional analysis, and we succeed at the cost of isolating our law from its values, we have gained nothing. I will claim, however, that it is precisely the fact (1) that particular modal approaches do not assure justice and (2) that in difficult cases these approaches *do* disagree, that enables us to make just decisions. Since these claims are so contrary to the assumptions of the usual debate I will spend some time setting out the customary ways of linking and legitimating models to justice before making my own argument. If I fail, if that is I am unable to satisfactorily show a non-foundational link between the forms of constitutional argument and our moral judgments, it would be bettter to abandon the methods I have sought to describe and return to the old debate.

That debate had a long run in 1987, the bicentennial year of the Constitutional Convention. Watching the performances, for I found them hard to listen to, seeing the dull pageantry and repetition in a hundred conferences and symposia, one is struck by the inexhaustible resources of that debate. There will never be a shortage, it seems, of persons willing to argue that the Constitution is what the framers meant it to be, and no more, or what the judges say it is, and no less. The Meese–Brennan debate,[3] with which the year began, pitted the United States Attorney General against the senior serving justice of the US Supreme Court. That combat was over the proper modes of interpretation. Roughly, one might say that the Attorney General is a strict constructionist, with a decided preference for historical argument, into which he appears to believe the other "strict" modes dissolve; the Justice, by contrast, inclines toward the prudential. What is it about these bicentennial performances that grates? Surely I, of all people, should be happy to see the issues of constitutional interpretation widely discussed, and even a "Constitution Minute" on network television.

First, there is an apparent unselfconsciousness about these presentations that aims to deceive the audiences and usually succeeds at deceiving the speaker. On the one hand, some speakers are so eager to disclaim any ideological motivation, other than their veneration of the Constitution, that they present themselves as above ideological conflict. Only their opponents, it seems, can be rightly portrayed as having a political agenda that their interpretive commitments serve. On the other hand, some speakers are so candid about their political reductionism as to imply that only *their* opponents can be so disingenuous as to *claim* to find guidance in the document and its conventional methods of interpretation as law. And thus none of the debaters, on either hand, seems to be aware of the ideological constraints imposed by the modality one wishes to predominate, only by the modalities one wishes to outlaw. The Bork hearings gave us many examples. Each of the various modalities was represented by someone's attack on Bork's strict constructionism.[4] Yet none suggested that his own argumentative commitments were also ideologically constrained. And Bork himself was at pains to persuade the committee that strict construction may serve a liberal political program, as in the 1930s, or a conservative one, as if his nomination by the most ideologically driven President since the Second World War was a mere coincidence.

Second, perhaps because the speakers are unaware of the palette of modalities from which they have taken their racing colors, there has been an intolerance in some quarters that is offensive to the spacious dimensions of the US Constitution. I was present in Chicago when a law professor felt compelled to leave a rather grand Bicentennial Dinner, something I do not think he would do lightly, owing to the vituperation of the US Assistant Attorney General for Civil Rights in his remarks about the US Supreme Court. And, on the other side of things, I was appalled to read in the most recent addition to constitutional theory to issue from the Harvard Press the charge that the claim to enforce the plain meaning of the text was "simply a lie."[5] I think this, too, arises in part from one's position inside a particular *mentality*, because it makes our adversaries appear to be either knaves or fools. Outside the modality one favors, the moves within another mode seem specious; they could only be taken, one thinks, according to some hidden rule, some ulterior motive or, perhaps, without a coherent view at all.

And this leads me to my third objection to the style of the debate: who would possibly be persuaded either way? Not the debaters, surely. They are merely confirmed in their views by these encounters. And not the audiences, I think. For, whatever attractive characteristics the speakers may have, the debates themselves require, in Tom Stoppard's words, "a degree of self-absorption that would glaze over the eyes of Narcissus."[6]

What are they all arguing about? They are disagreeing over the proper answer to a question each would pose to the other: how is it possible that a system of constitutional interpretation can assure justice? And what seems to irritate both parties is the manifest inadequacy of the other side's answers. In the following chapters I too will take up this question, because it is certainly as profound and insistent with respect to the descriptions I have given as it is regarding the conventional positions. I have organized my response in the following way:

1   I will describe the contradiction that is alleged to obtain between my description of legitimation (the system of incommensurate modalities) and any just system. I think it can be shown how this allegation is related to the objections usually posed to theories of interpreting the Constitution.

2   I will discuss some of the proposed "solutions" to the problem posed by my description. And I will show that these too, although done with infinitely greater polish and skill than the usual schemes, are related to them nevertheless in ways that reveal a common origin with the assumptions of the old debate.

3   I will dispute the felt need for such solutions. I believe this need results from an unstated conviction about meaning – namely, that a decision must correspond to a particular thought, and a just decision must derive from an ideal that guides our decisions and serves as the source of just rules. This conviction is, I believe, false.

4   Furthermore, I will argue that such a "meta-logic" – a general rule to tell us how to decide among the proposed outcomes generated

by the conventional modalities – is not only unnecessary but is positively harmful, and is incompatible with moral decision.

5   I will defend the constitutional system of legitimation in terms of its justice.

6   I will briefly describe the true role that hypothetical ideas and meta-rules play in the decisionmaking that the modalities, which depend upon no such rules, generate.

7   I will discuss some of the consequences of my analysis for a description of constitutional decisionmaking and its relation to justice and I will take up the implications of this kind of description for future work in this field.

Usually it is assumed that constitutional arguments are *means* to the *ends* of justice. In Books I and II, I have dispensed with this assumption. Moreover, although I have provided several accounts of legitimation – some, in Part II, in some detail – I have avoided claims that these accounts were *explanatory*.

The usual account of these matters is to explain the methods of interpretation as relating to justice, i.e., causally related to the real-world consequences of deciding in a certain way. A legitimate decision is a just one. It is the result of following particular rules that, taken together, form our ideas of justice.[7] In rejecting this approach (that the forms of argument are the instruments of justice), in claiming that a meta-logic[8] that would guide our choices among otherwise incommensurable modalities is in fact incompatible with moral choice, I must provide a different resolution of the question "How do we get justice from the construction of the US constitution?"

1

HOW CAN THE AMERICAN SYSTEM OF INTERPRETATION BE JUST?

Virtually no one, nowadays, is so unsophisticated as to believe that mere application of the Constitution – which I shall call, for reasons I shall explain in a minute, adherence to the rule of American law – is sufficient to assure justice. On the contrary, the partisans in the debate over constitutional interpretation are actually arguing about how to do that interpretation so that it can *be* justified. Liberals want to provide supplementary rules – such as the system of John Rawls[1] – to resolve difficult cases; conservatives like William Rehnquist want to ground interpretation in fixed references – like the structure and history of the constitutional text – that restrict the interpretive preferences available to judges;[2] progressives, like Robert Bork[3] or Mark Tushnet,[4] want to correct interpretation by reference to various social and political facts. But all agree on one thing: there are simply too many cases of different outcomes according to the legitimating methods to maintain that a just system can be comprehensive (able to cope with all forms of argument) and consistent (allowing for no correct but contradictory outcomes). This conclusion might be parsed as follows:

1 An outcome is either just or unjust.
2 Therefore a rule of decision that will determine a just outcome must constrain our choices to a class of consistent outcomes.
3 The system of American constitutional interpretation, by itself, does not dictate a particular outcome in every circumstance.
4 Therefore this system, by itself, does not assure justice.

It is true that usually the partisans of the constitutional debate approach this question from the other way around, that is, from the perspective of legitimacy. The claim is usually that we (or a judge) must know when to accept or reject a particular argument according to a comprehensive, consistent rule; that this is the only way that we can apply the law rather than our personal preferences; if we have no such rule, then the claim that we are acting from motives other than our preferences is a sham, and the respect due to our decisions – the legitimacy they enjoy – should be withdrawn.

But I think it can be seen that this issue, on which both Critical Legal Studies theorists and former Attorney General Meese agree,[5] is not necessarily about legitimacy. Indeed, on the view of legitimacy expressed in *Constitutional Fate*, and reiterated in the present work, this issue is not relevant to legitimacy at all. For I have endeavored to show that no such rule is necessary for a decision to be legitimate. And I believe I have shown many decisions, and how they are structured, without any reference to a meta-rule nor any demurrer, that I have detected, as to their legitimacy. It is sufficient if a decision can be rationalized in terms of the forms of argument. As to whether a judge was motivated to choose a particular form of argument owing to his or her preference for a particular outcome, one need not say (except perhaps to utter the caution that motive should not be confused with cause).

But perhaps we have been seduced. Perhaps, once we realize that we are according legitimacy to decisions that cannot be justified (that is, uniquely determined) by reference to the rules with which they are described, we will withdraw that legitimacy. Well, why would we? Because our goal is justice and not simply tranquility! Not necessarily. We might instead reject the idea that legitimacy is a by-product of justice, just as we learned to reject the notion that the methods that maintained legitimacy could be counted on to assure justice.

But if a decision is not made according to a determinate rule – and since not all outcomes are just, an indeterminate rule is therefore one that does not justify – what way do we have of ensuring that the decision will be just? Justice appears to require determinacy; but does it really? Of course, as J. W. Singer has observed, it is not hard to construct a system of determinate rules:

It is easy to create completely determinate legal rules and arguments.

For example, an absolutely determinate private law system could be based on the rule that no one is liable to anyone else for anything and that everyone is free to do whatever she wants without government interference . . . The plaintiff would always lose. The problem is that this or any other determinate system bears no relation to anything anyone would consider just . . . The reason is obvious. We cannot accept such a system because it would not protect other, important, competing values – security, privacy, reputation, freedom of movement. We invent more complicated rule systems to accommodate our contradictory values . . . Nothing tells us conclusively, when to accept or when to reject a particular argument.[6]

The difficulty, it would seem, is in constructing a determinate rule that invariably captures the ideal of justice we bring to the operation of such a rule. We cannot seem to design a rule, external to our preferences and therefore *legitimate*, that invariably yields results that match our internal ideal of justice, and is therefore *justifiable* on that ground.

To sum up thus far: the usual debate about legitimacy can be recast as a problem of justice; my treatment of legitimacy, with its apparent disjunction of legitimacy and justice, leads to the same question; so, how do we reconcile the need for a system that is just (and therefore determinate) with the constitutional system of interpretation, the American rule of law, that is apparently indeterminate, at least at crucial times?

A note on the rule of American law

The American system of constitutional interpretation which I have been discussing – that is, the six modalities that constitute the forms of constitutional argument in the United States – should not be confused with the notion of "the rule of law" and yet it is related to this idea in an important way. The "rule of law" is usually associated with adherence to doctrinalism, that is, the Anglo-American tradition of deciding appeals on the basis of neutral, general principles of law. This is only one form of constitutional argument.

It was the unique legal contribution of American constitutional law to place the state wholly under law. Perhaps this was only happenstance: having taken away sovereignty from the Crown and Parliament there was no state in which to vest it. It may be that the crucial years before the Constitution, and not those simply before the Revolution, determined this division of state and sovereignty.

I do not know; it does not matter. The important fact is that by this severance the power of the state, no longer sovereign, was put under law – the Constitution – and by so doing, put under the common law forms of argument. Historians, of whom Boorstin is perhaps the best known exemplar,[7] entirely miss this point even when they dwell on the lawyerliness of the framers, and especially when they contrast the provincial tidiness of the Americans with the passionate universalism of the revolutionists in France. In constitutional terms, one might well argue that France today has far more in common with the state it was before its revolution, which did nothing to disturb the sovereignty of the state, than the United States has with its pre-constitutional colonies. When Guizot remarked that the revolution in 1776 re-played the constitutional events of 1688,[8] he partly appreciated this dimension.

We might very well then call the constitutional system of interpretation I have been describing the "rule of American law" because that is its first rule: that the Constitution, and not the entities of the state that execute the Constitution, is supreme.

2

PROPOSALS TO CORRECT THE SYSTEM

This is the picture then that we usually have of the forms of argument and the role of justice: the forms determine a legitimate outcome, but not a particular result because the outcomes of different forms may be different; whereas a just outcome is one that matches our idea of what the outcome should be; when the outcomes differ, any of the outcomes might be just, but they cannot all be just. Therefore the forms of argument do not assure, and may undermine, achieving a just result. Let us look at an example.

Article I, section 8, clause 15 provides that the Congress shall have the power "To provide for calling forth the militia to execute the laws of the Nation, suppress insurrections and repel invasions."
[1] In August 1814, the governor of New York, in compliance with a request from the President, ordered companies of New York militia to assemble for the purpose of entering the service of the United States to repel an attack by the British that did not, ultimately, materialize. The President acted in accordance with a federal statute empowering him to call the militia whenever there shall be danger of invasion. A private in one of the companies refused to comply with the order; in 1818 a court martial imposed a fine and when he refused to pay, he was sentenced to a year in prison.[2] The question presented is, can the President call for the state militia when no invasion has taken place?

It would appear that either outcome can be rationalized according to the forms of constitutional argument. One might, quite reasonably, say that an invasion that has not yet occurred cannot be "repelled" (a textual argument); or one might, with perhaps more wisdom, maintain that, as a practical matter, the time to repel invasions is before the enemy reaches the nation's soil (a prudential argument). Either of these might yield a just result in the case of a civilian who conscientiously thought he was being unconstitutionally called up. Even though either result might be just, they cannot both be just. And therefore a system that can legitimate either outcome cannot be sufficient to assure a just result.

For this reason – on account of this picture of how things must be for our sense of justice to be vindicated by the system of law we operate – there have been a number of proposed "algorithms" in constitutional law. An *algorithm* is an explicit and finite step-by-step procedure for solving a problem in order to achieve a particular end. Most of these proposals were simply ways of pruning off some of the competing modalities. In the past this has taken place without any explicit acknowledgment that this was what was going on. Indeed much of the history of the theory of American constitutional interpretation is little more than the assertion of preferred modalities.

Recently, however, there have been scholars, mainly younger ones, who were sensitive to the possibilities of the modalities and sought to address the chief problem they pose, i.e., how do we choose among the modes when they disagree? Among the most thoughtful of these is the constitutional historian Jefferson Powell. In perhaps the most influential article of the decade, appearing in the Harvard Law Review,[3] Powell tried to assimilate the various modalities into historical argument, in the process enriching the latter so as to preserve the full range of modes. His argument went this way: if we take a careful look at the way in which the framers intended the Constitution to be interpreted, not simply at why it may be concluded they proposed a particular provision, we will see that they did not wish to abandon the customary modalities of legal interpretation in favor of historical argument. Powell produces numerous letters and essays from framers and ratifiers of the original Constitution to show that they expected doctrinal, structural, ethical and other modes to be used; indeed that they used these methods themselves. And thus the argument by the usual historicist in Constitutional law, that legitimate interpretation should be limited to applying the framers' intentions, invites rather than rejects the entire family of modalities.

This is a splendid achievement and it rightly deserves our attention. But is not the enterprise flawed at the conception? I once wrote,

"We don't know the original intent of the framers regarding their original intent, and we cannot know it,"[4] a passage that Powell correctly sees as opposed to his efforts at assimilation.[5] I meant, however, something other than simply it would be difficult to find out by what methods the framers intended courts to construe the Constitution. I meant that, as a logical matter, original intent – the term of art for the content of the purposes animating particular constitutional ideas – was opaque as to its own purposes, which were subsumed in it. Determining the "original intent" in this matter could add nothing to itself. To put it differently: we can have no "original understanding" (in this technical sense) of historical argument (not, as Powell thought I said, of constitutional argument). We have no argument, that is, based on the ratifiers' understanding of the issue that their intentions should govern interpretation. How could we? A statement, by the ratifiers, directing that their statements should be given weight could not be otherwise (i.e., it could not say "give our statements no weight") – and therefore it adds nothing. We cannot have an original understanding in support of the original understanding. In short, Powell may, as a practical matter, appear to obviate the conflicts about the legitimacy of non-historical modes by assimilating them into the historical mode. But just as less expansive historicists could produce no reason, outside that mode, why the other modalities should be rejected, so Powell can produce nothing to legitimize their use, beyond *his* single, unquestioned modal preference. So although we may embarrass the historicists with Powell's researches, we have not moved beyond the premises of historical argument.

A second, highly accomplished effort to resolve the problem of the modalities was published in 1987, also as a leading article[6] in the Harvard Law Review, by Richard Fallon. In this extensive piece he carefully reviews the various modalities and asks, "How are these different kinds of arguments related to each other? Are all entitled to influence in every case? Which take precedence in cases of conflict?"[7]

He sees clearly that the usual constitutional theories simply adopt a particular mode as the one true way. "Privileged factor theories give determinative significance to arguments within one or two of the categories and virtually ignore other kinds of arguments."[8] But he also rejects solutions, such as Laurence Tribe's,[9] that ratify a particular decision by subsuming one's instincts for justice within the forms of constitutional argument. Like a similar analysis proposed by

Stanley Fish,[10] such solutions do not account for the sense of constraint that judges feel, nor, more importantly, do they capture the
element of normative reflection that judges usually report. Like Fiss
and Fish, Tribe would appeal ultimately to practice. Fallon, on the
other hand, writes:

[I]magine the case of a Supreme Court justice who believes capital punishment to be not only inherently morally wrong, but also so empirically
random in its application that it arguably violates the constitutional prohibition against cruel and unusual punishment and the due process clause.
Suppose further, however, that this same justice finds that capital punishment is contemplated by the plain text of the Constitution and was approved
by the framers. I would expect this hypothetical justice to appeal to the
normative structure of the practice of constitutional interpretation, as she
understands it, to determine whether it is permissible for her to render a
judgment contrary to that indicated by what she initially takes to be the
best arguments from text and from the framers' intent. I would not expect
her inquiry to be merely ad hoc or addressed solely to others' "tacit" sense
of what the particular situation allowed.[11]

In my terms, one might say that the authors Fallon is criticizing
elide the distinction between legitimacy and justification.

Fallon also appreciates that the typology of arguments is in fact a
set of modalities. He rejects a "balancing" solution to the "commen-
surability problem" – the problem of competing modalities:

[A] defect of the balancing approach . . . inheres in the implicit assumption
that the five types of constitutional argument are substantially independent
– that it is possible to reach independent assessments of the balance of
arguments within reach of the categories, without looking at the others,
and to assign weights to the separate conclusions.[12]

I will not attempt to summarize Fallon's own effort at resolving
this issue. It is rich and complex and I could not fairly present it by
providing a digest only. Moreover, my objections are not related to
the ingenuity of the specifics but to the entire approach.

I am, of course, immensely encouraged that fine scholars are
turning to this problem. But their hope – that an algorithm can be
found that will undo the problem of competing modalities – is, in
my view, doomed. I will argue in chapter Three that the effort to
achieve this goal is unnecessary and, in chapter Four, that its effect
would be pernicious if achieved.

First, however, I must treat what is by far the most monumental effort to resolve the problem posed by incommensurate modalities, Mark Tushnet's *Red, White and Blue: A Critical Analysis of Constitutional Law*.[13]

Red, White and Blue observes that there is a pervasive presence in American constitutional law of five general theories. These theories correspond to the historical, textual, doctrinal, structural, and ethical approaches to interpretation. What makes the book interesting and important is that by firmly adopting a *prudential* perspective, it provides an unwitting or at least unselfconscious example of the general theorizing it wishes to explain. For this reason, its descriptions of the particular family of theories that characterize American constitutional jurisprudence are distorted, while it never acknowledges, indeed disclaims any account of the particular *set* of objections that the author poses to these theories.

Tushnet assesses these five general theories by analyzing the particular defense to the Countermajoritarian Objection to judicial review that can be inferred from each archetypal form of argument. This is a useful strategy because it enables the author to convey a good sense of the nature of each form of argument. But because he limits himself to instrumental, political explanations, not so much rejecting as ignoring the unquiet need for rationalization that underlies theorizing, he therefore sounds a little querulous when he complains, "The grand theorists have not explained how their theorizing activity actually serves their apparent political goals."[14]

For Tushnet tends always to reduce constitutional interpretation to tactical political manoeuvering. Each of the theories of constitutional interpretation he discusses fails, on his view, because it does not sufficiently constrain the discretion of judges. Historical argument is anachronistic, indeed impossible, because of its central task: one cannot really know what eighteenth century persons would have thought of a world in which they, by definition, cannot exist. Doctrinal arguments based on disinterested and principled grounds are also impossible because the precedents that are alleged to provide such grounds are manipulable, indeed require manipulation to generate principles and thus really do not constrain judges. And so on. These familiar arguments are organized in a similar way for each of the archetypal forms. Tushnet understands that "grand theory's primary function is to explain why the existing system of constitutional law deserves our rational respect,"[15] but he seems unaware that he falls neatly within its traditions himself, and thus evaluates other theories from within one of the classic modalities that define American constitutional theory. His standard – the "sufficient" constraint of judges – would have been quite at home with Bickel's, or Brandeis's (or Bork's!) prudential jurisprudence. What should we make of this ambitious attempt at reductionism? Let us examine its treatment of each of the forms of argument.

(a) Historical argument

Tushnet argues that

[A] problem with the [original] contract argument is that none of us entered the [original] contract. The framers did, and it might be fair treatment of James Madison to enforce the contract against him. But he died a long time ago.[16]

This reference to the framers suggests that Tushnet misunderstands historical argument. The framers' consent is of no more legal significance than the consent of the lawyer who drafts a will; perhaps less so, because the delegates to the Constitutional Convention were not authorized to do more than recommend changes to the existing Articles of Confederation.[17] When Tushnet writes that "most of us today – women, blacks, children and grandchildren of immigrants – are not successors in interest to the framers in any sense that makes the contract analogy compelling,"[18] he reflects this misunderstanding. The legally significant agreement – the "contract" – was between the people as endowing sovereign and government; the framers were no more than draftsmen. If the mere longevity of the settlors were to determine the legal status of a trust, we could scarcely have trusts – the Rockefeller Foundation, Princeton University, and countless other institutions would have ceased to exist with the demise of their original endowers. It is we who are the successors in interest to the *ratifiers* of earlier periods, including, of course, those who ratified the Twenty-Sixth Amendment in 1971. Since we retain sovereignty we can ratify new amendments – that is, we are *not* bound by the "framers" nor is this claimed according to historical argument.

Tushnet presses his prudential attack on originalism by saying that "the Bill of Rights provided protection, such as it was, against [acts by the federal government] not by the states. Because a genuine originalism would thus protect only against limited varieties of legislation, it fails its objective." But surely the proper "originalist" inquiry, on the matter of application of the Bill of Rights to the states, is whether the intentions of the ratifiers of the Civil War amendments[19] intended to provide such protection against the states. Even the most ardent proponent of historical argument does not confine himself to the eighteenth century text out of a distaste for everything that has happened since. The proper originalist construction of, for example, the Twenty-Second Amendment asks what the framers and ratifiers intended at the time of its adoption in 1951.

Although Tushnet is sometimes uncertain about the precise distinctions among the modes, he never varies from his own resort to the prudential. Even his defenses of historical argument – defenses one never encounters in the writings of those inclined to reply on historical approaches exclusively, like Raoul Berger[20] – are prudentialist. Thus, he writes:

[O]riginalists can argue . . . that originalism is *better* than the alternatives. It gives us a Constitution with many opportunites for legislative tyranny, some (though few) limits on legislatures, stringent limits on judges, and few opportunites for judicial tyranny. The alternatives provide many opportunities for judicial tyranny, few limits on judges, and an unknown mixture of opportunities for and limits on legislative tyranny.[21]

The prudentialist must rely on some standard external to the law to enable the measurement of the "better." Here, it is the constraint on judges. But the full-bore historicist would simply say that we rely on the original intent because that is the lawful way to act; whether it is practical to do so is not a constitutional question. Because Tushnet so resolutely refuses to see this, and thus overlooks the difference between historical argument and historical analysis, he can perhaps be acquitted of the charge of gross unfairness to Berger. Having given some of the rules of construction that Berger derives from his historical approach,[22] Tushnet at first mildly offers a purely pragmatic guess as to what usefulness they have ("they may be crystallized expressions of what more detailed inquiries have shown to have been usually true").[23] He then contrasts these highly reified rules with the detailed documentary and descriptive background that one finds in historical essays and contemptuously observes: "It is almost painful to read Berger's work after reading a far more subtle study by a serious historian J. R. Pole."[24]

But Berger's rules are legal rules, common law rules of construction that have little to do with historical analysis as practiced by professional historians, even when they are writing on legal events of great historical significance. It is as if, for Tushnet, historical argument is just something about the past. Thus Tushnet gives Justice Brandeis's classic expression of the purpose of the free speech clause in *Whitney* v. *California*[25] as "the best example in the case law of a hermeneutic effort to understand the past",[26] when it is really no such thing. Indeed, that is why Justice Brandeis gives us no citations to historical sources; it is a purely prudential expression of the purpose of the amendment. Although it associates the Justice's understanding with that of the founders of the Republic ("those who won our independence"),[27] it is by no means an historical argument. Had Justice Brandeis intended to make such an argument, he would have identified the views he was urging with those of the framers and ratifiers of the Fourteenth Amendment, on the basis of which he decided the case, for he was not careless about such things.

Tushnet's conclusion is that historical argument cannot achieve the necessary determinacy about past intentions without "smuggling in an implausible claim about the ability to retrieve meaning across time."[28] He thus evaluates the modality of historical argument prudentially, judging it against a standard of determinacy since determinacy is alleged to be a condition for achieving Tushnet's goal of judicial constraint.

(b)   Doctrinal argument

Tushnet correctly sees the general approach associated with doctrinal argument as relying on the search for disinterested and enduring principles of constitutional law that are *neutral* with respect to the parties or groups in society and are *general* with respect to *stare decisis*. But he offers a very non-doctrinal account of the "rule of law" as the basis of this approach:

The rule of law, according to the liberal conception, is meant to protect us against the exercise of arbitrary power. The theory of neutral principles asserts that a requirement of consistency, the core of the ideal of the rule of law, places sufficient bounds on judges to reduce the risk of arbitrariness to an acceptable level. The question is whether the concepts of neutrality and consistency can be developed in ways that are adequate for the task.[29]

Note that this is a prudential justification for doctrinal argument. Henry Hart, a genuine doctrinalist, put it differently:

[The Court] is *predestined* in the long run not only by the thrilling tradition of Anglo-American law but also by the hard facts of its position in the structure of American institutions to be a voice of reason, charged with the creative function of discerning afresh and of articulating and developing impersonal and durable principles of constitutional law.[30]

That is, the doctrinal approach is unavoidable for courts in the American system, not merely useful.

Tushnet does appreciate the claim of doctrinalists that it is the way in which they reach decisions that gives their holdings legitimacy; indeed, he finds this claim highly dubious:

It is implausible . . . that neutral application of principles is an important source of public acceptance of judicial decisions. The general public is unlikely to care very much about a court's reasoning process, which is the focus of neutral principles theory; its concern is with results.[31]

This observation supports the view that Tushnet is evaluating each of five various forms of argument from the point of view of the sixth, prudential argument. The standard he believes will determine legitimacy is that which the prudentialist sets for constitutional decision: the results. But if we were to take the doctrinalist claim seriously, is it so obvious that reasoned elaboration is irrelevant to legitimacy? I am inclined to think the public cares very much about how a judge reaches a decision, as we would discover if a judge rendered a decision saying that his astrologer told him to decide a certain way, or acknowledging that he had been paid by one of the parties to decide as he did. No doubt all Tushnet really means to say is that the public does not read judicial opinions, but is this unenviable luxury really indicative of their true concern?

Tushnet's chief complaint, however, is not that doctrinalism does not work – that it does not maintain the legitimacy of decisions made on that basis – but that it *cannot* work because it fails to provide the determinacy that, in his view, is required:

At the moment a decision is announced we cannot identify the principle that it embodies. Each decision can be justified by many principles, and we learn what principles justified Case 1 only when a court in Case 2 tells us.[32]

This can not be quite right, because if it were true, then it would apply to itself; that is, it would be a Case 2 for some other Case 1. But in any event, this is only a way-station to the conclusion that "[t]he theory of neutral principles thus loses almost all of its constraining force."

If it is only a consequence of the pressures exerted by a highly developed, deeply entrenched, homeostatic social structure that judges seem to eschew conclusions grossly at odds with the values of liberal capitalism, sociological analysis ought to destroy the attraction of the theory. Principles are "neutral" only in the sense that they are, as a matter of contingent fact, unchallenged, and the contingencies have obvious historical limits.[33]

But such jargon would shatter the faith only of a very naive believer – perhaps one who both demanded determinacy and was credulous enough to be persuaded that "sociological analysis" might supply it if reliance on precedent did not. In fact, principles are neutral, for purposes of doctrinal argument, to the extent that they are neutral as to the parties; that they are therefore contingent is a matter of course.

(c) Textual argument

By seeing constitutional interpretation as a form of politics only, Tushnet loses the ability to appreciate the constitutional sources of the modes of argument; instead the modalities of argument are, for him, merely instrumentally derivative of various political purposes or agenda.

In *Red, White and Blue*, Tushnet calls textualism "the contention that some provisions of the Constitution need not be interpreted but need only be applied, because they are entirely clear." What follows is an explanation of neither textual argument nor "textualism", a mode that prudentialists always find particularly hard to take seriously. Instead, Tushnet gives us a list of replies to the unstated query of how textual argument can possibly be made ("because the meaning of the text itself is directly available to courts without interpreting it, or because the text itself excludes enough possible interpretations.")[34] The textualist would say, however, that the provisions of the Constitution need not be interpreted according to an external referent (the intentions of the framers, the practicality of the outcome, etc.) "because" the Constitution does not say to do so, rather than because the texts are especially clear, exclusionary, etc. The words of the constitutional text represent an implicit contract, to which the people, every day, give their implicit consent. Were its terms interpreted according to any recondite algorithm, that implicit assent could not be taken for granted.

This is not the only instance of Tushnet's inability to state the textualist's case on its own terms. For example, he writes:

In such an unsophisticated form, textualism is obviously vulnerable in several respects. First, Frank Easterbrook has noted that the mathematical provisions, like all the others, have "reasons, goals, values, and the like," behind them . . . In this view the words "thirty-five Years" in the Constitution are simply the shorthand the framers used to express their more complex policies, and we could replace them by fifty years or thirty years without impairing the integrity of the constitutional structure.[35]

This confuses the intent of a provision with its expression in the text and confuses historical, textual, and even structural approaches. If by "thirty-five years" the framers sought a provision that would ensure a certain maturity and experience in the persons who held the office of president, the argumentative resort to this observation – in defense of the eligibility, for example, of an especially experienced thirty-year-old – is a resort to *historical* argument. One suspects that such carelessness simply reflects an inability to take this form of argument seriously. Thus he ends this section by saying:

Textualism in all its forms suffers from a fatal defect. It gives us a Constitution with the politics left out. At some level, that is its point. But if the Constitution is just another form of politics, the problem of social order recurs. I close with some textualism of my own. The Constitution provides that the Senate "shall be composed of two Senators from each State." For at least seven years, at least nine states had no Senators. How that came to be, and how the text of the Constitution came to accommodate that situation, tells us a great deal about textualism.[36]

This reference to the American Civil War is meant to be powerfully evocative, but amounts to no more than a *non sequitur*. It does not tell us "a great deal" about textual argument and the ideology of textualism[37] although it may perhaps tell us a lot about Tushnet's project. His observation shows that a sufficiently extreme political emergency – and for a constitution, a civil war must be the supreme crisis – will override even the clearest text. But if, in an emergency, facts override law, does not our awareness of this suggest that we know that something, something of importance, has been overriden?

(d) Structural argument

For each "grand theory" Tushnet adduces a model. He is surely right in noticing that each of the various approaches suggests a particular sort of rationale for judicial review and a particular sort of reply to the Countermajoritarian Objection. But such rationales are not in themselves a "theory of the constitution," rather they follow from one. Beginning with this fragment, Tushnet attempts to enlarge John Hart Ely's structural rationale for judicial review[38] (that judicial review is justified by its contribution to the enhancement of representation) into the entire structural approach, and accordingly misses its point. He makes this elemental mistake, I think because he is tone-deaf to the harmony between Ely and his great structuralist predecessors, Chief Justice John Marshall and Charles Black. And how *could* he see these connections, after all, when he has recast structural argument generally, and Ely's contribution in particular, in prudential terms? He sees the point of Ely's argument to be the constraint one can infer from it, i.e., that judges are limited to rationales and decisions that reinforce the representative structure.

The consequence of this is to alter structural argument to serve a superimposed prudential goal. Let me give a dramatic example of the confusion of these two approaches. Tushnet evaluates how structural approaches cope with the problem of guaranteeing free speech and reaches this surprising conclusion: "The theory is inadequate to guard against legislative tyranny" because it "justif[ies] invalidation of national sedition statutes, and nothing else."[39]

This is the argument:

The theory requires that policy result from the aggregation of revealed preferences. Disfranchisements prevent some people from using the vote to reveal their preferences whatever they are. Limitations on speech prevent people from revealing *particular* preferences, those for the policy about which speech is limited. For example, if a statute makes it unlawful to advocate racial segregation, those who prefer segregation will be unable to reveal that desire. The conclusion that only national laws can be attacked under the theory follows easily from the analysis of disfranchisements. Local restrictions on speech can be remedied by state or national legislation that prevents local legislatures from enacting such restrictions.[40]

That is, so long as Congress can override by statute any state or local law; and so long as Congress is well formed as a representative body, any statute or practice (save one that affects congressional representation) is beyond the justifying rationale of structural intervention that it enhances democracy.

First, one must observe that the "theory" does not require "that policy result from the aggregation of revealed preferences." That would be a prudential theory, that is, one justifying a particular argument by its contribution to an external value (maximizing the satisfaction of revealed preferences). The structuralist may indeed hold such assumptions. It may be that Madison thought that representation was a good thing because it allowed the preferences of voters to be reflected in government. But it is doubtful that Hamilton felt this way, and it is unlikely that either would have weakened his commitment to parliamentary representation if it had been shown that some other system, of opinion polls or councils of sociologists, for example, was a more effective means of translating revealed preferences into policy. The reason why the structuralist is *committed* to the particular system of representation we have – so unique among the societies that we recognize as "democratic" as to be almost idiosyncratic – is because the Constitution specifies such a system.

Second, instead of beginning with an external preference – maximizing consumer satisfaction, say – begin instead with the structures that the text provides: a national legislature constituted through elections, for example. Now contrast the following argument from Charles Black with the quoted passage from Tushnet regarding the implications of structural approaches for state restrictions on free speech:

From the very structure of the relation between the national representative and his constituency, there arises a compelling inference of some national constitutional protection of free utterance, as against state infringement. Is it conveivable that a state, entirely aside from the Fourteenth, or for that matter the First Amendment, could permissibly forbid public discussion of the merits of candidates for Congress, or for issues which have been raised in the congressional campaign, or which an inhabitant of the district – or of the state, where the election is senatorial – might wish to see raised in the campaign? I start with that as the hard core, because I cannot see how anyone could think our national government could run, or was by anybody at any time ever expected to run, on any less openness of public communication than that.[41]

Thus on a classically structural view, the "hierarchy of representation" leads to precisely the opposite of Tushnet's conclusion because the purpose of judicial constraint is not superimposed to govern the actual (structural) purpose for constitutional interpretation and decision.

There is no warrant for the inference that courts should, on representation-reinforcing grounds, desist from the review of state statutes. There appears to be one only if you confuse the prudential standard for judicial scrutiny with the substantive structural rationale for judicial review. If the latter arises from the constitutional structures created in the text, the courts could hardly refuse to decide matters on the ground that a perfectly representative body – the Congress – also had authority to remedy the matter, for it is Congress through its jurisdictional statutes that has given the courts a mandate for decisions in such cases in the first place.[42]

(e) Ethical argument

Tushnet begins with this characterization of the "theory" of ethical interpretation:

We have to distinguish between fundamental, basic, or human rights on the one hand, and nonfundamental, less basic rights on the other . . . Then, according to the present theory, courts can enforce the judgments of moral philosophy. First they must decide whether a fundamental right is implicated by the statute in question. If it is, courts must then decide whether the statute has reached a morally impermissible result . . . The positive case for relying on moral philosophy thus turns on the ability of judges to distinguish between fundamental and other rights and then to decide what moral philosophy requires.[43]

If courts could in fact apply moral philosophy in their judgments in this way, how would they go about reaching such judgments? Tushnet considers two possible methods: (1) by invoking the claims of a particular system, and (2) by reflecting the moral consensus of society. Notice that despite the use of terms like "fundamental rights," Tushnet neglects to say how the Constitution requires moral argument. We therefore cannot determine whether either of the two proposed methods would actually serve the constitutional requirement. And yet "neglects" is not the right word: Tushnet, like any thorough-going prudentialist, doesn't believe that there are any constitutional reasons for invoking a particular form of argument other than to promote a particular political agenda. That is why Tushnet does not address the constitutional basis for ethical argument, but rather proceeds directly to evaluate moral arguments as a means of serving prudential ends. And when, not surprisingly, moral argument is shown to be far too indeterminate for such a role, it is abandoned as insufficient on practical grounds.

Judicial review means that courts can sometimes displace judgments made by legislators. The theory being considered here would fail if judges were not better than legislators at working down from abstract principles to particular judgments. There are several reasons, though, to be skeptical about claims that judges are indeed systematically better than legislators.[44]

This would make the approach of ethical argument amount to: "Do good!" It would, as Tushnet suggests, turn on our real-world assessments of the likelihood that particular constitutional decisions are more or less likely to bring about a better world. This move transforms this form of argument (while retaining some of its aura) by introducing an extra-constitutional standard against which costs and benefits are measured, albeit a moral one.

By contrast, ethical approaches (using that phrase as a term of art to denote a particular mode of constitutional interpretation) hold that, whether better or not, judges are required to recognize arguments in an ethical modality because of the Constitution's role in society, its commitments (not simply those of judges), and so on.

Tushnet appreciates the problematic nature, however, of any prescription purporting to rely on the American ethos:

[There is another] way to invoke a community's commitment as the basis for judicial review. Instead of relying on "common values" widely shared in the society at the time of decision, courts could invalidate statutes because they are inconsistent with an enduring consensus about fundamental values, as reflected in the language of the Constitution, decided cases, and our society's cultural heritage. One might fairly wonder why we are not told that the deepest values of our society require us to adopt a form of Christian socialism. Or perhaps the enduring values of our society are what some would describe as racist, sexist, and generally inegalitarian and intolerant . . . Or finally, perhaps there is no "deep consensus" in the United States because the United States is simply the adventitious collection of people whose primary relationship is coresidence in an arbitrary defined territory.[45]

We can first dismiss the suggestion that the only thing in common in our national culture is "coresidence in an arbitrary defined territory." But what about the questions regarding the nature of our ethos? Why can't it be fundamentally Christian socialist, racist, or so forth? Some have said it is, and they are, of course, correct in some respects. The important point, however, is that these characterizations must link up with some legal commitment in the Constitution. The ethos in question is a constitutional one. Its elements are derived from the ethical choices manifest in the American Constitution. For example: because the Constitution rigorously and carefully puts certain matters beyond the reach of the powers allocated in Article I, ethical arguments can infer individual and group autonomy over these subjects. Such restraints on government do protect the racist, the socialist, and the sexist. An ethos that protects diverse private decisionmaking will accordingly be capable of characterization in many attractive – and not so attractive – ways. Now if one expects an ethos thus characterized to justify judicial review, one will naturally demand a single, complete, non-contradictory, determinate, and politically acceptable national ethos. Something like this ideology is reflected in Tushnet's hunger for a "republicanism of civic virtue." But if instead one is analyzing a modality of argument – that is, the way in which a particular constitutional argument is validated – one will expect no more of such characterizations than that they arise from the necessities and possibilities of the Constitution itself.

At the beginning of his chapter on this form of argument, Tushnet told this story:

One day, as Justice Oliver Wendell Holmes was leaving to go to the Supreme Court, a friend said to him, "Well, off to do justice again!" Holmes is said to have replied, "Sonny, I don't do justice; I just make sure that people play by the rules" . . . But the Justice's friend appealed to a deeply rooted sense that judges can do something else – they can provide justice. For our purposes "doing justice" means making sure that the legal process produces morally acceptable outcomes. In this view judges should uphold statutes that are morally permissible and strike down those that are morally impermissible.[46]

The contrast between this account and the actual anecdote is revealing on many grounds, but I will confine myself to one. The story comes from a reminiscence of Holmes by Learned Hand:

I remember once I was with him; it was a Saturday when the Court was to confer . . . When we got down to the Capitol, I wanted to provoke a response, so as he walked off I said to him, "Well, Sir, goodbye. Do justice!" He turned quite sharply and he said, "Come here. Come here." I answered, "Oh, I know, I know." He replied: "That is not my job. My job is to play the game according to the rules."[47]

There is a world of difference between, on the one hand, trying conscientiously to play by the rules and, on the other hand, seeing your task as making others do so. And there is an analogous difference between ethical arguments, with their mandate in the Constitution, and moral arguments generally. When the legal process is justified on the grounds that it produces morally acceptable outcomes it is being judged on a prudential basis, and all the other forms are merely sham. It is a pity that Tushnet, who is so clearly interested in the various modes, has so little feel for them.

(f)   Prudential argument

Tushnet never appreciates that he, along with the many writers he criticizes on this ground, is imprisoned within a particular approach. By the end of Part 1 of *Red, White and Blue*, the author has discussed five of the six modalities of argument: historical argument ("The Jurisprudence of History"), textual argument ("Textualism"), doctrinal argument ("Neutral Principles"), structural argument ("The Jurisprudence of Democracy"), and ethical argument ("The Jurisprudence of Philosophy"). Tushnet decides to call these forms of argument "formalisms" since they provide a "set of public criteria by which theorists, interested observers, and the judges themselves can evaluate what judges do."[48] When confronting his own ideological preference, he is at a loss to recognize the underlying similarity. This preference he decides to call "Anti-formalism,"[49] reflecting his assumption that prudentialist thinkers do not merely offer yet one more form of argument.

Tushnet's discussion of the "anti-formalists" is curiously truncated in light of his detailed descriptions of the partisans of other approaches:

Owen Fiss, Frank Michelman, and Cass Sunstein have attempted to ground constitutional theory in what they call public values ... [that] must be different from ones that merely happen to be commonly shared ... Sunstein and Michelman explicitly link their vision to the republican tradition, which conceives of the public interest as distinct from the aggregate of private interest. To Owen Fiss, "adjudication is the social process by which judges give meaning to our public values."[50]

Michael Perry, Laurence Tribe, Anthony Kronman, Alexander Bickel, and Edmund Burke are all mentioned[51] (but only just mentioned) as falling within this category of critics. Tushnet is right to group these disparate persons together; he has a good eye for his list. But it remains merely a list in the absence of the group's defining characteristic, a definition that would have swept in Tushnet as well: prudential argument is actuated by a political and economic program as to which the Constitution itself is agnostic, and thus the prudentialist must provide a standard external to the constitution.

For Tushnet, such agnosticism merely reinforces his view that law is politics. Rather pompously, he taxes the framers' refusal to constitutionalize a particular political program as naive: "[They] did not understand that courts are inevitably part of society's governing coalition."[52] He then sets up a political test as the rubric by which to judge constitutional theory: "An approach to constitutional law ... is indefensible if it would allow judges to uphold the worst and invalidate the best politically feasible programs."[53] Finally, he announces this agenda for future theorists: "The task of constitutional theory ought no longer be to rationalize ... It should be to contribute to a political movement that may begin to bring about a society in which civic virtue may flourish."[54]

Of course he is right that if you are certain of what civic virtue consists, you will be able to state a program that need not tolerate the contradictions of the multi-valenced scheme of competing modalities. Such virtue at the moment appears to have been discovered by many to reside in the "republican tradition."[55] But for the very reasons that have led him to reject other claims to overarching grand theory, Tushnet is compelled to concede that the simple adoption of the republican solution is not available to him. For if none of the classic modalities of interpretation could be relied upon to serve one prudential goal, what algorithm could Tushnet devise that would invariably serve another? He thinks this is because we have simply lost the knack of knowing what advances the republican tradition of civic virtue. And thus he concludes, in resignation: "The preceding chapters have . . . suggested that grand theory cannot be made coherent today because of the erosion of the republican tradition." [56] But I wonder whether this failure does, in fact, lie in ourselves – selves that Tushnet would like to reform – or whether it lies in the nature of knowledge, rules, and decisionmaking.

MISSOURI v. HOLLAND

252 U.S. 416, 40 S.Ct. 382, 64 L.Ed. 641 (1920).

Mr. Justice HOLMES delivered the opinion of the court.

1 This is a bill in equity brought by the State of Missouri to prevent a game warden of the United States from attempting to enforce the Migratory Bird Treaty Act of July 3, 1918, [on the ground] that the statute is an unconstitutional interference with the rights reserved to the States by the Tenth Amendment. [The District Court held the Act unconstitutional.]

2 On December 8, 1916, a treaty between the United States and Great Britain was proclaimed by the President. It recited that many species of birds in their annual migrations traversed certain parts of the United States and of Canada, that they were of great value as a source of food and in destroying insects injurious to vegetation, but were in danger of extermination through lack of adequate protection. It therefore provided for specified closed seasons and protection in other forms, and agreed that the two powers would take or propose to their law making bodies the necessary measures for carrying the treaty out. The [challenged Act] prohibited the killing, capturing or selling any of the migratory birds included in the terms of the treaty except as permitted by regulations compatible with those terms, to be made by the Secretary of Agriculture. [It] is unnecessary to go into any details, because [the] question raised is the general one whether the treaty and statute are void as an interference with the rights reserved to the States.

3 To answer this question it is not enough to refer to the Tenth Amendment [because] by Article II, § 2, the power to make treaties is delegated expressly, and by Article VI treaties made under the authority of the United States, along with the Constitution and laws of the United States made in pursuance thereof, are declared the supreme law of the land. If the treaty is valid there can be no dispute about the validity of the statute under Article I, § 8, as a necessary and proper means to execute the powers of the Government. . . .

4 It is said that a treaty cannot be valid if it infringes the Constitution, that there are limits, therefore, to the treaty-making power, and that one such limit is that what an act of Congress could not do unaided, in derogation of the powers reserved to the States, a treaty cannot do. [The fact that an] earlier act of Congress that attempted by itself and not in pursuance of a treaty to regulate the killing of migratory birds within the States had been held bad [in two lower court decisions] cannot be accepted as a test of the treaty power. Acts of Congress are the supreme law of the land only when made in pursuance of the Constitution, while treaties are declared to be so when made under the authority of the United States. It is open to question whether the authority of the United States means more than the formal acts prescribed to make the convention. We do not mean to imply that there are no qualifications to the treaty-making power; but they must be ascertained in a different way. It is obvious that there

may be matters of the sharpest exigency for the national well being that an act of Congress could not deal with but that a treaty followed by such an act could, and it is not lightly to be assumed that, in matters requiring national action, "a power which must belong to and somewhere reside in every civilized government" is not to be found. [We] are not yet discussing the particular case before us but only are considering the validity of the test proposed. With regard to that we may add that when we are dealing with words that also are a constituent act, like the Constitution of the United States, we must realize that they have called into life a being the development of which could not have been forseen completely by the most gifted of its begetters. It was enough for them to realize or to hope that they had created an organism; it has taken a century and has cost their successors much sweat and blood to prove that they created a nation. The case before us must be considered in the light of our whole experience and not merely in that of what was said a hundred years ago. The treaty in question does not contravene any prohibitory words to be found in the Constitution. The only question is whether it is forbidden by some invisible radiation from the general terms of the Tenth Amendment. We must consider what this country has become in deciding what that Amendment has reserved.

5 The State as we have intimated founds its claim of exclusive authority upon an assertion of title to migratory birds, an assertion that is embodied in statute. No doubt it is true that as between a State and its inhabitants the State may regulate the killing and sale of such birds, but it does not follow that its authority is exclusive of paramount powers. . . .

6 As most of the laws of the United States are carried out within the States and as many of them deal with matters which in the silence of such laws the State might regulate, such general grounds are not enough to support Missouri's claim. Valid treaties of course "are as binding within the territorial limits of the States as they are elsewhere throughout the dominion of the United States." No doubt the great body of private relations usually fall within the control of the State, but a treaty may override its power. . . .

7 Here a national interest of very nearly the first magnitude is involved. It can be protected only by national action in concert with that of another power. The subject matter is only transitorily within the State and has no permanent habitat therein. But for the treaty and the statute there soon might be no birds for any powers to deal with. We see nothing in the Constitution that compels the Government to sit by while a food supply is cut off and the protectors of our forests and our crops are destroyed. It is not sufficient to rely upon the States. The reliance is vain, and were it otherwise, the question is whether the United States is forbidden to act. We are of opinion that the treaty and statute must be upheld.
    Decree affirmed.
    Mr. Justice VAN DEVANTER and Mr. Justice PITNEY dissent.

3

WHY IT WAS THOUGHT SUCH PROPOSALS WERE NECESSARY

In this chapter I will first suggest why it was thought a rule, an algorithm, was needed to resolve the conflicting outcomes generated by the American system of constitutional interpretation (part I). Secondly, I will attempt to show why this is not, in fact, necessary (part II).

Part I

The following is my account of what I take to be the usual understanding of just decisionmaking in law.

A decision can be justified by reference to standards of justice; but the justification nevertheless depends on a rationalization of that decision. The rationalization acts as a kind of proto-justification, which is translated into the terms of the standards to be applied. For example, imagine how we might assess a decision to punish a thief. Suppose the victim who had been robbed proposed that the thief have his hand cut off. A decision to do so, if it can be justified, can only be justified according to some rationalization. The man who was robbed might say: such a punishment will prevent him from robbing again since a disabled, and marked, criminal will find it hard to steal again. Or he might say: I am entitled, by certain religious texts, to revenge (and this sentence will satisfy my entitlement). These rationalizations of the action are justified, or not, by testing them against the prevailing standards of justice. Perhaps, for example, the standards to be applied presuppose an absolute bar on the mutilation of any person by the state; in such a case, the proposed *rationalizations* will fail as claims of *justifications*.

I think it can be shown that such rationalizations are understood as depending on causal explanations. We can see this if we consider the role of reasons (the claims of deterrence and vindication, above) in rationalization. In order to understand how a reason rationalizes an action we have only to see that giving a reason for an action amounts to specifying its cause.

To take the example above: (1) The justification for the decision depends on comparing a rationalization of that decision with the standards of justice to be applied; the decision to punish the thief by cutting off his hand is justified because cutting off the hand will deter further thefts (the rationalization) and deterring theft is a conventional measure of justice. (2) A rationalization requires giving a reason for an action; "cutting off the hand will deter theft" rationalizes insofar as the *reason* for cutting off the hand is that it will deter theft. (3) A reason rationalizes the action by explaining it: "to deter theft" (the reason) explains why the hand is to be cut off (the explanation).

Let us go over this ground again. A *rationalization* amounts to the giving of reasons for an action. We say the reason accounts for the action (that it rationalizes it) if the reason explains the action; and it explains it by giving the person's reasons for acting as he did. Donald Davidson writes:

What is the relation between a reason and an action when the reason explains the action by giving the agent's reason for doing what he did? We may call such explanations rationalizations, and say that the reason rationalizes the action.

Because justifying and explaining an action so often go hand in hand, we frequently indicate the primary reason for an action by making a claim which, if true, would also verify, vindicate, or support the relevant belief or attitude of an agent. "I knew I ought to return it," "The paper said it was going to snow," "You stepped on *my* toes," all, in appropriate reason-giving contexts, perform this dual function. The justifying role of a reason, given this interpretation, depends on the explanatory role, but the converse does not hold. Your stepping on my toes neither explains nor justifies my stepping on your toes unless I believe you stepped on my toes, but the belief alone, true or false, explains my action.[1]

This is the picture we have of how a just decision is made: we are presented with facts that embody a conflict and we are called upon to resolve that conflict in a certain way (by requiring damages, fines, imprisonment, specific acts, etc.). In considering these facts, we appeal to certain rules which lie dormant, as it were, until they are brought to life by corresponding facts (is this parol evidence, is he a person of diminished responsibility, did she intend the harm she brought about). When the facts are brought into correspondence with the rules, we have a potential outcome (or outcomes): yes, the defendant landowner owed a general duty to maintain safe premises but the plaintiff was a trespasser. In a difficult case, the judge may find there is a conflict among opposing rules and so will have to appeal to principles that transcend such rules (e.g., no man may profit from his own wrong). The judge's rationale for the decision he renders (his rationalization of his action) consists in his giving reasons for having decided as he has.

How do we determine whether the outcome decided upon is just? We assess the rationalization offered in light of the most satisfactory moral theory at our disposal. We measure the rationalization to see if it states a proposition that can be inferred from the theory (that is, the rationalization acts as a proto-justification which is compared with our standards of justice.) For example: in *Watkins* v. *United States*[2] the United States Supreme Court dealt with the refusal of a former labor organizer, John Watkins, to answer questions put to him by a subcommittee of the Committee on Un-American Activities of the House of Representatives, which was investigating "Communist activities in the Chicago area." The Court overturned Watkins's conviction for contempt of Congress, giving as its reason the conclusion that neither the Congress nor its Committee had ever satisfactorily apprised Watkins whether the questions he had refused to answer were "pertinent to the subject under inquiry."[3] This failure was held to render the conviction void on the grounds of vagueness under the due process clause of the Fifth Amendment.[4] The decision can be defended as just if, on the basis of the most satisfactory moral theory, a man should not be held liable for acts when he has not been sufficiently informed of the legal consequence of his acts. Thus a person cannot be tricked into a crime. If this theory justifies the action taken (the decision) by the Supreme Court, it does so on the basis of a comparison of the rationalization given by the Court with the proposition just stated. The outcome – freeing Watkins – might be justified on many other grounds, as to which the Court's rationale is irrelevant. But the *decision* can be justified only by an examination of its reasons.

I believe this is the usual way that we depict just decisions to ourselves. I would draw attention to one aspect of this account of reasons as causes, and rationalization as explanation: Carl Hempel argued, rightly I think, that every explanation states or implies an empirical generalization.[5] An explanation unconditionally predicts what it explains. This requirement of reasons/explanations in justifying legal decisions – which is implied in the account I have given above, and is held very broadly among legal critics of many otherwise different views – is similar to that generally held regarding justification in the natural sciences. It is a view with respect to the justification of statements of fact about the world that imply empirical generalizations. It is *not* a view that arises from seeing legal statements as statements with a modal significance only. The reader of Book I who assumes that he or she is acquitted of the charge of confusing legal statements with statements about the world might reflect on the account given above of the justification of a legal decision. I surmise that such a view, or something essentially like it, is widespread across the Anglo-American community.

Part II

Four propositions appear to follow from the description I have given of the decision process: (a) there must be a rule (or principle) to guide the decision; (b) deciding is an instrument of justice, i.e., it is the means by which we bring about justice; (c) a just decision must therefore actualize a (just) rule or principle; (d) the justification for a decision consists essentially in recapitulating the decision process with its appeal to the just rule or principle. I believe none of these propositions is correct; and I hope I can show how their rejection leads also to the rejection of the need for a unifying or decisive algorithm to resolve conflicts among the modalities in order to assure justice.

(a)   There must be a rule (or principle) to guide the decision

This requirement is held by all of the authors discussed in Book III, i.e., by Fallon,[6] Post,[7] Powell,[8] Tushnet,[9] as well as by the premier Anglo-American legal theorists of our era, Ronald Dworkin[10] and H. L. A. Hart.[11] Although they have many differences among themselves, all would agree that a just legal system must provide determinate rules, either within itself (Hart)[12] or by an appeal to principles that are not autonomous to the system (Dworkin).[13] Indeed, the search for a constitutional algorithm, which we have seen in Fallon, Powell and Tushnet, arises from the fact that the modalities of interpretation in American constitutional law do not provide a determining rule themselves.

It would appear from this requirement that:

1   A decision is justifiable when a rule can be stated that corresponds with our notions of justice.

2   A rule must be capable of statement in advance of the decision if that decision is to be justified as having been taken on account of the rule.

3   When we can derive conflicting rationalizations for decisions there is no rule that can be stated in advance on which the decision necessarily depends.

It would appear that we must come up with either an algorithm (that tells us how to apply the rules of the modalities when they conflict) or some sort of meta-rule that refers us, for example, to political or moral theory outside the domain of the potentially conflicting modalities. But suppose we add a fourth proposition.

4   A decision is justifiable whether or not a rule is stated in advance of the decision so long as the decision itself corresponds to our notions of justice.

And surely this must be so: because the criteria for justification can be applied to the result. Consider, by contrast, this example drawn from immunology. Tumors transplanted from rats and mice rarely "take;" that is, the tumor grafts at first appear to grow but then, to the accompaniment of a sharp increase in the recipient's lymphocytes, the tumors dwindle away. Moreover, it seems that a mouse or rat in whom such a transplant has at first grown and then withered is absolutely refractory to further transplants of the same tumor. This evidence led many researchers to believe that an inoculation of cancerous cells would serve as a preventive measure. In fact, alas, the "immunity" thus stimulated is not an immunity directed at the tumor as such, but rather against the graft which the recipient's system treats as a genetically foreign cell.[14] What is the consequence of this error? It lies in the *explanation* of the event, and hence in our ability to predict on the basis of that event. But when we ask whether a particular legal decision is just, we are not trying to predict a future replay of the decision; we are evaluating a unique event. Thus if we are asked whether or not a particular decision is just and we have no idea of the thoughts of the decider, and we are unable to know what his intentions may have been, we do not suspend our judgment. If we can justify a decision without knowing on what basis it was made then a decision is justifiable whether or not a rule is stated in advance of the decision. So long as the system of deciding produces just results, it does not matter if an erroneous rule, and thus it does not matter if no rule, guides the decisionmaker. It is not the pre-existent rule that justifies the decision – that would amount to circularity – and therefore the pre-existent rule is not necessary to that justification.

(b) Deciding is an instrument of justice

This is the usual view of the relationship between deciding and justice – that the former "implements" the latter. We bear in mind certain parameters as a result of our experience in the world (these are rules and principles); we are presented with a question; we decide the question by referring to these rules or to new rules we have derived from them, and in applying them:

> Two conditions are essential to the realization of justice according to law. The law must have an authority supreme over the will of the individual, and such an authority can arise only from a background of social acquiescence, which gives it the voice of indefinitely greater numbers than those of its expositors.[15]

This account, I am afraid, plays real havoc with the modal perspective I have been urging. For if we accept that the modes are incommensurable, then they cannot serve either as the rules, or principles from which new rules are derived, that would decide among the various outcomes they legitimate, i.e., that would subordinate the will of the individual. But if they – the rules of the modalities – are not the basis for the decision, then they cannot legitimate, because they are the only modalities that are sanctioned by the Constitution.

Under Hand's account, which I have just quoted, we assume the view that to decide is to engage an inner state, with respect to which we bring the matter to be decided into agreement. Making the decision happens "inside us" and we externalize it when we undertake behaviour that is in agreement with this inner state of mind. So when we say: "[I have decided that] a minor may not be executed consistent with the terms of the Constitution" we are merely giving expression to an inner event. Moreover, under this account, our sense of justice is presumed to be the source of the event. We may be wrong, our sense may be distorted, etc. but the decision – if it aims to be a just one – proceeds from our notions of justice, and is actualized by our behaviour. Cardozo, in this celebrated passage from *The Nature of the Judicial Process*, exemplifies this view:

Let me take as an illustration of such conflict the famous case of *Riggs v. Palmer*, 115 N.Y. 506. That case decided that a legatee who had murdered his testator would not be permitted by a court of equity to enjoy the benefits of the will. Conflicting principles were there in competition for the mastery. One of them prevailed, and vanquished all the others. There was the principle of the binding force of a will disposing of the estate of a testator in conformity with law. That principle, pushed to the limit of its logic, seemed to uphold the title of the murderer. There was the principle that civil courts may not add to the pains and penalties of crimes. That, pushed to the limit of its logic, seemed again to uphold his title. But over against these was another principle, of greater generality, its roots deeply fastened in universal sentiments of justice, the principle that no man should profit from his own inequity or take advantage of his own wrong. The logic of this principle prevailed over the logic of the others. I say its logic prevailed. The thing which really interests us, however, is why and how the choice was made between one logic and another. In this instance, the reason is not obscure. One path was followed, another closed, because of the conviction in the judicial mind that the one selected led to justice.[16]

If this is right, then there must be some way in which our inner state (our sense of justice) is related to our expression, our decision: and thus the decision is the instrument of justice.

But suppose instead that justice is sometimes an instrument of deciding; that it is created out of the process of deciding and, having been created, can then be referred back to. In the law, justice arises from law practices; in the absence of legal practices there would be no just legal decisions, as in the absence of the discipline of physics, no engineering solution could be "technically sweet." This makes justice useful all right – since it provides standards against which we can test alternative decisions – but it does not depend on an idea that must *necessarily* exist prior to our deciding.

Is it so obvious that we must have a specific idea of justice before we can decide? I think I can show in this section that it is not even necessary to have any inner state of mind whatsoever before we can "give" expression to it. Sometimes we simply decide. The expression is all there is. And when we are asked to justify it, we use the vocabulary of justification that had not really occurred to us prior to our decision. Sometimes we reserve the epithet "rationalization" for just this phenomenon, but I am not concerned with the spurious psychological claims of inauthenticity in this context. When a parent is asked to justify a decision to a child, the parent *may* give good reasons for the decision that had not in fact occurred to the parent prior to the child's demand for a justification. One cannot say that justification is never about the past, but one can say that it need not be, and that whether it is a true account of the past need not determine whether it is justificatory.

(c) A just decision actualizes a just rule or principle

It is usually said that legal language functions by capturing an inner state of its drafter that, once expressed, causes the same inner state to occur in a reader. Legal language is functioning correctly when the relevant reader will be affected by it in the way the drafter intended, which is presumed to be a recapture of the thought in the mind of the drafter at the time of the composition. And of course this works in reverse: the interpretation of a provision seeks to affect this recapture of meaning. With respect to *constitutional* interpretation, this may be the meaning that the draftsman conceived and attempted to capture in his drafting; or it may be the meaning that a court would conceive when called upon to interpret the provision; or the meaning that would lead to the most efficient outcome; or the meaning that the average reader might give it; and so on. An accompanying notion regarding the Constitution seems to be that the interpretation of a provision *infuses* it with meaning. Persons working within a particular method, it may be said, are trying to capture the same thoughts (of the drafters, of earlier courts, of economic analysts, etc.) The "correct" decision within one of these modes is the one that correctly actualizes the appropriate thoughts.

Decisions based on different modal approaches often disagree. How can we know which one is right? If we apply this same general approach, i.e., if we assume that a decision must actualize a principle (as, for example, the decision to refuse to seat an elected twenty year-old Congressman actualizes the principle that the text of the Constitution, as interpreted by contemporary native speakers, is paramount to any political decisions), then a just decision would have to be, on this view, the result of an interpretation that actualizes a just rule or principle.

A putatively just decision therefore seems to require a means of comparing it with a just rule or principle. If one knew the rule (or principle) then one would know whether the decision corresponded to it; and thus it often appears to us that there must be a rule for us to be able to decide justly; and that in so deciding we are bringing into reality what was hitherto the pregnant form of a just idea.

But is this so? Does the drafter have to have anything at all in mind, necessarily, when he drafts a provision? Consider this: he receives a direction to draft a declaration of complaint against the government's ministers. He writes up this bill of complaint, as he has been trained to do, putting into formal expression each of the wrongs that the government has done. He may think of some of these and reflect on their intolerableness; but others he may simply copy from earlier texts he has drafted for other occasions. Is it necessary that he have an idea in mind as a preliminary to his drafting and must this idea be the one to which his writing aspires? Is the idea *in words* (so that the drafting is simply a kind of dictation) and if not, or if only partially so, how can it frame a rule sufficient to guide the choice among words, since a wordless rule is only the knowledge of how to proceed, how to decide, and not a principle (in the sense of a directive). Consider this famous passage from Jefferson's initial draft of the Declaration of Independence:[17]

When in the course of human events it becomes necessary for

one *dissolve the political bands which have connected*
{a} people to {advance from that subordination in which they

                        them with another, and to
have hitherto remained, & to} assume among the powers of the

                 separate and equal
earth the {equal & independent} station to which the laws of

nature & of nature's god entitle them, a decent respect to the

opinions of mankind requires that they should declare the

                        the separation
causes which impel them to {the change}.

                           self-evident
We hold these truths to be {sacred & undeniable}; that all men

                              they are endowed by their
are created equal {& independent}; that {from that equal

       creator with {equal rights, some of which are}
creation they derive in rights} inherent & inalienable among

    these
{which} are {the preservation of} life, {&} liberty, & the pursuit

of happiness . . .

Notice that the changes in the first paragraph apparently fit the
standard model of composition: "a people" becomes "one people,"
"equal and independent" becomes "separate and equal." These are
felicitous changes. They simplify while enriching; the meaning is
unchanged and so, it may be concluded, is the correspondence
between the words and the ideas Jefferson was expressing.

But now consider the changes in the second paragraph. "Self-
evident" does not mean "sacred and undeniable." A *self-evident*
truth is one that a people will recognize; it is undeniable, perhaps
even sacred in a secular sense, but it is much more than that. It is
manifest in the nature of things. "All men are created equal and
independent" is not the same thing as the assertion that "All men
are created equal" because "equality" does not subsume independence. Being "endowed by [our] creator with inherent and inalienable rights" is by no means the same as *deriving* rights from our

equal creation, which is itself a very different matter from possessing "equal rights, some of which are inherent and inalienable" (the changed language that was changed again in the final version).

The decisions that are reflected in the alterations to the second paragraph may of course be the result of a change in Jefferson's principles. But then what idea governed *that* change? Suppose instead that Jefferson's principles were broad enough to tolerate either language – his drafting did not *violate* them – but that he decided among them precisely because the decision was not made for him in advance. The principle that emerged did not dictate one form of expression in advance but was a consequence of changes in expression. Does that not show that a just decision need not necessarily actualize a *prior* just principle or rule?

(d) The justification for a decision recapitulates the decision

This is the standard paradigm for an appellate opinion: that the court tells how it reached its decision so that we may judge its rightness. But that word "rightness" conceals two different ideas: legitimacy and justification. We have already seen that a judge does not refer to the forms of argument to achieve legitimacy: he or she simply reasons according to those forms. Just as I do not refer to a measure of the distance between my drawn bowstring and the target, or refer to the height of someone when I look upward (or downward) at her eyes, the judge does not *refer* to the forms of argument in analyzing a constitutional question. The judge uses them; indeed their use is all a legitimate opinion consists in. Reference is neither necessary nor sufficient for such legitimacy.

What about justification? Do we need an explanation from a court as to how it reached its decision so that we may judge whether it is justified in doing so? Are "reasons" in a constitutional opinion the same as "reasons" in the natural sciences, i.e., are they *causes*? If they are, then in order to understand how a reason in an opinion rationalizes a decision, we must see how the action (the decision) for which the reason is given was caused; and the reason must be the cause.

But why? Why can we not rationalize an act whose cause we do not know? Contrast these two cases:

1   When President Abraham Lincoln signed the Emancipation Proclamation in 1863, he freed the slaves resident in the states of the Confederacy; but the Proclamation does not deal with those slaves in states that were not in rebellion, notably Maryland and Kentucky.[18] To justify such a decision – to evaluate the rationalization provided for it by measuring that rationalization against our moral standards – it would seem necessary to know something about Lincoln's state of mind. For example, if we offer the rationalization that partial emancipation was undertaken as a pragmatic way of engineering total eventual emancipation we will evaluate the decision according to one set of moral premises; but if we offer the rationalization that the aim of the Proclamation was to stimulate slave rebellion in the rear of the Confederate lines and thus was partial simply because Lincoln wished to confine unrest to the South, then the decision appears in a different light. A different set of questions becomes relevant. It seems that we want to know why the decision was taken before we can proceed with justifying it.

2   Suppose a federal district judge is called upon to decide the constitutionality of the War Powers Act,[19] which requires the President to withdraw troops from a war zone in the absence of Congressional approval, after sixty days; and suppose that the judge's decision in favor of the Act's constitutionality has the effect of preventing an attack on a US vessel that a foreign power now believes (as a result of this judicial decision) will be withdrawn. Finally, suppose that the judge's decision rejects the textual argument that because the President is the sole Commander-in-Chief and can therefore order the disposition of troops as he chooses, Congress cannot interfere with such orders by statute. What is the rationalization proffered for the decision? That will be found in the opinion. It might have been concluded that, for structural reasons such as the concurrent role Congress and the executive play in declaring and making war, the War Powers Act has a sound constitutional basis. Is the decision justified in light of this argument? Or in light of the result that an attack was avoided? Well, that depends on the moral rules one brings to bear on the decision. But note that in neither case does it matter whether the judge actually knew about the attack, or, *a fortiori*, was motivated to decide by fear of the attack on the American ship. An account of the judge's motivation may excuse the decision but it cannot justify it. It is the outcome of the decision

that must be justified (even if some moral systems do so on the basis of its cause).

The standard account holds that the rule to which we refer as the *reason* we decided a certain way provides a rationalization of the decision. But this formulation obscures the distinction between the reason we have for doing something and the reason we actually did something. In the law we can sharpen this distinction by saying it is between the reasons we give and the reasons we decided.

In the standard account the reasons motivating our decision enable a justification of the decision if the reasons are in accord with our moral theory. If we are content to evaluate the reasons we gave in this way they too will enable a justification (albeit from a different frame of reference than that of legitimacy). Justification does not require a rule of decision.

If the cause of a decision does not bear any necessary relationship to justification, how is a constitutional decision to be judged as just (or not)? In the same varied ways we evaluate other social decisions as just. The rules for moral reasoning are used in a way that is analogous to the use of rules for legal reasoning (though there may be less consensus on what rules are to be used) – in an interplay between a moral act and a hypothetical moral ideal. As such, moral analysis cannot be "plugged into" the legal decision – as a sort of super rule – because it has no status as legal reasoning (just as the legal reasons, the uses of the forms of argument, have no special moral status). So one learns to think in moral terms just as one learns to think in legal ways: the "thoughts," and the ideals, are the consequence, not the cause, of this process.

Unlike the example Davidson gave above – "You stepped on *my* toes" – the justifying role of the legal reason given does not depend on its explanatory role. The fact that the War Powers Act can be legitimately held constitutional on structural grounds – that such a decision can be rationalized in this way – does not necessarily tell us anything about why the decision was reached. Nor, as a matter of justification of the decision, do we necessarily care. For if we learned that the rationale given, though just in light of the moral theory applied, had been selected on the basis of motives having nothing to do with that rationale, that fact would not thereby necessarily render it unjust. As far as justice goes, it will be a matter for an analysis that does not depend on whether the judge knew he was, for example, choosing the most efficient outcome when the micro-economist/moral analyst assesses the decision (to take one moral framework). It is true that one must provide an account that rationalizes the decision. But one never further demands of a legal opinion "why this rationale rather than another one on *moral* grounds?" For these reasons we may say that justice arises from decisions; it does not necessarily precede them.

This, then, is an account of why it is thought that an algorithm is needed: because it has been believed that a rule (or principle) had to be provided on which a decider must rely. The erroneous need for a causal explanation is widely held, I suspect, to be a requirement of justice. It is not so. In the next chapter I will argue that such a requirement is actually pernicious.

I should like to close this discussion with a brief passage from the Postscript to Franz Kafka's *The Trial*.[20] Kafka left his executor Max Brod careful and explicit instructions that his unpublished manuscripts be burned unread. It is owing to Brod's refusal to obey these categorical instructions that we have *The Trial*, *Amerika*, *The Castle*, and other posthumously published works. The Postscript to the first edition is largely devoted to a justification of this decision. The passage I will quote, however, deals with the decision *per se* rather than the reasons that may be offered to support it. It reads like a confession:

My decision does not rest on any of the reasons given above but simply and solely on the fact that Kafka's unpublished work contains the most wonderful treasures . . . In all honesty, I must confess that this one fact of the literary and ethical value of what I am publishing would have been enough to decide one to do so, definitely, finally, and irresistibly.[21]

In this Postscript, notice that Brod has severed the account of the decision from its rationalization. More importantly, which do we look to for justification: whether Brod sincerely believed *The Trial* to be a masterpiece, or whether it is?

4

THE POSSIBILITY OF JUSTICE

In the previous chapter I attempted to show why it was thought that an algorithm – a meta-rule, as it were – was required to resolve the different outcomes generated by the modalities of constitutional interpretation. And I tried to show that the assumption on which this belief rested, namely the view that deciding necessarily depended upon matching a decision with an idea (the meta-rule), was wrong. Nevertheless, it might be argued that such a meta-rule would be helpful, even if not strictly necessary. It would tell us what to do in doubtful cases when we found ourselves unable to decide, for example, and would give us a basis on which to determine the justice of the decision. In the present chapter I will argue that such a rule is not helpful, indeed that it is utterly destructive of constitutional decisionmaking. Finally, I will maintain that such meta-rules are incompatible with moral choice (whereas it is usually thought that they enable moral thought by providing a moral guide to decisionmaking).

These are my initial objections to the enterprise of providing a meta-rule that would resolve conflicts among the modalities. First, the effort to find a trans-modal decision procedure collapses the structure of legitimation that is the whole point of the operation of the modalities. For if the various modes legitimate constitutional argument within their forms, what legitimates the new decision procedure? To say, for example, "The implicit norms of our constitutional practice . . . require that the claims of the different kinds of arguments be ranked hierarchically"[1] is but to create another modality or give a privileged position to one pre-existing. (To "rank hierarchically" here means that, for example, a textual argument trumps a prudential argument – "no matter how effective a deterrent to political corruption we cannot employ the bill of attainder in the face of explicit prohibition against doing so" – or perhaps the other way around – "no matter what the text says the President can declare and enforce martial law without Congressional authorization if civil disorder is severe enough," the prudential trumping the textual.) To use this new "mode" as a trans-modal algorithm (a meta-rule) is simply to revert back to the privileged status moves of other modal preferences. It reminds me of a serious flaw in Robert Bork's strict constructionism: he would have judges rely on historical argument and when this is unclear, leave the decision in the hands of the legislature.[2] But then legislatures too must make decisions about the constitutionality of their own acts. If they also are confined to historical argument, what can they be presumed to have relied upon in those very instances in which the courts are directed to defer to them? If there is a hierarchy of modes, which mode supports this hierarchy? And how will we choose among competing hierarchies, that are also "implicit" in the Constitution?

Second, there is often conflict within a single mode, so that even if a hierarchical meta-rule were available, it would not always be clear when such a rule would apply, and it may also be unclear whether and to what extent the modalities are actually in conflict. Fallon recognizes that arguments from the various modalities often interlock,[3] as we saw in *Missouri* v. *Holland* and the Iran–Contra analysis. This interlinkage, however, is far from inter-operability. In fact, it defies the operation of a meta-rule to resolve the incommensurability of the various modes if they are interdependent but not fungible. Even if we assume that a textual argument trumps a prudential one, how do we rank the *Griswold* majority (the textual rights of the First, Third and Fourth Amendments depend, as a prudential matter, on preventing the surveillance and intrusion required to enforce anti-contraception laws);[4] the Stewart dissent in that case (no text provides a right of privacy);[5] and the Goldberg concurrence (the text of the Ninth Amendment is evidence of the constitutional ethos that sequesters certain unenumerated powers from government exercise)?[6]

Third, the choice of the meta-rule would depend on the type of opinion to be crafted; so there would have to be another meta-rule to govern *that* decision. A doctrinal opinion, for example (as we

saw in *Missouri* v. *Holland*) forms a different precedent from a
prudential opinion, and is therefore more or less appropriate to a
particular function of constitutional review.[7] So it is possible that
before we choose a particular form of argument (which the meta-
rule would rank relative to other choices) we would first have to
choose the function the opinion is to serve; and that choice would
require another rule or re-introduce the incommensurability issue.

Fourth, I am sure that such enterprises ought to fail. Look at
what is lost by such a solution. The incommensurate modalities give
us various possible worlds against which to measure our sense of
justice and fitness. Consider the case of *Furman* v. *Georgia*.[8] In
Furman the Court held that capital punishment, at least as it was
then administered, violated the Eighth Amendment, which prohibits
"cruel and unusual punishments." The five Justices in the majority
each wrote a concurring opinion that approached the issue from a
different perspective. Two Justices concluded that the death penalty,
however administered, was "cruel and unusual" because the execution
of a human being "does not comport with human dignity"[9] or
because it is "morally unacceptable" and "excessive" in light of
prevailing American standards.[10] One Justice decided that because
the death penalty is inflicted on the poor in vastly greater proportion
than on the well-off, the penalty, as it works out in practical life,
amounts to a violation of the equality of treatment that is implicitly
promised in the Eighth Amendment.[11] Two Justices concluded that
capital punishment was both "cruel" and "unusual" because it was
applied in an arbitrary, standardless way such that its actual
occurrence was "freakish" and "wanton" and thus could serve no
purpose.[12]

Because a majority of the Court was not committed to holding
the death penalty unconstitutional *per se* it could be predicted that
state legislatures would attempt to re-fashion their statutes. This, of
course, happened. In *Jurek* v. *Texas*,[13] and *Gregg* v. *Georgia*,[14] the
Court confronted statutes that purported to provide procedures
and standards sufficient to remove the arbitrary elements that were
offensive in *Furman*. The invitation to uphold these statutes meant
contemplating a number of possible legal worlds. In one of these
possible worlds, capital punishment is impermissible, on constitutional grounds, because it cannot be administered consistently with
the relationship between persons and the state that the Constitution
requires, a relationship that assumes that the state's procedures for

action against persons will be calibrated approximately to the risks it imposes. In that world, there is no procedure that is adequate to take life. In another possible world, capital punishment is permitted, indeed cannot be struck down by the Fourteenth Amendment's due process clause, because the text of that amendment explicitly contemplates the taking of life. (The amendment forbids the taking of "life" without due process, thus implicitly validating some executions, i.e., those that comport with due process.) In another possible world, capital punishment statutes, like the Texas statute in *Jurek*, are not consistent with *Furman* v. *Georgia* and either must be struck down, and *Jurek* reversed, or *Furman* overruled. In another possible world, the practices of the ratifiers of the Eighth and Fourteenth Amendments, which included state executions, might be dispositive. The multiplicity of modes gives us a way to measure a possible legal world against our sense of rightness, going back and forth between a proposed interpretation and its world, and ourselves.

The multiplicity of incommensurate modalities has other benefits. It allows different groups in America to claim the Constitution as their own in the face of reasoned but adverse interpretations. It also allows changes to come without requiring that the Constitution be repudiated, when a precedent has been rightly decided within a particular mode, but has come to mean something unacceptable in the world within which it must operate.

Consider the celebrated case of the *Erie Railroad Co.* v. *Tompkins*.[15] For almost one hundred years Justice Story's opinion in *Swift* v. *Tyson*[16] had stood for the proposition that in the federal courts the law to be applied in diversity cases – suits between parties from different states – was a federal common law. Tompkins, a citizen of Pennsylvania who was injured while walking along a railroad right-of-way, sued in the federal court for Southern New York, where the railroad corporation was located. Neither party suggested overruling *Swift*, although the railroad doubted it applied. Justice Brandeis, in an opinion for the US Supreme Court, held that there could be no federal general common law because Congress has no enumerated power to substitute its law for that of the states in diversity cases.[17] Brandeis argued that *Swift* had failed to bring the uniformity of decision that its authority had promised,[18] and that the application of *Swift* discriminated against citizens of a state (by allowing non-citizens to remove to federal court if they found the law there more favorable).[19]

Despite his conclusion that section 34 of the Judiciary Act,[20] which provided that "the laws of the several states . . . shall be regarded as rules of decision . . . in the [federal] courts," could not constitutionally be limited to the *statutes* of the several states (but must also include state common law), Justice Brandeis did not strike down the federal statute which had been held, in *Swift*, to apply in this way. Rather he decided that the Court had erred in *Swift* and so left the statute in place. This is a rather dramatic example of the virtue I am calling attention to, since not only the Constitution but the statute is left unblemished despite the utter repudiation of the provisions of both as previously interpreted.

Finally, a trans-modal rule would deny to judicial review its very basis in law and thus re-introduce a problem that the modalities had resolved. Recall that the argument for judicial review ran this way:

The working of the arguments maintains legitimacy. These arguments are predicated on the operation of judicial review; that is how they arise. Therefore a legitimate judiciary, in the American constitutional context, must review.[21]

But if there were an ultimate decision procedure governing or ranking the forms of argument, then judicial review could be legitimate only if *that* decision procedure were indispensable to the legitimate resolution of a case according to law. And that argument we do not have (precisely because the forms of argument alone engage the constitutional basis for decisionmaking, the subordination of the acts of the state to law). Moreover, by making such a ranking incumbent upon the decider – for if it were not so, if it were merely discretionary, we would then need yet another rule to know when to apply it – the meta-rule denies to judicial review its legitimating role with respect to government practices generally, since the court could not properly decide otherwise. If you can only say "Yes" your consent cannot really matter, cannot add anything to what is being done.[22] If judges are free to decide, which they must be in order to legitimate the practice of judicial review, then the meta-rule cannot dictate the outcome. If the rule *causes* the judge to decide, then the judge was not free and cannot legitimate the acts of others.

Despite my genuine admiration for these efforts, arising from my recognition of how superior the scholarship discussed in the previous chapter is to much of the current debate, I think these efforts are still somehow pulled by the expectations of that debate. That is why their authors are looking for a single decision procedure. That is the way the old disputants solved the question of how we know when the judge was right. Having discredited the old reply that privileged a single modality, we should not reiterate that mistake by inventing a super-rule to do the same job.

Perhaps most important, however, such a meta-logic[23] (i.e., a system that would provide an overarching explanation that resolved the incommensurabilities of the modalities of interpretation) is incompatible with moral choice because, in constitutional decisionmaking, the *choice* presented to the decider is a choice among incommensurate possibilities. Eliminate that and the only choice – moral or political or otherwise – that remains is whether to decide the case on legitimate grounds at all.

Of course, every choice among modal options *could* be governed by an overarching rule; in such a world, the constitutional decider would obviously cease to be legitimately free to introduce moral concerns into the choice among options. Consider the following rather rudimentary logical argument.

First a few definitions:

A *"possible world"* is a way things could have been; it is a state of affairs of some kind.[24]

A proposition *"p"* corresponds to a state of affairs *"S"* if it is impossible that p be true and S fail to obtain, and impossible that S obtain and p fail to be true.

Some states of affairs that do not obtain are impossible; the propositions that correspond to these states of affairs are necessarily false.

Now consider the following hypothetical:

Imagine: Chief Justice Taney must decide whether the Missouri Compromise, which provided that certain states could enter the Union as legally tolerating or prohibiting slavery,[25] should be held constitutional (or to put it somewhat more technically: whether a lawsuit will lie that is based upon a statute that embodied that compromise). *"S"* is a state of affairs that contains a conflict of the forms of constitutional argument such that some forms support a conclusion that the statute is unconstitutional, and others go the other way. (From a structural point of view, the congressional compromise is an appropriate exercise of the national scope of congressional representation: new states should be admitted according to national rules; from an ethical point of view, the compromise violates the security of private property by creating states that might imperil the possession of previously owned slaves.) All other conditions in the world are reflected in *S* except that Taney has not decided the matter. Thus the following propositions are, as yet, unknown:

(1)   If *S* obtained, Taney would legitimately hold the statute unconstitutional.

(2)   If *S* obtained, Taney would legitimately hold the statute constitutional.

One of these conditionals is true; neither is specified within *S* – which is only to say that Taney could legitimately hold either way. Now consider the following propositions:

(3)   *S* obtains.
(4)   Taney legitimately holds the statute unconstitutional.
(5)   Taney legitimately holds the statute constitutional.

So there are possible worlds in which (3)&(4), and (3)&(5) are true. Since either (1) or (2) is true (that is, since both cannot be true) it follows that there are worlds – either (3)&(4) or (3)&(5), for example, that no meta-logic could specify since we cannot know which of either (1) or (2) is true prior to the actualization of (3). If a meta-logic could specify such an outcome, then we could know that prior to the actualization of any specific state of affairs; and this could happen only if Taney were not legitimately free to decide either way.

So if (1) is true, then no meta-logic could have been created such that (3) and (5) are true; if (2) is true, then no meta-logic could have dictated that (3) and (4) are true.[26]

Or to put it the other way around: if a meta-logic were created that would govern the outcome of the decision, then Taney would not be morally free to legitimately decide either way. In the very incommensurabilities of the forms of argument lies the possibility of moral choice.

In summary: the algorithm that some critics are searching for, and others would impose, is not only not necessary to decision and to justice but is inimical to the legitimacy and justification of constitutional review in America. It would collapse the system of legitimation of judicial review; it would be incoherent as regards the modalities themselves; it would be recursive and lead to a regress of meta-rules; it would sacrifice the political stability and pluralistic allegiance afforded by the present system of interpretation; it would change the nature of overruling and thus of constitutional change itself; it would undo the way in which review validates the practices of government. Finally, the provision of a meta-rule would disable moral choice. Such meta-rules would make the art of decision into a kind of placid pornography, and for much the same reason, i.e., to assure a completely anticipated outcome. As Nabokov once observed:

Old rigid rules must be followed by the pornographer in order to have his patient feel the same security of satisfaction as, for example, fans of detective stories feel – stories where, if you do not watch out, the real murderer may turn out to be, to the fan's disgust, artistic originality (who for instance would want a detective story without a single dialogue in it?). Thus, in pornographic novels, action has to be limited to the copulation of cliches. Style, structure, imagery should never distract the reader from his tepid lust. The novel must consist of an alternation of sexual scenes. The passages in between must be reduced to sutures of sense, logical bridges of the simplest design, brief expositions and explanations, which the reader will probably skip but must know they exist in order not to feel cheated (a mentality stemming from the routine of "true" fairy tales in childhood). Moreover, the sexual scenes in the book must follow a crescendo line, with new variations, new combinations, new sexes, and a steady increase in the number of participants (in a Sade play they call the gardener in), and therefore the end of the book must be more replete with lewd lore than the first chapters.[27]

5

JUSTIFYING AND DECIDING

In this chapter I should like to address the issue of how we justify the system of constitutional interpretation I have been describing. I will treat this in two parts: first (part I) how do we justify a particular decision that is the legitimate result of such a system – how do we know when a result is just? – and secondly (part II), how do we justify the system generally – that is, is the fundamental system of American law just?

I will argue that we assess the justice of a particular decision by reference to some external standard, a system of evaluation outside the operation of the modalities of argument. That is how *justifying* is done; but not, I will argue, *deciding*. Whether a particular painting is an accomplished work of art is a matter judged by the standards of art criticism. One could study Berenson for a lifetime, however, and never be able to paint; nor is mastery of such criticism necessary to the art. Indeed some works that were once disparaged by the critics of an earlier period are praised later. It is the same with deciding a matter according to law. Whether a particular decision is just is a matter judged by the critical standards of the day; but the employment of those standards is a part of the decision only to the extent that the modalities of argument incorporate them by reference.

I will then argue that the importance of the American system of constitutional interpretation is that it permits a legitimate role for conscience. Thus I conclude that the system is just, not because it produces just outcomes, but because it permits an opportunity for justice consistent with the freedom of the conscience to decide matters. I will also argue, therefore, that this – not the ratio of right decisions to wrong ones – justifies the system. And I will suggest that moves to modify the system – the way in which we make constitutional decisions – in order to increase the number of just outcomes are misguided. We cannot assure a just result without doing away with the moral freedom to decide; yet I think it can be shown that the persistent efforts, by partisans on all sides, to increase the number of just decisions by confining interpretation to a favored mode – the transition of a form of argument into an ideology – makes precisely this mistake.

Part I

If there is no conclusive mode, no trans-modal standard, how do we know when the judge is right? How do we justify the result of a constitutional decision in a particular case? It would appear that the incommensurate nature of the various modalities of argument that enable legitimation makes such an assessment impossible. For if these modes lead to different outcomes, we have no rule that enables us to choose among them; and yet they cannot all be right. How can it be just for the plaintiff to win and the defendant to lose and for the same plaintiff to lose and the same defendant to win? This is the "contradiction" so beloved of law professors generally, and especially the theorists of the Critical Legal Studies group.[1]

In the following passage, from the most eloquent of those theorists, Roberto Unger, I will include a comment on private law because, as we have seen, the forms of constitutional argument are taken from private law and because Unger's criticism of American constitutional decisionmaking is more clearly understood with this predicate.

The generalization of contract theory revealed, alongside the dominant principles of freedom to choose the partner and the terms, the counterprinciples: that freedom to contract would not be allowed to undermine the communal aspects of social life and that grossly unfair bargains would not be enforced. Though the counterprinciples might be pressed to the corner, they could be neither driven out completely nor subjected to a system of metaprinciples that would settle, once and for all, their relation to the dominant principles . . . Which of these classing conceptions provides the real theory of contract? . . . The development of constitutional law and constitutional theory throughout the late nineteenth and the twentieth centuries tells a similar story of the discovery of indeterminacy through generalization. This discovery was directly connected with its private law analogue . . . The doctrines of protected constitutional interests and of legitimate ends of state action were the chief devices for defining the intrinsic legal-institutional structure of the scheme of ordered liberty. They could not be made coherent in form and precise in implication without freezing into place, in a way the real politics of the republic would never tolerate, a particular set of deals between national government and organized groups . . . Thus a cadre of seemingly harmless and even toadying jurists partly authorized the insight required to launch the attack . . . the discovery of the indeterminate content of abstract institutional categories . . .[2]

Notice how Unger assumes that these "toadying jurists" refused to freeze into place a particular set of holdings that the real politics would never tolerate. Why, one might ask, did they not simply ask their masters for the constitutional theory that the "real politics" would tolerate? My answer, I fear, will never be the same as Unger's. Of course his assessment is overstated: the rules of American constitutional law are coherent, and their implications are precise; that is why one can derive contradiction. But has he not captured something here – in his Mephistophelean and glamorous prose – that is relevant to our problem? Decisions in American constitutional law _do_ oscillate between equally plausible rationales; and we are never willing to enshrine one single generative form of these rationales as our determinate ideology. How then can we say a particular decision is just if either rationale (and thus either outcome) would have done? And how can we be guided to that decision if the rationales are equally plausible?

Unger gives this answer: speaking for the Critical Legal Studies Movement, he says:

We have approached the critique . . . in an equally distinctive way. The starting point for our argument is the idea that every branch of doctrine must rely tacitly if not explicitly upon some picture of the forms of human association that are right and realistic in the areas of social life with which it deals. For example, a constitutional lawyer needs a theory of the democratic republic that describes the proper relation between state and society or the essential features of social organization and individual entitlement that government must protect come what may. Without such a guiding vision, legal reasoning seems condemned to a game of easy analogies . . . [E]very thoughtful law student or lawyer has had the disquieting sense of being able to argue too well or too easily for too many conflicting solutions. Because everything can be defended, nothing can; the analogy-mongering must be brought to a halt.[3]

I trust I have shown that, in this regard at least, this approach is far from distinctive. Moreover, I have endeavored to show that a "guiding" theory is neither necessary nor desirable to decisionmaking. Is it necessary (or desirable) for justice? And without it, how can we decide whether a particular decision is just?

How do we determine that a decision is just? We measure it against our values. Our values justify our practices. Throughout the Iran–Contra hearings, when there was much righteous indignation flourished with the Polonial phrase "The ends don't justify the means!"[4] I would often think instead of Paul Porter, who is alleged to have remarked, "If the ends don't justify the means, I'd like to know what-the-hell does."

If our values justify our law (and its operations) then does this mean that our legal practices are merely the means by which we carry out our moral and political commitments? The way in which these questions are answered will, I believe, determine also our answer to the questions posed here in this first part of this chapter.

Our values do not necessarily precede our choices; rather, making decisions actualizes and in some cases even precipitates our values. Before all choices, there are no values, only vague attractions, repulsions, attitudes. A human being is thus not a set of ordered preferences, even though, from time to time, he or she must act and thereby create a preference. So it is not that values are a pre-condition for making choices, but rather the other way around. (And this must be so: otherwise that essential feature of our values, that they are reflected in our preferences, could never come into being, since there are always some choices as to which we have, hitherto, attached no values. The study of how values are actualized is the domain of the psychologist, not the political economist who infers values from choices; but neither discipline depends on maintaining that values are anterior to choice.)

It is true that when we have decided something, we may then assess it in terms of the justice of the result we have reached. Judge Henry Friendly once told the following story that seems suggestive of the account I have given of decisionmaking. Judge Learned Hand, at the time the events of this story took place, had been a federal judge for fifty years. He was the nation's leading appeals judge, a mantle that would in time go to Judge Friendly. Like Friendly he had been a superb student at Harvard College (Hand had been valedictorian of the class of 1893), and an equally impressive law student at the Harvard Law School (where Friendly had been the valedictorian of the class of 1927). Hand had urged Friendly's appointment to the Second Circuit; when Friendly retired it was generally held that, with Holmes and Brandeis, Hand and Friendly had been the leading federal jurists of the century. When this story occurs, however, Friendly had just assumed his judgeship. He was not young, but he was new. In the first few weeks, when assailed by self-doubt, he had secretly gone back and read the first few opinions of Hand, hoping to find that his great colleague had achieved the polished practice of this craft over time, only slowly beginning to display the mastery which Friendly hoped he could learn but believed himself without. Hand was a handsome man, stylish in his manners and his prose; Friendly noticed these things, and was appreciative of them, though he did not flatter himself that these qualities were his. He knew he was brilliant, and he knew he could work very hard; but he did not know whether he could be a great judge.

Judge Friendly was assigned the duty of writing an opinion in a case that appeared straightforward enough during the conference of the panel that heard the case. But, as sometimes happens, particularly with very conscientious judges, once the drafting began new complexities appeared. A simple problem had turned into a quite difficult one and Judge Friendly went to Judge Hand's chambers for advice. Friendly carefully laid out the problem, outlined the various options and precedents and then asked for Hand's views. To which request, Learned Hand replied, "Damn it, Henry, just decide it! That's what you're paid for."[5]

A judge who never felt the constraints of the various modalities, who felt that any decision could be satisfactorily defended, would be very very foolish or very very unimaginative. Only a law student or law professor could say that "everything can be defended" or that "it will always be possible to find" convincing ways of making a set of distinctions look credible. Indeed the law reviews and law journals are filled with articles and notes that refute this claim by their implausibility. And yet, in the difficult cases, these constraints are not determinative. The case must be *decided*.

What justifies the sensibility that makes such a decision if, as I have claimed, it is not made according to a rule? There are no grounds independent of the sensibility that is judging those grounds. We can say only: these are the sensibilities we have. They are all we have. We can of course change them and they might have been different. Our reading and living and deciding other matters will change us and then we will be different and the results we now desire may appear quite differently to us. But even the conscious decision to alter our sensibilities is made according to their force. The decisions we make will ultimately be judged according to their consequences, not according to the motives that drove them. The particular decisions made by a constitutional decider will be deemed just or unjust according to ways of evaluation that are as complex and conventional as those that determine the forms of argument.

The United States Constitution formalizes a role for the conscience of the individual sensibility by requiring decisions that rely on the individual moral sensibility when the modalities of argument clash. We are tempted to think that, in a just *system* (a subject I will take up presently), we can presume that a particular outcome is just if there is no contradiction within the system. And most cases in the American system, despite the rhetoric of indeterminacy, are not deeply conflicted cases. When these conflicts occur, however, the system of constitutional interpretation prescribes a role for the individual conscience: it does not prescribe a particular outcome. Therefore, even if the system is just we may not presume that every outcome is just.

To summarize: a particular decision will be deemed just according to the prevailing practices of moral theory. These *may* legitimately influence a constitutional decider when faced with a modal conflict but such a role is irrelevant to their role as evaluative standards once the decision has been made. A particular theory *could* assure "just" results but at the price of its legitimacy. Such a cost I think would be most intolerable to the American people. Even then, the application of such a theory would, of necessity, be bounded by decisions as to its appropriateness, judgments for which there is no theory to guide. Simply because we use such "theories" to map our acts of conscience we should not be led to conclude that they bear any causal relationship to the terrain thereof.

The US Constitution strictly avoids mandating such a theory. Rather it requires moral choices by refusing to enshrine any particular comprehensive morality. One might say that it reflects an incomplete, institutional morality that requires a decision, requires a choice. Therefore the question I have addressed in this chapter – when is a particular decision just – quickly becomes: Is the system of constitutional interpretation itself just?

Part II

We have seen that decisions may precipitate values. The ratification of the US Constitution was a profoundly value-creating decision. With a single exception – the Thirteenth Amendment that forbids slavery, the outcome of a terrible struggle to forge constitutional law that was both legitimate and just – the terms of the Constitution do not express commitments _vis-à-vis_ individuals and their relationships in common, but among governments, or between governments and individuals. As a consequence, the adoption of the Constitution crystallized values around governmental relationships. The "morality" of the American constitutional system is, broadly speaking, that of the values of limited government, forbearance and pluralism. It expresses a liberal, tolerant vision of the organization of society, and thus can be juxtaposed with the antiliberalism of the counter-Enlightenment.

If there is a constitutional morality, it is not the same as the morality that governs individual relationships. Moreover, such a morality cannot amount to merely the superimposition of a political program or ideology onto constitutional practice. That would amount to a displacement of the constitutional morality, which is studiedly incomplete.

The moral commitments of the Constitution do not usually appear in opinions as such, and are not fashioned as arguments. Rather, the US Constitution is a series of decisions to give abstract rules priority over substantive moral values, to pursue the ideal of the rule of law (and thus judicial neutrality), to maintain respect for individual conscience, to reject preferential status for particular communities. In short, the US Constitution does not endorse communal values, nor, with the one exception noted above, particular individual values. And thus when a constitutional decision is made, its moral basis is confirmed if the forms of arguments can persuasively rationalize the decision, and the decision is not made on grounds incompatible with the conscience of the decisionmaker. That is constitutional decision according to law. Whether this system is "right" – or the outcome to which it has given rise – is a matter of the moral analysis to which it may be subjected. The US Constitution engages our moral sensibilities by the clash of its interpretive modalities, which require the moral instance of our judgment. The justice of the system lies in the extent to which it is able to confer legitimacy on the right moral actions of its deciders. It is thus the very fact that legitimate rationales *do* conflict that enables justice to be done.

It is not enough, therefore, for the critic to describe a possible world in which there is less injustice than in the present. He must also show that it is possible to actualize such a world in which the system of interpretation is legitimate or acknowledge that he is simply proposing the destruction of our fundamental civil institution. The former task is made somewhat more difficult than might at first appear when we realize that just results do not legitimate themselves.

Because we live in a period when the essential respect for art seems to have been lost, along with, perhaps inspired by, a feeling that, with a little training in acquiring what is only a disguise or facade anyway, each of us could do as well, indeed even better for our lack of practiced facility, it is quite possibly not a welcome proposition to be told that doing justice requires a mastery of the art of deciding and not of the principles of a theory of justice.

6

THE ROLE OF IDEAL SYSTEMS

The structure of constitutional decisionmaking I have described, which leaves a crucial role for moral decision, naturally provokes us to try to systematize the decider's values. This, it may be thought, would give us *only* just and right decisions, or at least a calculus so that we would be able to instruct someone how to render just and right decisions. I hope that I have to some extent cast doubt on this enterprise, but I would certainly be remiss if I did not mention the various schools of thought that are currently engaged in this effort.

The standard view, which I think continues to dominate American jurisprudence, is that of the Legal Process school.[1] If one plays by the rules – if, that is, one decides according to the legitimate forms of argument – then justice will out. Sometimes the adherents of this school find it necessary to supplement the legitimate forms of argument with certain additional principles that are thought to be reflected in the morals of the community and as such can be introduced as ethical arguments. Fundamental values that are reflected in the language of the Constitution, in caselaw and the society's cultural traditions are adduced. The doctrinal distinction between law-making and law-applying is crucial to this school, since it admits for constitutional bases of decision only the standard forms, while the scope of legislative decision is held to be unconstrained (or not similarly constrained).

Against this dominant view three jurisprudential movements currently hold the field: they are the schools of law and economics,[2] critical legal studies,[3] and law and hermeneutics,[4] dominated, respectively, by a secular interest in the work of micro-economists,[5]

Frankfurt School political scientists,[6] and Deconstructionist literary critics.[7] The scholars in these movements have usually read the main texts of the philosophers whose work inspired their campaigns; or at least they have read the commentaries by the lawyer-generals who lead them.[8] They are united by the deflation that was felt after Legal Realism made it impossible to believe in the natural justice of the legal system; and, perhaps also by the drop in heroic status for lawyers and law professors that accompanied this deflation. There is perhaps also a feeling that association with more fundamental disciplines, and more fundamental thinkers, will ground our efforts in a way that mere legal analysis cannot do. I will return to this alleged fundamentality and conclude this chapter with a description of what I take to be the useful role of apparently cognate systems.

These three schools rely on efforts to translate legal problems into the informal proof structures of other disciplines. I am not competent to say whether this is really a move to more manageable disciplines, but I am of the conviction that it is so distorting that the original problem vanishes in the translation not because it is solved but because it cannot tolerate the move. I do not wish to add to the vast literature explaining and in some cases criticizing these approaches;[9] I have collected a few citations in the notes for readers who wish to pursue this subject further. Rather, I wish to note that in their search for fundamental authority outside legal methods they are addressing a different, and jurisprudentially ineffectual issue. They would there-fore sacrifice legitimacy much as the legal process school, to which they are justifiably reacting, has sacrificed justice. There is no warrant that these disciplines can provide for a privileged constitutional status for their solutions to legal problems.

These efforts are most problematic when the scholar simply tries to supplant legal criticism by appropriating wholesale the criticism accomplished in another discipline. Sometimes this is simply reductionism – wherein, for example, law "turns out" descriptively (and usually normatively) to be no more than welfare economics – and as such is misleadingly easy to ridicule. What satisfies us in legal craft is simply left wanting within another discipline; that, in part, is why there are different disciplines. To take a simple example: it is not hard to show that every regulation of property is a "taking" – that is, an unacknowledged tax on the individual holding the property whose rights are diminished by the regulation, as when a zoning change restricts lawful uses – and from this vantage point, to show that the constitutional caselaw that comprises takings juris-prudence is an absolute hash. This caselaw appears to rely instead on common sense,[10] traditional views of the role of property that have no sharp defining characteristic. What is a judge to do when called upon to enforce the provision of the Fifth Amendment "that no private property shall be taken for public use without just com-pensation?"[11] Whatever she does, her task is not satisfied by the consensus in the economics profession that a regulation is a tax.

What is the proper use of these coordinate disciplines? I will make three points: (1) that doing law by reference to the standards of a coordinate discipline, like economics, say, is not doing economics; (2) that the importing of a theory from a coordinate system can be a useful heuristic, *provided* the coordinate prototype is specified as such; (3) that the desire to find a clearer and sharper model arises from a mistaken impression about law and philosophy.

The first of these points is, I hope, obvious enough. Imagine a judicial opinion with sets of simultaneous equations. It is not the mathematical illiteracy of the judiciary that makes this so implausible; rather it is the idea that law could grapple with human behaviour in such a highly reified way. The standards of mathematics – technique, economy, rigor – have much in common with those of legal argu-ment. But a mathematical argument does not convince unless it is a mathematical question that has been put. It follows from this obser-vation that someone doing law, with the assistance of arguments stolen from other disciplines, is not acting within those other disci-plines. Lawyer's history is not just shoddy history; it is the use of historical methods that have been fabricated, re-made for a purpose that is not the historian's purpose.[12]

The second point is more important. If we import a model – economic, political, etc. – into law we invariably carve away those aspects of the legal situation to which the model is inapplicable. We forget that the model is merely a prototype, and so we resist the reality of the divergence of the actual from our model. In this way we do not enrich legal analysis by resort to coordinate disciplines; we impoverish it. Thus a jurist trying to apply the principles of John Rawls tends to bend the legal analysis to "rights" and inevitably away from the historical claims of the state.

There is nothing wrong with this, so long as the role of the imported model is recognized for what it is: a heuristic object of comparison and not a rule of decision. For if it were taken as the latter, it would de-legitimate the analysis, replacing the legal approach with one for which there is no constitutional authority. And yet have I not argued earlier that one must resolve conflicts by reference to one's conscience? Well, suppose my conscience attempts to track the ideas of John Rawls. How can that be illegitimate? Because deciding to rely on Rawls is not deciding a case.[13] This truism exposes the fact that (1) the decision to rely on Rawls is not itself "Rawls-governed" and therefore the imported system is never decisive and cannot replace the function of conscience, and (2) a system of analysis is not a conscience. Of course one can proceed by testing an ideal system against the possible outcomes of one decision. But our decisions do not arise from ideal systems and therefore such tests are one-way, heuristic, only.

The third point has something to do with the first two. It is because we are inclined to believe the law is "applied philosophy" that we are tempted to resort to cognate disciplines. Sometimes this almost seems a sort of "philosopher envy," excited in some cases no doubt by the hope of stature by association. But one may also see this drive for fundamental association in this passage from the eminent Ronald Dworkin: "I end simply by acknowledging my sense that politics, arts, and law are united, somehow, in philosophy."[14] Or this, from the former Solicitor General of the United States, the distinguished Harvard law professor Charles Fried:

The picture I have, then, is of philosophy proposing an elaborate structure of arguments and considerations which descend from on high but stop some twenty feet above the ground. It is the peculiar task of law to complete this structure of ideals and values, to bring it down to earth.[15]

The implicit assumption is that law, in principle, could be reduced to a more basic structure, but the links are never made. It is never shown just how, for example, the mathematical treatment of probability in micro-economics really captures the human sense of risk *in law*, much less how the ways of applying the rules of law, rather than the rules themselves, could be legitimately developed from the prototype. (One sees an example of this failing when a teacher of Evidence accounts for the Hearsay rule by reference to contemporary psychology.)[16]

This is no less obvious with respect to the law and hermeneutics movement where one may encounter the unguarded observation that legal analysis is no more than the study of language. Thus one finds, in a recent article in the Yale Law Journal, the view that "legal theorists hope to find foundations for legal meaning in the analogy to literary interpretation."[17] And similarly, with respect to Critical Legal Studies, whose most interesting (and amusing) theorist, writes:

Teachers teach nonsense . . . when they persuade students that legal reasoning is distinct, as a method for achieving correct results, from ethical and political discourse in general (i.e. from policy analysis) . . . There is never a "correct legal solution" that is other than the correct ethical and political solution to that legal problem.[18]

It should be plain from these passages that they have much in common; and that it is their belief that legal statements depend upon some factual state of affairs that is their foundation. There *is* a lesson in contemporary philosophy for the legal critic, but it is a cold one. Twentieth century philosophy discredits many of the epistemological assumptions of natural law and positivism, of formalism and realism, but it does not replace these schools (which partly accounts for the curious isolation of political philosophy from the developments in logic and epistemology). The message of such philosophy is: you are on your own; we've done enough harm already.[19] Until legal critics absorb this important lesson we will be trapped in problems that have their origins in philosophy's once-proposed solutions; like minotaurs within mazes we await new maps from our captors but are given only new victims.

As I was completing the preparations for the lectures that form the core of this book, I received an invitation to a conference sponsored by the American Association of Law Schools, to be entitled "The Constitution as Law." The brochure described the topic of the conference in these terms:

Many argue that the constitution has served us well for 200 years because its text is treated like any other legal text and interpreted through a methodology that, like the methodology used to interpret a stop sign, often makes possible agreement on its meaning among adherents of different political/moral philosophies.

The problem with the Constitution interpreted through such a methodology is that the Constitution turns out to be imperfect from the point of view of practically anyone's political and moral ideals. It permits – and may even require – considerable injustice and imprudence. But if that is so, then one wonders how the Constitution can be regarded as authoritative.

This sounded promising. Indeed it is the subject I have been addressing in this book and that I have claimed is the next question in constitutional theory, to replace that of judicial review. I glanced at the list of participants and reacted much as Zhivago did when he confronted the new board of commissars, to find that they were the old Tsarist bureaucrats in different clothes.[20] Would So-and-So, I wondered, have exchanged his tweed jacket for the dark linen coats with padded shoulders one sees in Paris? Had So-and-So shaved off his beard? So my glance returned to the invitation. It continued, describing the two approaches to the problem that participants would take:

[M]any reject as ultimately impossible the interpretative methodologies of hard law. Relying upon Continental deconstructionists or upon Wittgensteinian critiques of rule-following, they deny that the hard law methodologies can ever succeed in constraining the political/moral choices of the present decisionmaker. Hard law is a theoretical impossibility.

Those who regard the Constitution as hard law believe that by undermining the hard law view of the Constitution, we undermine the Constitution's efficacy. For the rejectionists, the Constitution amounts to no more than the redundant entreaty to do what's just, good, and wise.

This is indeed the problem, or rather, the problem lies in a structure that claims these two views are alternatives, moreover, as *the* alternatives. Putting aside the barbarisms about Wittgenstein, such a description actually perpetuates the difficulties of the old debate around judicial review, with a veneer of the up-to-the minute glamour of high culture and intellectual fashion.

The rearrangement of the issues, as I have urged it in the preceding chapters, abandons the assumptions that are the basic sources of the two so-called alternatives. As a consequence, I distinguish between legitimacy and justification. The forms of argument do legitimate review; the necessity for legitimation therefore requires review by constitutional decisionmakers; that will justify the occasion of review generally, but not the system of interpretation we employ that makes this necessary nor its results in a particular case.

A critic would be mistaken, therefore, to describe the system as unjust if, as seems inevitable, it produces unjust results; rather the system would be unjust if it can be shown that *systemic* changes would bring about fewer unjust decisions *and* that these changes would not compromise (or would adequately replace) the methods of legitimation.

This system, as I have observed, requires individual decision precisely because the modalities conflict. The result is not any less law because the outcome is not the same for all deciders; indeed it could not really be law, it could not follow the forms of argument and recognize their character as modalities, if it were any other way. The space for moral reflection on our ideologies is created by the conflict among modalities, just as garden walls can create a space for a garden.

THE ROLE OF MORAL DECISION

In his most famous passage, Clausewitz says that war has its own grammar, but not its own logic. In the preceding pages I have been making a similar point about American constitutional interpretation. Whether Chrétien de Troyes's romance *Le Chevalier de la Charrette*[1] is an earnest presentation of courtly love or a self-parody, whether a lion with stripes is a tiger or simply another lion, is a matter of judgment. And whether or not the Constitution permits Congress to determine under what rules the President can use nuclear weapons[2] is also a matter of judgment, we may say, but with this decision other matters are determined that carry very heavy stakes. The decision has a legal purpose, and is thus not merely a matter of judgment, and it has a legal grammar, a grammar surprisingly like that of "reasonable care," "malice aforethought," "notice," "unconscionability," and not at all like that of "pro-choice" or "right-to-life." I have relied on essentially logical arguments to display the grammar of constitutional interpretation. What are the implications of this sort of analysis?

(1) The price for creating a constitutional system of interpretation in which individual deciders are given a crucial role is a world in which they can produce "legitimate" injustice. The efforts of many thinkers to improve this state of affairs typically consist in trying to impose a meta-rule to resolve the indeterminacy of the various forms of argument along lines of which the critic approves.

In traditional constitutional jurisprudence this has taken the form of transmuting the modalities of argument into ideologies. This provided a precise set of rules to which the decider was supposed to conform, a calculus that linked the form of argument and its legitimating role with a particular justification for a single set of non-contradictory results.

Judges have resisted this, as Unger pointed out,[3] not because they were corrupted by "real politics" but because of the nature of real life. Determinant rules are simply incapable of protecting our values because they sacrifice the very means by which values come into being, namely, the exercise of moral choice. No human society of any moral stature would long consent to this.

(2) We do not learn the forms of argument by studying them as forms, but by legal practice; they do not presuppose mental entities to which they conform and which can be handed over to the student (including such entities as "sovereignty" or "consent"). Accordingly, we cannot replace (or supplement) the operation of such forms by reference to an external code, however internally consistent it may be. Within a culture, legal rules operate to actualize many possible worlds, some of which are inconsistent with others. I endeavored in another, collaborative, work (*Tragic Choices*[4]) to show that by this process we preserve our values. It is only because one has a mistaken view of those values – that they proceed from an ideal – that one could possibly have thought otherwise.

(3) Does this mean we can be educated to do better, make wiser and more just decisions? Yes: it is only if one conflated legitimacy and justification (perhaps by narrowing one's focus to a single mode) that one would conclude that this was the best of all possible worlds. But let us be clear about how this improvement might come about. The study of history – which includes of course the history of ideas – poetry and fiction, drama and biography, enriches the daily experience of legal practice. But the latter is the soil from which justice must grow. Our consciences did not arise from the ideal and they cannot be replaced by it. A theory of justice is a wonderful artifact, like a vase. Any case it could decide would be a travesty of human responsibility.

(4) Why then do these theories arise, not as descriptions but as "explanations?" The source of this phenomenon lies in a widely shared view of law that I have tried to discredit in my work. Consider this passage from Ronald Dworkin:

I think that many positivists rely, more or less consciously, on an anti-realist theory of meaning. They think that no sense can be assigned to a proposition unless those who use that proposition are all agreed about how the proposition could, at least in theory, be proved conclusively. Lawyers are agreed, according to positivism, about how the existence of a law or legal rule can be proved or disproved, and they are therefore agreed about the truth conditions of ordinary propositions of law that assert rights and duties created by rules. But controversial propositions of law, which assert rights that do not purport to depend upon rules, are another matter. Since there is not agreement about the conditions which, if true, establish the truth of such propositions, they cannot be assigned any straightforward sense ... According to [my] theory, controversial propositions of law are true just in case the political theory that supplies the best justification for non-controversial propositions of law provides for the right or duties which the controversial proposition describes.[5]

Put aside for one moment the "anti-realist" critique. Notice instead that Dworkin's theory asserts a meta-logic, a system that embraces both law and politics (a political theory), the application of which verifies propositions of law (tells us when they are "true"). This *requirement* – for how else can the propositions of law be assigned any straightforward sense – is something he shares with H. L. A. Hart, whose position he is criticizing; indeed the quoted passage recapitulates the core of the critique (that positivism cannot deal with controversial or novel propositions of law).

What Hart and Dworkin share (indeed what a great many constitutional commentators share) is an empiricist idea about how our thoughts are derived (and thus what is required so that they can be "assigned any straightforward sense"). This idea, this metaphysics, is taken from the explanatory methods of science (or sometimes indirectly through the social sciences). And it is the usual way most intellectuals, perhaps most people generally, today, think of our ideas.

This metaphysics holds that our concepts are the results of our experiences. We have an experience and – depending on how we react to it, and we might react in different ways, depending in part on our cultural frameworks – we develop a concept, on the basis of which we act (we think we decide, we judge). For this reason, these writers of jurisprudence hypothesize a justificatory calculus regarding law of the sort we once read about science by empiricists like Russell.[6]

If political theory is required to justify the operations of a legal system – because such theories "explain" the operations of the system – then the just outcomes of that system are predicted by the theory. Legal systems of this kind simply never exist outside the seminar room, in part because the values society labors to preserve are contradictory. I have tried to show in earlier chapters how such explanations are neither in fact necessary to justice nor helpful to decisionmaking. I mention the underlying metaphysics here only to suggest a reason why such system-making appeals to us in the first place. The belief that interpretive statements in law (such as: "the Constitution requires that a state cannot be sued in federal court by its own citizen without its consent") are statements about the world, though widely if unacknowledgedly shared, is false. Such statements are descriptions; they are not about things (like the Constitution) but are about interpretations. Thus they are modal descriptions, not empirical ones. Whether they are true or false depends upon a human choice, not a correspondence with facts in the world. It is a measure of the strong grip the false metaphysics has on us that such a distinguished academic should think that to believe otherwise is to be an "anti-realist" or nominalist.[7] One who expects a further thought to lie behind a decision, and that that thought is determined by a meta-logic, would conclude that in its absence there appears to be no link between the thought and the real world.

(5)   It is true that ideological statements about the Constitution – such as "because the US Constitution was consented to by sovereign ratifiers, their expectation that a state cannot be sued in federal court without its consent is dispositive of the issue" – purport to be explanatory. But ideological statements of this kind are built out of interpretive descriptions (modal statements) and are greatly misleading. They are like similar scientific "explanations," such as "Man's vestigial large toe has ceased to be prehensile because when he left off tree-climbing such dexterity was no longer necessary to survival" or even statements like "the apple falls because of gravity."

Yet we would not regret the loss of such misleading explanations in the law if we did not believe they were necessary for justice. When we accept the moral usefulness of rationalizations that are merely descriptive, that is, that give reasons for a decision without purporting to be re-enactments of the thought processes of the decider, we will lose our taste for constitutional ideologies.

(6)   Is law then a science, nevertheless, because science itself is not metaphysical, that is, it is "ethical," to use Richard Rorty's term?[8] This view holds that the basis for science is "ethical" in that it consists in various familiar virtues of inquiry – intellectual honesty, open-mindedness, willingness to accept and even seek criticism, skepticism about one's own views, and a reliance on persuasion rather than force. These are the same virtues, Mark Sagoff has observed,[9] that guide constitutional decisionmaking (and indeed he would argue, any sort of legitimate inquiry). Langdell was right therefore (though for the wrong reasons) when he thought law was a "science."

I am not competent to write with any confidence about scientific inquiry. I realize that Sagoff's position is compatible with mine: the "scientific" model could be wrong for both law and science. But I am inclined to think that the nature of physical accounts is entirely different from that of legal statements. The causal descriptions of things in the world are explanations in the sense that they need not hypothesize any other causes to wholly account for the descriptions they provide. These "descriptions" therefore are much more limited than those of the humanities, that is, of statements that are not part of a deterministic calculus. The fact that in science, as in the humanities, there is simply no way to get out of the concepts and vocabulary of a theory to see where it corresponds with something unconceptualized (the fact that, alas, even Euclid did not see beauty bare), is not embarrassing to the scientist as it is fatal to the social theorist, because statements about the world are precisely those to which a causal description is not misleading. Whether scientific statements are true is thus subject to the framing of hypotheses and tests, in a way that is not the case with whether law statements are true. A sociology of coercion can account for the latter; but no vote of scientists will slow the speed of light, or quicken the decay of a nucleus.

(7)   Wittgenstein once wrote that the empiricist theory of meaning rests on a confusion, or conflation, of motive and cause.[10] One could say the same thing of the various jurisprudential views I have implicitly (and sometime explicitly) criticized. How is the present work different from these?

I treat constitutional interpretation as a conceptual problem, not a factual one. This book is a collection of agreements about the use of the American constitution in practice. It describes, by examples, what sorts of combinations and strategies are possible. It is, in Wittgenstein's words, "a gathering of recollections about rules," about the operation of the modalities of constitutional law. This work does not tell us how law must be constructed in order to fulfill some purpose, in order to have a particular effect on human beings. Indeed I have tried to replace the world of the thought (or the intention), within which the decisions about law are believed to reside (and to which they must retreat to consult "principles") with the world of legal practice and actual decision.

This approach has implications for legal scholarship and theory. It suggests that analyses that strive to discover and expose inconsistencies in doctrine – whether the conventional stage material of the law professor or the equally narcissistic sarcasm of the commentator – can simply miss the point. Clear, consistent rules can generate equally plausible claims for mutually exclusive results; they may be used to legitimate a variety of actions. In this apparently contradictory method, not in spite of it, our values are created, endure, and prevail.

In my Mellon Lectures at Oxford, which were drawn from the material that has, belatedly, been formed into this book, I closed with eight lines from Rilke.[11] Here, I should like to end with a quotation from another poet, who is also a distinguished American constitutional lawyer, Charles L. Black, Jr. He wrote as a conclusion to a partly autobiographical essay entitled "Reflections on Teaching and Working in Constitutional Law:"

You may remember that I also started off disliking, and of course, fearing, the "artificial reason," the *technicality* of law. Well, you live and learn. I have before now confessed that I have lived in law long enough to learn that, like the technicalities of any true art, those of law are emancipating. The traditions of law, the shop-work and shop-talk of law, its rules of precision and its rules of thumb – these can be made means of coming to think naturally and creatively. I have discovered lately that some younger people especially look on me as a traditionalist – not in result but in modes of thought. I hope they are right.[12]

"Decisions according to law," to use Black's felicitous phrase,[13] inevitably require conscience – that is, they require a *decision*, not a calculation or an interpretation, or even a passionate conviction.

We may suppress our consciences in the certain knowledge that they are corrupt and ill-informed. We may try to anesthetize them with a routine adherence to ideology, frequently reinforced by the adroit characterization of every phenomenon as an event that instantiates or confirms our ideological outlook. This sort of addiction ultimately makes coping more difficult. We may even persuade ourselves of the reality of our own mythologies, and the mythopoeic nature of our actual lives. Yet this process finally yields the bitter and brittle irony for which our century is so notable. The "hermeneutics of suspicion" – the constant awareness that every proposed solution is merely an excuse for maintaing the status quo – is not a very nourishing diet for solving problems. Mythologies can never decide moral questions; they can only pose ironic dilemmas.

What then should we rely on? In his lecture "The Coming Victory of Democracy" Thomas Mann insisted that constitutional systems such as ours would only prevail if democracy preserved a "deep and forceful recollection of itself" by "constantly renew[ing] its spiritual and moral self-consciousness."[14] The recursion to conscience is the crucial activity on which the constitutional system of interpretation that I have described depends. It is the purpose of this book to remind the Reader of this fact. This particular sort of recollection is the very thing that the current commentary on constitutional decisionmaking seeks to dispense with by insisting on the illegitimacy of our practices and the need for a particular decision process.

The cultivation of our constitutional traditions requires, as I have endeavored to show, the cultivation of our consciences and the rejection of systems and systematic approaches that, for all their idealism, are finally conscienceless. I am well aware that the notion of "cultivation", indeed the very idea of "conscience" in our post-Freudian world, concedes the charge that our values are not fundamental or privileged because they cannot be shown to be "objectively" superior. For in judging their superiority we must bring to bear as part of the examining apparatus the very values we are examining. But it scarcely follows from this concession that our values are not worth defending. If values are ever worth defending – and, in the end, what else could be if not the ground and measure of what we wish to protect – then the fact that all values are privileged only by our decisions to make them so does not subtract a millimeter from the justice of their defense. Rather this agnosticism imposes on us the responsibility to constantly engage in a self-conscious examination of the premises of our decisions. That is the method of American constitutional interpretation, arising no doubt from the agnosticism of the Constitution itself, which studiedly refrains from endorsing particular values other than the structures by which our values are brought into being and preserved.

But if we are agnostic as to all values, one might ask, how can we privilege this choice, i.e., the decision to protect the way in which we bring our values into actuality? The reply that *that* is the law, that it is provided for in the Constitution, is, as we have seen, only a valid reply within the system of legal interpretation. And yet once we appreciate that the validity of all such answers depends on the particular discipline within which the question makes sense, we may be less inclined to insist that only the "fundamental" is worthy of our allegiance. "To realize the relative validity of one's convictions," Schumpeter wrote, "and yet stand for them unflinchingly is what distinguishes a civilized man from a barbarian."[15]

It has been suggested that this observation cuts the ground from beneath the Constitution: for who would stand "unflinchingly" for values that are no more ultimate than those against which one feels one must stand? But this argument is as circular as the one it pretends to attack: it assumes that there must be *some* values that are not relative to our assessment of them in order that they may be regarded as worthy of defending. Moreover, such an attack misses the point of American constitutional interpretation – that it is worth defending precisely because, in our culture, it enables our values to be brought forth and assessed. For this reason I quoted this epigram of Nietzsche's in *Constitutional Fate*: "We should not let ourselves be burnt for our opinions: we are not that sure of them. But perhaps for this: that we may have and change our opinions."[16] It may be that the principal worth of this book, if it has worth, is the connection it describes between the legitimating forms and moral decision. Any proposed utopian scheme must show, not only that it will lead to more just results, but that these will be achieved by means that are legitimate to the culture.

We should be especially vigilant therefore to answer attacks on the legitimacy of our constitutional forms – forms that are likely to be the most enduring and admirable of the American contributions to human history. Often these arguments come from quarters where "solutions" abound, and persons are only too willing to take up the responsibilities of decision that the rest of our people have put aside in perplexity. The constitutional puzzle is not solved, any more than the problem of earning a living is ever solved; it begins again each day. But it should be clear, now, that the puzzling elements of the problem of constitutional interpretation are largely illusory. We do not need a "solution" to go forward. Having decided, we are ennobled or debased through practices whose highest recommendation is that they are all we have.

"The prestige of political philosophy is very high these days," wrote Michael Walzer in the early 1980s.[17] It is difficult to see why. All across the world the doctrinaire ideals of political theorists are in rout and what seemed like the perpetual oppression of the individual conscience now appears to be loosened by the interaction between doctrines and the realities they claimed to explain. One of these realities has proved to be the enduring self-consciousness of the conscience. The "democracy" that students who were massacred in Tianenmen Square were fighting for has been perplexing to Western political commentators: it did not seem, in the words of one, as if the students had "a coherent theory of democracy." But isn't that the point?

It is the illusion of our Age, to which we relentlessly cling, that men and women can create tools to solve moral and political problems, much as we have created technologies that solve physical problems. And yet, as ever, when one goes to the room where such tools are kept, one finds only the shards and artifacts of ideas broken in earlier tasks. We are incapable of making something that will obviate (rather than suppress) the requirement for moral decision. Then each person must go back out, armed with what he has found, to defend what he wants to survive ultimately when the one thing he knows for certain is that he himself will not ultimately survive.

Theory can describe but it cannot explain our fates. Knowing this does not diminish our hunger for explanation in the slightest; but it locates where our understanding will be found. Decision according to law is an ideal, but it is also an art and finally it is our piety, our "service to God."[18]

NOTES

BOOK I

Chapter 1   The Written Constitution

1   Which would hardly have seemed surprising to the British audience that first heard these lines.

2   There is a superb discussion of the competing claims of Athens to have been governed by a series of constitutions at about the fifth century in Dennis Proctor, *The Experience of Thucydides* (1980), 46–57, but I take these to have been more in the nature of codes in that they did not require amendment for change but could be supervened by ordinary political action that did not disturb the overall structure of the state.

3   At the request of Hugh de Payens, founder of the Order of the Temple, Bernard of Clairvaux wrote the *"Liber de laude novae militiae."* 9 *New Catholic Encyclopedia* (1967), Military Orders, 846.

4   "The *formula vitae* written by Francis for Clare and her nuns was composed mainly of Gospel texts. Although it was in no sense a documentary rule, it sufficed for the early years." *11 New Catholic Encyclopedia* (1967), Poor Clares, 566.

5   The answer I propose to this question is not an explanatory one. That is, it was the fact of each of the colonies having been governed according to a written charter that, perhaps as much as anything, accustomed the Americans to the idea: but this causal explanation is the sort that historians or political analysts might give. In the present work, I am interested in the possibilities available to history and politics, the constraints within which their ideas play out. And so my answer to the question "why" is a descriptive one.

6   From the Mayflower Compact – "This day before we came to harbour,

observing some not well affected to unitie and concord, but gave some appearance of faction, it was thought good there should be an association and agreement, that we should combine together in one body, and to submit to such government and governours, as we should by common consent agree to make and chose, and set out hands to this that follows word for word." *A Relation of the Beginning and Proceedings of the English Plantation Settled at Plymoth in New England* (1622;1974 reprint), at 3.

7 "As no contract could be made with a sovereign, so no contract could bind a sovereign. The holder of sovereign power was a mortal god absorbing, with this one qualification about their lives, the personality, the property rights and the conscience of his subjects. This power could not be limited or divided in any mixed form of state. For Hobbes as for Bodin, if there was a contract with or a contract limiting the government this only created a different form of government – only placed the sovereignty elsewhere without, on the other hand, limiting it. In every form of state, sovereignty inexorably absorbed all public right." F. Hinsley, *Sovereignty* (2nd edn, 1986), 143.

8 This sits uneasily with classical international law. For example, "Grotius rejected the view that sovereignty everywhere belongs to the people and that all government exists for the sake of the governed, not the rulers." E. Dumbauld, *The Life and Legal Writings of Hugo Grotius* (1969), 65–6, n. 51, citing *De Jure Belli ac Pacis* 1.3.8.1 and 1.3.8.14.

9 "I consider the people who constitute a society or nation as the source of all authority in that nation; as free to transact their common concerns by any agents they think proper; to change these agents individually, or the organization of them in form or function whenever they please; that all acts done by these agents under the authority of the nation are the acts of the nation, are obligatory to them and enure to their use, and can in no wise be annulled or affected by any change in the form of the government, or of the persons administering it, consequently the treaties between the United States and France, were not treaties between the United States and Louis Capet, but between the two nations of America and France; and the nations remaining in existence, though both of them have since changed their forms of government, the treaties are not annulled by these changes." T. Jefferson, "Opinion on the Question Whether the United States have a Right to Renounce Their Treaties with France, or to Hold them Suspended till the Government of the Country shall be Established," in *Basic Writings of Thomas Jefferson* (P. Foner ed., 1944), 316.

10 Letter from Thomas Jefferson to Wilson C. Nicholas (September 7, 1803), reprinted in *The Political Writings of Thomas Jefferson* (E. Dumbauld ed., 1955), 144.

11 See Jefferson, *Basic Writings supra*, n. 9.

Chapter 2   The Problem of Legitimacy

1   Philip Bobbitt, "Constitutional Fate," 58 Texas L. Rev. 695 (1980) (The Dougherty Lectures). Subsequently published as *Constitutional Fate: Theory of the Constitution* (1982).

2   "[W]hen the Supreme Court declares unconstitutional a legislative act or the action of an elected executive, it thwarts the will of representatives of the actual people of the here and now; it exercises control, not in behalf of the prevailing majority, but against it." A. Bickel, *The Least Dangerous Branch* (1962), 17.

3   For an elegant, but none the less deeply misleading account, see Robert McCloskey, *The American Supreme Court* (1960), 40–4.

4   Newspaper accounts in the wake of *Marbury* reveal little concern over the Court's exercise of judicial review. Except for some commentary in a series of letters from "An Unlearned Layman" in the *Washington Federalist*, "there was no other meaningful published discussion or criticism of the Supreme Court's claim that it had the power to declare acts of Congress unconstitutional. In terms of quantity and quality this response is remarkable considering the nature of the power claimed by the Court. The fact that the decision was announced during the time surrounding the Repeal Act controversy, where the power of judicial review was heatedly supported and denied, makes the failure of significant public commentary disputing the opinion on this point even more salient." See Burris, "Some Preliminary Thoughts on a Contextual Historical Theory for the Legitimacy of Judicial Review," 12 Okla. City U. L. Rev. 585, 641 (1987) (hereinafter, "A Contextual Historical Theory"). See also the contemporary newspaper accounts collected by Burris at 630ff.

   Federalist newspapers used the opportunity to criticize President Jefferson for withholding the commissions; the President was "guilty of an act not warranted by law, but violative of a vested right." *New York Evening Post*, March 23, 1803, reprinted in "A Contextual Historical Theory," at 635. The same paper characterized Jefferson as hypocritical for acting beyond the allowable scope of his office, even though he claimed to believe in limited government.

   The reaction of the Republican press was also muted; there were no calls for impeachment of the Supreme Court justices. One paper questioned "whether there is any analogy between what is called the *independence of the judges* in England and the *independence of the judges* in America – and whether making the former independent of the *king* justifies the making of the latter independent of the people." *Aurora General Advertiser*, March 31, 1803, reprinted in "A Contextual Historical Theory," at 636.

The Court was also criticized for its unnecessary resolution of the first two questions: "[The reports state the Court held it] . . . had no constitutional jurisdiction of the subject, and accordingly dismissed it [the mandamus], for want of such jurisdiction; and yet, as solemnly undertook to give a formal opinion upon the merits of them; and that, without a hearing of the adverse party, and in opposition to the executive department of government. . . [I question whether this is not a libel of the Court if it is not truly reprinted.] I make this enquiry, because I take it for granted that the Supreme Court of the nation would not from party motives volunteer an extrajudicial opinion for the sake of criminating a rival department of government, and yet, in all my reading I have not been able to find either principle or precedent for such a practice." *Independent Chronicle*, June 16, 1803, reprinted in "A Contextual Historical Theory," at 637.

The most detailed attack identified by Burris is in the form of seven letters addressed to the Chief Justice from "Littleton," published in the *Aurora General Advertiser*. These letters are silent on judicial review: "While Littleton ridiculed the Court's attempt to review the acts of the President, at no point during his lengthy discourse on the opinion did he attack the claim by the Supreme Court that it had the power to declare acts of Congress void when inconsistent with the Constitution. A permissible inference from the general lack of commentary is that the invocation of the power of judicial review to declare acts of Congress unconstitutional appears to have been silently accepted as a legitimate part of the judicial power under article III of the Constitution." Id. at 640.

5 McCloskey explains this by saying that the Republicans were not inclined to complain about the striking down of a law that had been passed by a Federalist Congress, as though it would not have occurred to the new Republican Congress that such a power could be directed against *their* statutes as well (by the Federalist judiciary).

6 "The interpretation of the laws is the proper and peculiar province of the courts. A constitution is, in fact, and must be regarded by the judges, as a fundamental law. It therefore belongs to them to ascertain its meaning, as well as the meaning of any particular act proceeding from the legislative body. If there should happen to be an irreconcilable variance between the two, that which has the superior obligation and validity ought, of course, to be preferred; or, in other words, the Constitution ought to be preferred to the statute, the intention of the people to the intention of their agents." *The Federalist* (B. Wright ed., 1961) no. 78, at 492 (A. Hamilton).

7 Early circuit cases regularly cite *Marbury*. See *U.S.* v. *Smith*, 27 F. Cas. 1192, 1198 (C.C.D.N.Y. 1806) (no. 16, 342); *Gilchrist* v. *Collector of*

Charleston, 10 F. Cas. 355, 360 (C.C.D.S.C. 1808) (no. 5,420); *U.S.
v. The William*, 28 F. Cas. 614, 618 (Dist. C.D. Mass. 1808) (no. 16,
700); *Averill v. Tucker*, 2 F. Cas. 239, 240 (C.C.D.C. 1824) (no. 670);
Baker v. Biddle, 2 F. Cas. 439, 444 (C.C.E.D.Pa. 1831) (no. 764);
Johnson v. U.S., 13 F. Cas. 868, 873 (C.C.D.Me. 1830) (no. 7,419);
Bonaparte v. Camden & A.R. Co., 3 F. Cas. 821, 828 (C.C.D.N.J.
1830) (no. 1617).

Casebooks anxious to make this non-problem the subject of genuine
classroom debate uniformly collect *Eakin v. Raub*, 12 Serg & Rawle,
330, 344 (Pa. 1825) (Gibson, J., dissenting). See, e.g., Mason, Beaney,
and Stephenson, *American Constitutional Law: Introductory Essays
and Selected Cases* (7th edn, 1983), 50. The *Eakin v. Raub* decision
that is cited is an opinion in dissent from a state supreme court. This
speaks volumes for the lack of materials on this side of the argument.
Indeed, Justice Gibson himself is reported to have said to counsel in
1845, "I have changed that opinion". *Norris v. Clymer*, 2 Pa. 281. His
opinion in *Eakin v. Raub* is not cited by any federal court.

Marbury was not the first time a statute had been struck down by
the Court and indeed was not the first time the federal courts had
struck down a congressional act. See *Ware v. Hylton*, 3 U.S. (3 Dall.)
199 (1796) (invoking the Supremacy Clause to hold a Virginia statute
invalid as inconsistent with the 1793 Treaty of Peace). "Our Federal
Constitution establishes the power of a treaty over the constitution
and laws of any of the States; and I have shewn that the words of the
4th [treaty] article were intended, and are sufficient to nullify the law
of Virginia . . ." Id. at 245 (opinion of Justice Chase); *Cooper v.
Telfair*, 4 U.S. (4 Dall.) 14, 19 (1800). *Cooper*, three years before
Marbury v. Madison, reflects a broad acceptance of judicial review:
"It is indeed, a general opinion, it is expressly admitted by all this bar,
and some of the judges have, individually, in the Circuits, decided
that the Supreme Court can declare an act of congress to be unconstitutional, and, therefore, invalid; but there is no adjudication of the
Supreme Court itself upon the point. I concur, however, in the general
sentiment, with reference to the period, when the existing constitution
came into operation . . ."

8 Action by the First Congress, whose members included many of the
framers and whose constituencies were virtually identical with the
ratifiers, are usually taken as indicative of the historical intentions of
the framers and ratifiers. Section 25 of the Judiciary Act of 1789
allowed the Supreme Court to review decisions from the highest state
courts in which the validity of a state statute or an exercise of state
authority was attacked as "being repugnant to the constitution, treaties,
or laws of the United States." Judiciary Act of 1789, ch. 20 sec. 25,

1 Stat. 73, 85–7 (approved September 24, 1789); current version at 28 U.S.C. 1257 (1987).

9   *Marbury* v. *Madison*, 5 U.S. (1 Cranch) 137, 175 (1803).

10 "[Justice Sutherland] dismisses declarations favorable to minimum wage legislation by saying that 'they reflect no legitimate light upon the question of its validity, and that is what we are called upon to decide,' adding that 'The elucidation of that question cannot be aided by counting heads.' It is judicial heads that count. Five Supreme Court heads of the particular moment voted the condemnation although thirty-five of the forty-five judges who sat in all courts on the question voted for validity. It was Selden in his *Table-Talk* who said: 'They talk (but blasphemously enough) that the Holy Ghost is President of their General Councils, when the Truth is, the Odd Man is still the Holy Ghost.'" T. Powell, *Vagaries and Varieties in Constitutional Interpretation* (1956) (on the Court striking down an act of Congress establishing a minimum wage for women factory workers in *Adkins* v. *Children's Hospital*, 261 U.S. 525 (1923).

"[W]hen is authority legitimate? I find it convenient to discuss that question in the context of the Warren Court and its works simply because the Warren Court posed the issue in acute form. The issue did not disappear along with the era of the Warren Court majorities, however. It arises when any court either exercises or declines to exercise the power to invalidate any act of another branch of government. The Supreme Court is a major power center, and we must ask when its power should be used and when it should be withheld." R. Bork, "Neutral Principles and Some First Amendment Problems," 47 Ind. L. J. 1, 1–2 (1971).

11 Article VI of the US Constitution is commonly referred to as the Supremacy Clause: "This Constitution, and the Laws of the United States which shall be made in Pursuance thereof; and all Treaties made, or which shall be made, under the Authority of the United States, shall be the supreme Law of the Land; and the Judges in every State shall be bound thereby, any Thing in the Constitution or Laws of any State to the Contrary notwithstanding."

A textualist would argue that the Supremacy Clause compels courts to determine the constitutionality of state acts because any state law "to the contrary" of the Constitution cannot be given legal effect. A similar argument holds that courts must determine, according to the text, whether the federal laws of the United States are in fact "in pursuance" of the Constitution before they can be given effect.

12 See, e.g., the current debate over the Eleventh Amendment which precludes federal jurisdiction in suits brought against a state. "The Judicial power of the United States shall not be construed to extend

to any suit in law or equity, commenced or prosecuted against one of the United States by Citizens of another State, or by Citizens or Subjects of any Foreign State." U.S. Const. Amend. XI. In *Hans v. Louisiana*, 134 U.S. 1 (1890) the Supreme Court held that the amendment also bars citizens from suing their own state in federal court. Lately, much has been written on whether *Hans* is in fact consistent with the framers' intent. See, *Atascadero State Hospital* v. *Scanlon*, 473 U.S. 234, 247–302 (1985) (Brennan, J., dissenting); *Welch* v. *Texas Dep't of Highways & Pub. Transp.*, 107 S. Ct. 2941, 2958 (1987) (Brennan, J., dissenting); L. Marshall, "Fighting the Words of the Eleventh Amendment," 102 Harv. L. Rev. 1342 (1989); W. Marshall, "The Diversity Theory of the Eleventh Amendment: A Critical Evaluation," 102 Harv. L. Rev. 1372 (1989); Amar, "Of Sovereignty and Federalism," 96 Yale L. J. 1425, 1473–92 (1987); Fletcher, "A Historical Interpretation of the Eleventh Amendment: A Narrow Construction of an Affirmative Grant of Jurisdiction Rather than a Prohibition against Jurisdiction," 25 Stan. L. Rev. 1033 (1983); Gibbons, "The Eleventh Amendment and State Sovereign Immunity: A Reinterpretation," 83 Colum. L. Rev. 1889 (1983); Jackson, "The Supreme Court, the Eleventh Amendment, and State Sovereign Immunity," 98 Yale L.J. 1 (1988); See also, Nowak, "The Scope of Congressional Power to Create Causes of Action Against State Governments and the History of the Eleventh and Fourteenth Amendments," 75 Colum. L. Rev. 1413 (1975); L. H. Tribe, "Intergovernmental Immunities in Litigation, Taxation, and Regulation: Separation of Powers Issues in Controversies about Federalism," 89 Harv. L. Rev. 682, 683–99 (1976); Amar, "*Marbury*, Section 13, and the Original Jurisdiction of the Supreme Court," 56 U. Chi. L. Rev. 443, 493–9 (1989); Massey, "State Sovereignty and the Tenth and Eleventh Amendments," 56 U. Chi. L. Rev. 61 (1989).

13 This passage was written in 1987.

14 Scalia, "Originalism: The Lesser Evil," 57 U. Cin. L. Rev. 849 (1989); Pollak, "'Original Intention' and the Crucible of Litigation," 57 U. Cin. L. Rev. 867 (1989); Hatch, "Modern Marbury Myths," 57 U. Cin. L. Rev. 891 (1989); "Book Notes Commemorating the Bicentennial of the Constitution," 101 Harv. L. Rev. 849 (1988); "A Bicentennial Celebration of the Constitution: The Third Circuit Judicial Conference in Philadelphia," 49 U. Pitt. L. Rev. 685 (1988); "A Symposium on Constitutional Law," 12 Okla. City U. L. Rev. 431 (1987); "Symposium: In Celebration of the Bicentennial of the Constitution," 72 Iowa L. Rev. 1177 (1987); "Symposium: 'To Endure for Ages to Come': A Bicentennial View of the Constitution," 65 N.C.L. Rev. 881 (1987); "Bicentennial Constitutional and Legal History Sym-

posium," 24 Cal. W. L. Rev. 221 (1987); Kniec, "Of Balkanized
Empire and Cooperative Allies: A Bicentennial Essay on the Separation
of Powers," 37 Cath. U. L. Rev. 73 (1987) (The Brown Lecture);
Symposium: "A Constitutional Bicentennial Celebration," 47 Md. L.
Rev. 1 (1987); "The Constitution as an Economic Document." A
Symposium Commemorating the Bicentennial of the United States
Constitution, 56 Geo. Wash. L. Rev. 81 (1987); Special Constitutional
Issue, 72 Mass. L. Rev. 3 (1987); Bicentennial Symposium: "The
Constitution and Human Values: The Unfinished Agenda," 20 Ga. L.
Rev. 811 (1986); Amar, "Our Forgotten Constitution: A Bicentennial
Comment," 97 Yale L. J. 281 (1987).

Chapter 3   *The Modalities of Constitutional Argument*

1   Antony Flew, *A Dictionary of Philosophy* (1979), 235.
2   For possibility can be stated in terms of necessity: if a proposition is
    necessarily true, then it is impossible that it is false.
3   I am aware of course that some persons have taken the view that modal
    sentences can be re-defined in terms of ordinary propositions. Carnap,
    for example, seems to have taken the position, at an earlier period, that
    modal sentences are translatable into propositions about the syntactical
    properties of those same sentences. See R. Carnap, in *Die Logische
    Syntax der Sprache* (1934; English trans. *The Logical Syntax of Lan-
    guage*, 1937), sec. 69. Bertrand Russell took the view also that modal
    statements were extensions of propositions about propositional func-
    tions. See Russell, *Logic and Knowledge, Essays 1901–1950* (R. C.
    March ed., 1956), 231; see also *Introduction to Mathematical Philos-
    ophy* (1919), 165: "if 'qx' is an undetermined value of a certain pro-
    positional function, it will be necessary if the function is always true,
    possible if sometimes true, and impossible if never true."
4   S. Levinson and S. Mailloux, *A Hermeneutic Reader* (1988), 11: cf.
    P. Brest and S. Levinson, *Processes of Constitutional Decisionmaking*
    (2nd edn, 1983), 35–6.
5   Schauer, "An Essay on Constitutional Language," 29 UCLA L. Rev.
    797 (1979).
6   The judicial Power shall extend to all Cases, in Law and Equity,
    arising under this Constitution, the Laws of the United States, and
    Treaties made, or which shall be made, under their Authority; – to all
    Cases affecting Ambassadors, other public Ministers and Consuls; –
    to all Cases of admiralty and maritime Jurisdiction; – to Controversies
    to which the United States shall be a Party; – to Controversies between
    two or more States; – between a State and Citizens of another State;
    – between Citizens of different States; – between Citizens of the same

State claiming Lands under Grants of different States, and between a State, or the Citizens thereof, and foreign States, Citizens or Subjects." U.S. Const. Art. III, sec. 2, cl. 1.

7 *Dred Scott* v. *Sandford*, 60 U.S. (19 How.) 393, 407 (1856).

8 "The right of the people to be secure in their persons, houses, papers, and effects, against unreasonable searches and seizures, shall not be violated, and no Warrants shall issue, but upon probable cause, supported by Oath or affirmation, and particularly describing the place to be searched, and the persons or things to be seized." U.S. Const. amend. IV.

9 *Olmstead* v. *U.S.*, 277 U.S. 438, 464 (1928).

10 *Berger* v. *New York*, 388 U.S. 41, 59 (1967).

11 In *I.N.S.* v. *Chadha*, 462 U.S. 919 (1983) the Court struck down a legislative veto, a provision authorizing Congress (or a portion of its membership) to invalidate a decision of the Executive branch, as unconstitutional. The provision at issue in *Chadha* was sec. 244(c)(2) of the Immigration and Nationality Act, which authorized either House, by resolution, to invalidate the decision of the Attorney General, allowing a particular deportable alien to remain in the United States.

In *National League of Cities* v. *Usery*, the Court struck down provisions of the 1974 amendments to the Fair Labor Standards Act that extended the Act's minimum wage and maximum hours provisions to most employees of states and their political subdivisions.

In *Morrison* v. *Olson*, 108 S. Ct. 2597 (1988), the Court upheld the authority of the Special Prosecutor appointed under provisions of the Ethics in Government Act. The appointment of a Special Prosecutor, created to investigate high-ranking executive branch officials, is triggered when the Attorney General decides to seek investigation by a special counsel. The Special Division (a special court created by the Act) appoints the Special Prosecutor and defines her jurisdiction. The office is terminated either by the Special Prosecutor or by the Special Division.

In *Bowsher* v. *Synar*, 478 U.S. 714 (1986) the Court struck down the Gramm – Rudman – Hollings Amendment to the 1985 Balanced Budget and Emergency Deficit Control Act. The Court held that powers vested in the Comptroller General (who may be removed only at the initiative of Congress) under the reporting provisions of the Act violated the Constitutional injunction that Congress play no direct role in the execution of the laws.

12 *Ex Parte Yarbrough*, 110 U.S. 651 (1883).

13 Id. at 651, 657, 658, 663, 666.

14 The argument in *National League of Cities* v. *Usery*, 426 U.S. 833

(1976) (which was emphatically *not* a Tenth Amendment case), went essentially like this. (1) We have a federal system, composed of a supreme federal state and member states. (2) It follows that, to have such a system, there must be at least one thing that the national legislature cannot order the states to do; otherwise, we would not have a federal system but would instead have replaced it with the regions and departments of a unitary system. (3) Determining the wages and hours of state employees is a function crucial to the preservation of a state as a state; if Congress could manipulate the costs of such items, it could control state policies generally. (4) Therefore, Congress cannot be permitted to exercise such control.

15 See *Ashwander* v. *Tennessee Valley Authority*, 297 U.S. 288, 346–56 (1935) (Brandeis, J., concurring) (courts are without the authority to decide the constitutionality of statutes when the controversy can be resolved on other grounds). In *Ashwander*, Justice Brandeis develops a set of seven rules that require the Court to forbear deciding a case on constitutional grounds. The Court will not pass upon the constitutionality of legislation in a friendly, non-adversarial proceeding: *Chicago & Grand Trunk Ry.* v. *Wellman*, 143 U.S. 339 (1892). The Court will not decide questions of constitutional law unless absolutely necessary to a decision of the case: *Burton* v. *United States*, 196 U.S. 283 (1905). The court will not "formulate a rule of constitutional law broader than is required by the precise facts to which it is to be applied": *Liverpool, N.Y. & P.S.S. Co.* v. *Emigration Commissioners*, 113 U.S. 33, 39 (1885). The Court will not decide a case upon constitutional grounds if it can be decided on the grounds of statutory construction or general law: *Siler* v. *Louisville & Nashville R. Co.*, 213 U.S. 175 (1909). The Court will not pass upon the validity of a statute on the complaint of one who fails to show that he is injured by its operation: *Tyler* v. *The Judges*, 179 U.S. 405 (1900). The Court will not pass upon the validity of a statute on the complaint of one who has availed himself of its benefits: *Great Falls Mfg. Co.* v. *Attorney General*, 124 U.S. 581 (1888). "When the validity of an act of the Congress is drawn in question, and even if a serious doubt of constitutionality is raised, it is a cardinal principle that this Court will first ascertain whether a construction of the statute is fairly possible by which the question may be avoided:" *Crowell* v. *Benson*, 285 U.S. 22, 62 (1932).

16 *Home Building and Loan Asso.* v. *Blaisdell*, 290 U.S. 398, 444 (1934). The Contracts Clause provides: "No State shall . . . pass any . . . Law impairing the Obligation of Contracts . . ." U.S. Const. Art. I, sec. 10.

17 *Bowles* v. *Willingham*, 321 U.S. 503, 519, 521 (1944).

18 A. Bickel, *The Least Dangerous Branch* (1962), 116.
19 "Congress shall make no law respecting an establishment of religion
    . . ." U.S. Const. amend. I.
20 *Everson v. Board of Education*, 330 U.S. 1 (1947).
21 Id. at 17.
22 *Lemon v. Kurtzman*, 403 U.S. 602 (1971).
23 Philip Bobbitt, "When Courts Refuse to Follow: Incidents of lower
    court overruling of Supreme Court Precedent" (unpublished mss).
24 I ignore for the moment elements of this ethos, such as the Thirteenth
    Amendment, that are not confined to such inferences.
25 *New York Times*, November 29, 1983 at 30, col. 1. Also see *Austin
    American-Statesman* of May 26, 1988 in which it was reported that a
    superior court judge in Phoenix had ordered an eighteen-year-old
    woman to practice birth control for the rest of her child-bearing years
    as a condition of probation. In Indianapolis, a man who pleaded guilty
    to dealing in cocaine was forbidden to marry or father a child for
    four years as a condition of his reduced sentence. *Austin American-
    Statesman*, July 15, 1989.
26 *Meyer v. Nebraska*, 262 U.S. 390 (1923).
27 *Pierce v. Society of Sisters*, 268 U.S. 510 (1925).
28 *Moore v. City of East Cleveland*, 431 U.S. 494 (1977).
29 *In re Quackenbush*, 156 N. J. Super. 282, 383 A. 2d 785 (1978).
30 *O'Connor v. Donaldson*, 422 U.S. 563 (1975).
31 Philip Bobbitt, *Constitutional Fate: Theory of the Constitution* (1982),
    57–8.

Chapter 4   The Usefulness of this Approach

1 A. de Tocqueville, *Democracy in America* (P. Bradley Knoff ed.,
   1948), 280.
2 P. Bobbitt, "Is Law Politics?" 41 Stan. L. Rev. 1233 (1989) (reviewing
   M. Tushnet, *Red, White and Blue: A Critical Analysis of Constitutional
   Law*, 1988).
3 "And yet legal argument – the analysis of the Constitution to which
   so many able minds have devoted themselves this last quarter century
   – cannot establish independent legitimacy for judicial review, for its
   debates and its analyses are conducted by means of arguments that
   themselves reflect a commitment to such legitimacy. So although a
   general theory of constitutional law may appear to establish the legitimacy of certain kinds of arguments – as when a social contract theorist
   might wish to confine courts to a textual analysis of the Constitution
   – it is in fact the other way round. It is because we are already
   committed to the force of an appeal to text that such an argument can

be used in support of a court's role. When one argues that a court's experience with parsing documents, or its time for reflection, or its relative insulation from political pressure, and so forth, fit it as an institution for the task of assessing the constitutionality of legislation, one is already committed to the view that enforcing rules derived from the constitutional text is the legitimate task at hand" Philip Bobbitt, *Constitutional Fate: Theory of the Constitution* (1982), 5.

4 Regarding the historical approach, cf. (1) "The model . . . calls for judges to apply the rules of the written constitution in the sense in which those rules were understood by the people who enacted them." Kay, "Adherence to the Original Intentions in Constitutional Adjudication: Three Objections and Responses," 82 Nw. U. L. Rev. 226, 230 (1988). (2) "There is fairly strong evidence that the enactors were familiar with and expected judicial enforcement of the Constitution." Id. at 283, n. 289, citing R. Berger, *Congress vs. the Supreme Court* (1969). (3) R. Berger, "Federalism: The Founders' Design – a Response to Michael McConnell," 57 Geo. Wash. L. Rev. 51 (1988); Simeone, "An Essay on the Original Philosophy of the American Constitution," 6 St. Louis U. L. Rev. 313 (1987).

5 Compare Simeone, "Original Philosophy" (a rather undifferentiated historical approach) with Jaffa, "What Were the 'Original Intentions' of the Framers of the Constitution of the United States?" 10 U. Puget Sound L. Rev. 351 (1987). Both of these approaches can be distinguished from one that relies strictly on a political theory that would give effect to the Federalist Papers and the First Judiciary Act: "[h]istory cannot prove – or disprove – that legitimate constitutional interpretation must be intentionalist because that is a legal, not a historical question." Powell, "The Modern Misunderstanding of Original Intent" (Book Review), 54 U. Chi. L. Rev. 1513, 1532 (1987).

6 See Powell, "Modern Misunderstanding". R. Berger cites *Federalist* no. 78 to argue that legitimate judicial review is limited to policing constitutional boundaries between the branches of government. R. Berger, *Government by Judiciary* (1977), 293.

7 Re textual approaches, cf. (1) "Once text and intent are seen as separable, the former comfortably assumes authoritativeness in a way the latter cannot. Only the text is adopted. The problem of 'summing' individual intentions to find the relevant one that vexes any search for original constitutional intent does not exist for the text. We know exactly how to sum the votes necessary to promulgate constitutional language. In the amendment process, we also have a well-established, well-understood, and universally accepted mechanism for altering the constitutional text. There is nothing comparable for constitutional intention." Bennett, "Objectivity in Constitutional Law," 132 U. Pa.

L. Rev. 445, 459 (1984). (2) "[The] general intelligibility of language enables us to understand immediately the mandate of numerous constitutional provisions without recourse to precedent, original intent, or any of the other standard interpretive supplements." Schauer, "Easy Cases," 58 S. Cal. L. Rev. 399, 418 (1985); see also Schauer, 'An Essay on Constitutional Language', 29 U.C.L.A. L. Rev. 797, 809 (1982).

8   "Constitutional judicial review . . . is intentionally antimajoritarian.
. . . I do not believe that this reality undermines the legitimacy of judicial review. Rather what is necessary is a theory which explains why it is desirable to have an institution, like the judiciary, identifying and protecting important values from the majority of society." Chemerinsky, "Wrong Questions Get Wrong Answers: An Analysis of Professor Carter's Approach to Judicial Review," 66 B.U.L. Rev. 47, 49 (1986).

   "A central aspiration of the tradition has been to achieve justice, and justice has generally been seen to lie partly in the direction marked out by the more particular aspirations symbolized by the various constitutional provisions regarding individual rights." Perry, "The Authority of Text, Tradition, and Reason: A Theory of Constitutional Interpretation," 58 S. Cal. L. Rev. 551, 577 (1985).

   For a *tour de force* in prudentialism, see, M. Tushnet, *Red, White and Blue: A Critical Analysis of Constitutional Law* (1988).

9   J. Choper, *Judicial Review and the National Political Process* (1980), 60–70; Sandalow, "Judicial Protection of Minorities," 75 Mich. L. Rev. 1162 (1977).

10   See, e.g., editorial commentary comparing the Supreme Court's decision on flag-burning (*Texas* v. *Johnson*, 109 S. Ct. 2533 (1989)) and legislation introduced in reaction to that decision: "The Supreme Court acted with monumental strength and wisdom when it decided that the first amendment protects even the young man who doesn't comprehend why his childish burning of a flag on a Dallas street is being tolerated. Courageous political leaders, in Congress if not in the White House, could say that to the public . . . [but] Having already decided to demagogue rather than educate, Congress now rushes to do so needlessly. The only fire is in Congress, and it threatens arson against the Constitution." *New York Times*, September 19, 1989, at A24, col. 1.

11   "No doubt it is in the interest of the majority to obtain the acquiescence of the minority as often and in as great a degree as possible. And no doubt the Court can help bring about acquiescence by assuring those who have lost a political fight that merely momentary interest, not

fundamental principle, was in play." A. Bickel, *The Least Dangerous Branch* (1962), 30.

12   C. MacKinnon, *Feminism Unmodified: Discourses on Life and Law* (1987).

13   Tushnet, *Red, White and Blue*, 160, 162–3.

14   "This decision by the people to limit themselves by law – not only by the idea of law but by the actual processes of law in courts of their own establishing – is part of the distinctive essence of American democracy. . . . Living, vigorous judicial review . . . cannot be justified as something that thwarts and contradicts popular desire – but it can be justified as something that fulfills popular desire. All people everywhere desire to know that the acts of government possess the vital quality of legitimacy; judicial review . . . serves this need. The American people specifically, have stated their desire that certain acts be forbidden to government, and they need means to bring this about; though judicial review in the past has doubtless fallen short of expectation in this regard, it has done something, and it could do more." C. Black, *The People and the Court* (1960), 117. C. Black, *Decision According to Law* (1981), 17–19, 37–9. J.H. Ely, *Democracy and Distrust: A Theory of Judicial Review* (1980), 120–5.
Amar, "Of Sovereignty and Federalism," 96 Yale L. J. 1425 (1987); "Philadephia Revisited: Amending the Constitution Outside Article V," 55 U. Chi. L. Rev. 1043 (1988): "A Neo-Federalist View of Article III: Separating the Two Tiers of Federal Jurisdiction," 65 B.U. L. Rev. 205 (1985); Blasi, "Checking Theory of the First Amendment," 1977 Am. B. Found. Res. J. 521 (1977).

15   "The original document, before addition of any of the amendments, does not speak primarily of the rights of man, but of the abilities and disabilities of government. On reflecting upon the text's preoccupation with the scope of government as well as its shape, however, one comes to understand that what this text is about is the relationship of the individual and the state. The text marks the metes and bounds of official authority and individual autonomy. When one studies the boundary that the text marks out, one gets a sense of the vision of the individual embodied in the Constitution." Brennan, "The Constitution of the United States: Contemporary Ratification," 27 S. Tex. L. Rev. 433, 439 (1986).
     "I want to claim that the source or basis of our Constitution's authority is in what might be described either as a shared moral consciousness or identity, or as a deeply-layered and shared consensual attitude toward certain stories about and norms of political morality that are understood by a sizable number of our people as representational of the value and importance of the Constitution." Simon, "The

Authority of the Constitution and its Meaning: A Preface to a Theory of Constitutional Interpretation," 58 S. Cal. L. Rev. 603, 614 (1985). Wellington, "Common Law Rules and Constitutional Double Standards: Some Notes on Adjudication," 83 Yale L. J. 221 (1973).

16 "By demonstrating that its judgments were indeed the authentic voice of a body of principles reaching back through the past to the sacred instrument, the Court, despite false starts and a few egregious blunders, was able down throughout the years to resolve the great divisive constitutional issues in ways that commanded the assent of the country yet also met its current needs and aspirations." Cox, "The Role of the Supreme Court," 47 Md. L. Rev. 118, 120 (1987).
Paul M. Bator et al., *Hart & Wechsler's The Federal Courts and the Federal System* (Foundation, 3rd edn, 1988).

17 *Marbury* v. *Madison*, 5 U.S. (1 Cranch) 139 (1803).

18 "It is emphatically the province and duty of the judicial department to say what the law is. Those who apply the rule to particular cases, must of necessity expound and interpret that rule. If two laws conflict with each other, the courts must decide on the operation of each. So if a law be in opposition to the constitution; if both the law and the constitution apply to a particular case, so that the court must either decide that case conformably to the law, disregarding the constitution; or conformably to the constitution, disregarding the law; the court must determine which of these conflicting rules governs the case. That is of the very essence of judicial duty." Id. at 177–8.

19 "That the people have an original right to establish, for their future government, such principles as, in their opinion, shall most conduce to their own happiness, is the basis, on which the whole American fabric has been erected. . . . The powers of the legislature are defined, and limited; and that those limits may not be mistaken or forgotten, the constitution is written. To what purpose are powers limited, and to what purpose is that limitation committed to writing, if these limits may, at any time, be passed by those intended to be restrained? The distinction, between a government with limited and unlimited powers, is abolished, if those limits do not confine the persons on whom they are imposed, and if acts prohibited and acts allowed, are of equal obligation. It is a proposition too plain to be contested, that the constitution controls any legislative act repugnant to it; or, that the legislature may alter the constitution by an ordinary act." Id. at 176–7.

20 "It must be well recollected that in 1792, an act passed, directing the secretary at war to place on the pension list such disabled officers and soldiers as should be reported to him, by the circuit courts, which act, so far as the duty was imposed on the courts, was deemed unconstitutional. . . . This law being deemed unconstitutional at the

circuits, was repealed, and a different system was established; but the question whether those persons, who had been reported by the judges, as commissioners, were entitled, in consequence of that report to be placed on the pension list, was a legal question, properly determinable in the courts. . . . That this question might be properly settled, congress passed an act in February, 1793, making it the duty of the secretary of war, in conjunction with the attorney general, to take such measures, as might be necessary to obtain an adjudication of the Supreme Court of the United States on the validity of any such rights, claimed under the act aforesaid. . . . When the subject was brought before the court the decision was, not that a mandamus would not lie to the head of a department, directing him to perform an act, enjoined by law, in the performance of which an individual had a vested interest; but that a mandamus ought not to issue in that case – the decision necessarily to be made if the report of the commissioners did not confer on the applicant a legal right. The judgment in that case, is understood to have decided the merits of all claims of that description; and the persons on the report of the commissioners found it necessary to pursue the mode prescribed by the law subsequent to that which had been deemed unconstitutional, in order to place themselves on the pension list. The doctrine, therefore, now advanced, is by no means a novel one." Id. at 171–2.

21 I should warn any reader who is tempted to conclude that this simply amounts to a re-statement of the is/ought distinction – it doesn't. See Book III or bear with me.

22 G. Gilmore, *The Ages of American Law* (1977).

23 *Thompson* v. *Oklahoma*, 108 S. Ct. 2687 (1988).

24 Constitutional law plays at least as great a role in the operation of the Presidency as it does in the life of the Court.

Chapter 5   *The Problem of Indeterminacy*

1 Levinson, "Law as Literature," 60 Tex. L. Rev. 373, 391 (1982).

2 "The Judicial power of the United States shall not be construed to extend to any suit in law or equity, commenced or prosecuted against one of the United States by Citizens of another State, or by Citizens or Subjects of any Foreign State." U.S. Const. amend. XI.

3 "It seldom happens in the negotiation of treaties, of whatever nature, but that perfect *secrecy* and immediate *despatch* are sometimes requisite. There are cases whether the most useful intelligence may be obtained, if the persons possessing it can be relieved from apprehensions of discovery. . . . The convention have done well, therefore, in so disposing of the power of making treaties, that although the President must,

in forming them, act by the advice and consent of the Senate, yet he will be able to manage the business of intelligence in such a manner as prudence may suggest." *The Federalist* (B. Wright ed., 1961), no. 64 at 422 (J. Jay).

4 R. Bork, "Original Intent: The Only Legitimate Basis for Constitutional Decision Making," Judge's J. 13, 14 (Summer 1987).

5 Singer, "The Player and the Cards: Nihilism and Legal Theory," 94 Yale L. J. 1, 6 (1984).

6 See, Powell, Book Review 54 U. Chi. L. Rev. 1513 (1987) (reviewing R. Berger, *Federalism: The Founders' Design*, 1987).

7 See, e.g., the continuing debate over the meaning of the Eighth Amendment which provides that "excessive bail shall not be required, nor excessive fines imposed, nor cruel and unusual punishments inflicted." In a death penalty case, Justice Stewart interpreted "cruel and unusual" to mean bizarre, *outré*: "These death sentences are cruel and unusual in the same way that being struck by lightning is cruel and unusual." *Fairman* v. *Georgia*, 408 U.S. 238, 309 (1971). Other justices disagreed; indeed, all nine justices filed separate opinions. Justice Burger criticized the Stewart and White concurring opinions on specifically textual grounds: "[t]o be sure, there is a recitation cast in Eighth Amendment terms: petitioners' sentences are 'cruel' because they exceed that which the legislatures have deemed necessary for all cases; petitioners' sentences are 'unusual' because they exceed that which is imposed in most cases." Id. at 398 (Burger, C.J., dissenting).

8 See chapter 4, pp. 23–30.

9 O. Fiss, "Objectivity and Interpretation," 34 Stan. L. Rev. 739, 742 (1982). See also, O. Fiss, "Comment, Conventionalism," 58 S. Cal. L. Rev. 177 (1985).

10 Fiss, "Objectivity and Interpretation," 739.

11 Id. at 742.

12 Id. at 743.

13 Id. at 744, 745.

14 Id. at 747.

15 S. Fish, "Fish v. Fiss," 36 Stan. L. Rev. 1325, 1325 (1984). See also, S. Fish, "Working on the Chain Gang: Interpretation in Law and Literature," 60 Tex. L. Rev. 551 (1982).

16 Fish, Fish v. Fiss, at 1333.

17 Id. at 1335, 1336.

18 Llewellyn, "The Constitution as Construction/Creation," 34 Colum. L. Rev. 1 (1934).

19 R. Cover, "The Supreme Court, 1982 Term – Foreword: Nomos and Narrative," 97 Harv. L. Rev. 4 (1983).

20 R. Cover, *Justice Accused: Antislavery and the Judicial Process* (1975).

21 For example, "America first realized [during the Depression] that it had been fragmented into separate rural and urban cultures, and that the rural poor belonged to a world so vastly different from the world of the urban elite as to merit close artistic and scholarly attention. . . . Among the better-known works of the era that have retained their power to shock the reader . . . *The Grapes of Wrath*." "Comment: *Hood* v. *Dumond*: A Study of the Supreme Court and the Ideology of Capitalism," 134 U. Pa. L. Rev. 657, 664 n. 24 (1986).

22 *Maher* v. *Roe*, 432 U.S. 464 (1977).

23 Fiss, "Objectivity and Interpretation," 739, 749 (1982).

24 Fish, "Fish v. Fiss," 1325, 1337.

25 Fiss, "Objectivity and Interpretation," n. 23 at 763.

26 Fish, "Fish v. Fiss," n. 24 at 1346.

27 *Korematsu* v. *U.S.*, 319 U.S. 432 (1943).

BOOK II

Chapter 1   The Case Method

1 The quotation is from an address to the Harvard Law School Association in 1886, quoted by G. Gilmore, *Ages of American Law* (1977), 42.

2 C. Langdell, *Cases on Contracts* (2nd edn, 1879), viii–ix.

3 C. Langdell, *Selection of Cases on the Law of Contracts* (1871), vi.

4 "After encountering an initial but short lived campaign of resistance, the case method swept through the world of legal education in the United States, bringing with it tremendous changes in legal education." 40 Hastings L. J. 771.

5 Compare, P. Brest and S. Levinson, *Processes of Constitutional Decision-Making* (2nd edn, 1982); G. Stone, L. Seidman, C. Sunstein and M. Tushnet, *Constitutional Law* (1986).

6 P. Freund, A. Sutherland, M. Howe and E. Brown, *Constitutional Law* (4th edn, 1977); G. Gunther, *Cases and Materials on Constitutional Law* (11th edn, 1985).

Chapter 2   Missouri v. Holland

1 P. C. Bartholomew, *Leading Cases on the Constitution* (1960), 177.

2 *Missouri* v. *Holland*, 252 U.S. 416, 417–24 (1920).

3 Id. at 418, 420, 421.

4 Id. at 417; Brief for Appellant at 27–8, *Missouri* v. *Holland*, 252 U.S. 416 (1920) (no. 609).

5 *Missouri* v. *Holland*, n. 2 at 417, 420.

6 Brief for Appellant, n. 4 at 56, 59–60.

7 *Missouri* v. *Holland*, n. 2 at 424–29.

8 Id. at 424; Brief for Appellee, n. 4 at 8–13, *Missouri* v. *Holland*, 252 U.S. 416 (1920) (no. 609).

9 *Cohens* v. *Virginia*, 19 U.S. (6 Wheat.) 264 (1821).

10 *The Legal Tender Cases*, 79 U.S. (12 Wall.) 457 (1870).

11 *Missouri* v. *Holland*, n. 2 at 424, 425.

12 Brief for Appellee, n. 4 at 13–14.

13 Emphasis added.

14 *Holmes–Pollock Letters*, vol. 2 (M. Howe ed., 1941), 13. See also, P. Bobbitt, *Constitutional Fate* (1982) at 70.

15 *United States* v. *Shauver*, 248 U.S. 594 (1919).

16 *United States* v. *McCullagh*, 54 U.S. (13 How.) 216 (1851).

17 *Geer* v. *Connecticut*, 161 U.S. 519 (1896). Missouri had relied on these cases in its brief for the proposition that the regulation of migrating game was a state, and not a federal, power. Rather than merely distinguishing them away, however, Holmes uses the distinction to set up his own argument. This is the hand of the master.

18 "Aside from the authority of the State, derived from the common ownership of game and the trust for the benefit of its people which the State exercises thereto, there is another view of the power of the State in regard to the property in game which is equally conclusive. The right to preserve game flows from the undoubted existence in the State of a police power to that end . . ." Id. at 534. A careless judge or advocate would simply quote this language and rely on it.

19 U.S. Const. Art. VI, cl. 2. This section is commonly referred to as the Supremacy Clause.

20 Compare such fastidiousness with the less careful readings of *McCulloch* v. *Maryland* that describe it as holding that the Necessary and Proper Clause provides an enumerated power that is the basis for Marshall's upholding of the constitutionality of the federal bank. See, J. Nowak and R. Rotunda, *Constitutional Law* (3rd edn, 1986), 117.

21 "The office of a postmaster is so essentially unlike the office now involved that the decision in the *Myers* Case cannot be accepted as controlling our decision here. . . . The actual decision in the *Myers* Case finds support in the theory that such an officer is merely one of the units in the executive department and, hence, inherently subject to the exclusive and illimitable power of removal by the Chief Executive, whose subordinate and aid he is. Putting aside dicta . . . the necessary reach of the decision goes far enough to include all purely executive officers. It goes no farther; much less does it include an officer who occupies no place in the executive department and who exercise no part of the executive power." *Humphrey's Executor* v.

U.S., 295 U.S. 602, 627 (1935). (The President may not remove a Federal Trade Commissioner from office even though he may remove a Postmaster under the rule of *Myers* v. *U.S.*, 272 U.S. 52 (1926).)

22 Compare, e.g., H. Monaghan, "Our Perfect Constitution," 56 N.Y.U. L. Rev. 353 (1981), D. Laycock, Book Review, 59 Tex. L. Rev. 343 (1981), and Perry, "The Authority of the Text, Tradition, and Reason: A Theory of Constitutional 'Interpretation'," 58 S. Cal. L. Rev. 551, 556 (1985), with F. Schauer, "An Essay on Constitutional Language," 29 UCLA L. Rev. 797 (1982), F. Schauer, "Easy Cases," 58 S. Cal. L. Rev. 399, 418 (1985) and T. Grey, "A Constitutional Morphology: Text, Context, and Pretext in Constitutional Interpretation," 19 Ariz. St. L. J. 587 (1987).

23 Holmes's reference to the events of 100 years ago is not an obscure reference to events in 1820, but as the context shows, a reference to the adoption of the Constitution, rendered with poetic license.

24 "It is clear that if the President had authority to issue the order he did, it must be found in some provision of the Constitution." *Youngstown Sheet & Tube Co.* v. *Sawyer*, 343 U.S. 579, 587 (1952); "I get nowhere in this case by talk about a constitutional 'right of privacy' as an emanation from one or more constitutional provisions. I like my privacy as well as the next one, but I am nevertheless compelled to admit that government has a right to invade it unless prohibited by some specific constitutional provision." *Griswold* v. *Connecticut*, 381 U.S. 479, 509–10 (1965) (Black, J., dissenting).

25 "No State shall make or enforce any law which shall abridge the privileges or immunities of citizens of the United States; nor shall any State deprive any person of life, liberty, or property, without due process of law; nor deny to any person within its jurisdiction the equal protection of the laws." U.S. Const. amend XIV, sec. 1.

Incorporation is a strategy whereby the protections that individuals enjoy *vis-à-vis* the national government through the Bill of Rights are applied against state governments: "My study of the historical events that culminated in the Fourteenth Amendment, and the expressions of those who sponsored and favored, as well as those who opposed its submission and passage, persuades me that one of the chief objects that the provisions of the Amendment's first section, separately, and as a whole, were intended to accomplish was to make the Bill of Rights, applicable to the states." *Adamson* v. *California*, 332 U.S. 46, 71 (1947) (Black, J., dissenting).

26 "Valid treaties of course 'are as binding within the territorial limits of the States as they are elsewhere throughout the dominion of the United States.' *Baldwin* v. *Franks*, 120 U.S. 678, 683. No doubt the great body of private relations usually fall within the control of the State,

but a treaty may override its power. We do not have to invoke the later developments of constitutional law for this proposition; it was recognized as early as *Hopkirk* v. *Bell*, 3 Cranch. 454, with regard to statutes of limitation, and even earlier, as to confiscation, in *Ware* v. *Hylton*, 3 Dall. 199. It was assumed by Chief Justice Marshall with regard to the escheat of land to the State in *Chirac* v. *Chirac*, 2 Wheat. 259, 275. *Hauenstein* v. *Lynham*, 100 U.S. 483. *Geofroy* v. *Riggs*, 133 U.S. 258. *Blythe* v. *Hinckley*, 180 U.S. 333, 340. So as to a limited jurisdiction of foreign consuls within a State. *Wildenhus's Case*, 120 U.S. 1. See *Ross* v. *McIntyre*, 140 U.S. 453. Further illustration seems unnecessary, and it only remains to consider the application of established rules to the present case." *Missouri* v. *Holland*, n. 2 at 434–5.

27 For example, "[T]he sanity and safety of the judicial doctrine of the earlier decisions regarding proper limitation upon the treaty-making power were more or less swept away by the language of Mr. Justice Holmes in *Missouri* v. *Holland*." Holman, "Treaty Law-Making: A Blank Check for Writing a New Constitution," 36 A.B.A. J. 707, 709 (1950).

28 Whitton and Fowler, "The Bricker Amendment – Fallacies and Dangers," 48 Am. J. Intl L. 23, 25 (1954).

29 Holman, "Treaty Law-Making," n. 23; Ober, "The Treaty-Making and Amending Powers: Do They Protect Our Fundamental Rights?" 36 A.B.A. J. 715 (1950).

30 Id.

31 S. J. Res. 1, introduced by Senator Bricker in 83rd Cong., 1st Sess., 99 Cong. Rec. (Feb. 7, 1953); text proposed by the Committee on Peace and Law through United Nations of the American Bar Association and approved by the House of Delegates Feb. 26, 1952.

32 *Reid* v. *Covert*, 354 U.S. 1 (1957).

33 Id. at 16.

Chapter 3 The Iran–Contra Affair

1 An example is a form of outsourcing known as a *maquiladora* – typically a US firm exports raw materials to a Mexican assembly plant and then reimports the finished product into the United States. Another example common on the US/Mexican border is twin plants, under the same management. The capital-intensive part is on the US side to take advantage of US tax benefits; the labor-intensive part is on the Mexican side, to avoid US minimum wages, workers' compensation insurance requirements, occupational safety and health regulations, and

environmental laws. Notes, "An Investor's Introduction to Mexico's Maquiladora Program," 22 Tex. Intl L. J. 109 (1987).

2　American executives frequently argue that their international competitiveness is hampered by the Foreign Corrupt Practices Act (FCPA) (Pub. L. no. 95–213, 91 Stat. 1494). The Act makes it illegal for US persons or their agents to make, offer or authorize, either directly or indirectly, payments to foreign political candidates with the intent of influencing official action to obtain business. And, bribes that are illegal under the FCPA are subject to tax penalties under the tax code. See, Parriott, The Tax Treatment of Bribes, Kickbacks, and Other Payments to Foreign Officials, reprinted in R. Kaplan, *Federal Taxation of International Transactions* (1988), 512.

3　Of course, it would clearly be unethical for the attorney to advise setting up such a shell corporation. A more difficult ethical question for the attorney is how to advise a corporate client on what constitutes an illegal bribe without providing instructions on evading the law. Under the FCPA, not all bribes are illegal: "only payments to foreign governments designed to influence official action to obtain business are illegal, whereas, payments to foreign government employees to expedite ministerial action are not illegal." Id. at 512.

4　"The term 'covert action' refers to a specific type of clandestine activity that goes beyond the collection of secret intelligence. It is an attempt by a government to influence political behavior and events in other countries in ways that are concealed." *Report of the Congressional Committees Investigating the Iran–Contra Affair*, S. Rept. no. 216; H. Rept. no. 433, 100th Cong., 1st Sess., 375 (1987) (hereinafter, *Report*).

5　From 1936 to 1979, Anastasio Somoza Garcia and then his son, Anastasio Somoza Debayle, ruled Nicaragua. In 1961, opponents of Somoza formed the National Liberation Front (FSLN), popularly known as the Sandinistas. Somoza was overthrown in 1979. Between 1979 and 1981, the Sandinistas consolidated their hold on Nicaragua and a new Nicaraguan rebel movement – anti-Sandinista "Contras" – emerged. Id. 25, 27.

6　The Administration's fears were not entirely fanciful: Senator Patrick Leahy (D Vt) submitted his resignation from the vice chairmanship of the Senate Intelligence Committee in 1987 after admitting that he had leaked the Intelligence Committee's draft staff report on the investigation into the Iran–Contra scandal to one of the television networks. United Press International, August 3, 1987.

7　In 1982 the first Boland Amendment was adopted as an amendment to the Defense Appropriations Bill for fiscal year 1983. Introduced by Representative Edward P. Boland, the amendment prohibited CIA use of funds "for the purpose of overthrowing the Government of Nicaragua." In 1984, the second Boland Amendment was adopted to an omnibus appropriations bill and similar provisions were adopted as parts of the Defense and Intelligence Authorization bills. It provided: "no funds available to . . . any . . . agency or entity involved in intelligence activities may be obligated or expended for the purpose or which would have the effect of supporting, directly or indirectly, military or paramilitary operations in Nicaragua by any nation, group, organization, movement or individual." The prohibitions contained in the second Boland Amendment were incorporated by reference in the Supplemental Appropriations Act of fiscal year 1985. The third Boland Amendment, which permitted certain agencies to support the Contras only in specified ways, e.g., the provision of communications equipment, related training, and intelligence information and advice, was attached to various statutory provisions from 1985 through 1986. *Report*, at 33, 31, 395–407.

8 "Under the law, covert actions may be initiated only by a personal decision of the President. A *Finding* is an official document embodying that decision. By signing a *Finding*, a President not only authorizes action, but accepts responsibility for its consequences." Id. at 32.

9 *Iran–Contra Investigation*, Joint Hearings before the Senate Select Committee on Secret Military Assistance to Iran and the Nicaraguan Opposition and the House Select Committee to Investigate Covert Arms Transactions with Iran, 100th Cong., 1st Sess., pt. I, 317–18 (1987) (hereinafter, *Investigation*) (testimony of Oliver North).

10 Id.

11 Id. at 109.

12 *Report*, at 59, 327.

13 "Secretary Shultz warned that solicitation of third-country funds that the Government could control might be an 'impeachable offense,' attributing this opinion to Chief of Staff James Baker." Id. at 414.

14 The Tower Commission was a special review board created by Executive Order to investigate the Iran–Contra affair. The Commission's conclusions are published in *Report of the President's Special Review Board*, John Tower, Chairman (Washington: Government Printing Office, February 26, 1987).

15 Some representative newspaper topics during the summer of 1987:
"New York Times/CBS News Poll finds the majority of Americans still think Pres. Reagan lied when he said he did not know that money from Iran arms sales was channeled to Nicaraguan rebels." *New York Times*, July 18, 1987 at 1, col. 4.
"North Tells Panel that He Assumed President Knew." *Los Angeles Daily Journal*, July 8, 1987 at 1, col. 6.

"News analysis of first stage of Congressional investigation on Iran–Contra Affair; key question, what Pres. Reagan knew or did." *New York Times*, June 10, 1987 at 1, col. 3.

16 *Report*, at 4, 38, 118.

17 Id. at 31.

18 Id. at 133.

19 Id. at 157–61.

20 Id.

21 Id. at 333. Congress had prohibited CIA involvement in the Angolan civil war in the 1970s.

22 I believe this account to be an accurate description, but the reader should also know that Mr McFarlane has consistently denied any participation in the Enterprise. See, *Investigation*, pt. II at 210.

23 *Report*, at 331.

24 Id. at 367.

25 Id. at 78, 327.

26 U.S. Const. Art. I, sec. 9, cl. 7.

27 *The Federalist* (B. Wright ed., 1961), no. 26 at 218 (A. Hamilton).

28 J. Nowak, R. Rotunda, and J. Young, *Constitutional Law* (2nd edn, 1983), 136.

29 Id.

30 U.S. Const. Art. I, sec. 8, cl. 11.

31 U.S. Const. Art. I, sec. 8, cl. 1.

32 U.S. Const. Art. I, sec. 9, cl. 7.

33 First as a Visiting Fellow at the International Institute for Strategic Studies and since 1984 as a Fellow of Nuffield College, Oxford and a member of the Modern History Faculty of Oxford University.

34 "Plausible denial" means structuring an authorized covert operation so that, if discovered by the party against whom it is directed, United States involvement may plausibly be denied. *Report*, at 16.

35 *New York Times*, September 23, 1984, sec. 4, at 22, col. 4.

36 C. Read, *Lord Burghley and Queen Elizabeth* (1960).

37 This refers to the policy of several Presidential administrations of the 1970s which sought to strengthen relations with China as a way of applying pressure on the Soviet Union.

38 *Report*, at 412. See also, K. Stith, "Congress' Power of the Purse," 97 Yale L. J. 1343 (1988).

39 "For two years, before Pearl Harbor . . . Roosevelt pressed against such limits [the Neutrality Act] to the utmost. He exchanged American destroyers for British bases by executive agreement, sent American troops to Greenland and Iceland, and instituted a convoy system in the North Atlantic, issuing 'shoot on sight' orders to the United States Navy." Biden and Ritch, "The War Power at a Constitutional Impasse:

A 'Joint Decision' Solution," 77 Geo. L. J. 367 (1988). The first US Neutrality Act was passed in 1794; the current provisions are codified at 18 U.S.C. secs. 951–70 and 22 U.S.C. secs. 401–65.

40 "[P]aradoxical was the action of this strict constructionist who, although operating under a Constitution with no provision for the purchase and assimilation of foreign territory, boldly initiated and carried through the Louisiana Purchase, at one stroke of his pen doubling the size of the United States . . . Historians of subsequent generations have been as busy as politicians of his own in quoting strict constructionist statements from Jefferson in order to prove that he betrayed his philosophy because he could not resist the temptation to double the area of the United States." A. Mapp, *Thomas Jefferson: A Strange Case of Mistaken Identity* (1987), 402, 404.

41 Jefferson to Breckinridge (August 12, 1803) in Paul L. Ford (ed.) *The Writings of Thomas Jefferson:8* (1897), 244.

42 See n. 13 above.

Chapter 4   The Nomination of Robert Bork

1 The committee held twelve days of hearings, lasting about eighty-seven hours and heard from 112 witnesses. The committee heard from legal scholars, lawyers, and the representatives of various organizations and interest groups. Among the witnesses were President Gerald Ford, former Chief Justice Warren Burger, and five former Attorneys General of the United States. The committee scrutinized the nominee's qualifications and credentials, including his record as a Judge on the United States Court of Appeals for the District Circuit, as Solicitor General of the United States, and as a law professor at Yale University. On October 6, 1987, the committee voted nine to five to report the nomination with an unfavorable recommendation; the nomination was later defeated by a vote of the Senate. *Nomination of Robert H. Bork to be an Associate Justice of the United States Supreme Court.* S. Rep. no. 7, 100th Cong., 1st Sess. 1 (1987) (hereinafter, *Senate Report*).

2 U.S. Const. Art. II, sec. 2, cl. 12.

3 "[T]he practice of calling on a nominee to appear before the Judiciary Committee did not begin until 1939." Freund, "Appointment of Justices: Some Historical Perspectives" 101 Harv. L. R. 1146, 1157 (1988).

4 See Ross, "The Questioning of Supreme Court Nominees at Senate Confirmation Hearings: Proposals for Accommodating the Needs of the Senate and Ameliorating the Fears of the Nominees," 62 Tul. L. Rev. 109 (1987).

5 *Senate Report*, at 1008.

6 Id.
7 Id. at 1009 (emphasis omitted).
8 Id.
9 Id. at 1010.
10 1 *Annals of Congress* (1st Cong.) (J. Gales ed.), 520 (statement of Rep. Madison, June 17, 1789).
11 Nomination of Robert H. Bork to be Associate Justice of the Supreme Court of the United States: Hearings before the Senate Committee on the Judiciary. 100th Cong., 1st Sess. 260 (1987) (hereinafter, *Senate Hearings*).
12 Id.
13 Id.
14 Id.
15 Id. at 103.
16 Id. at 104.
17 Id. at 105.
18 Id. at 114–15. Emphasis added.
19 Id. at 115.
20 Id. at 116.
21 Id. at 116–17. Bork is mistaken: these apparently rhetorical flourishes are in fact crucial to the rationale in *Griswold*, which is that as a practical matter, the right to privacy must be protected in order to protect other less controversial rights.
22 Id. at 117. Emphasis added.
23 See also exchanges at 118 ("I hate to keep saying this, Mr. Chairman, much of my objection is to the way some members of the court have gone about deriving these things") and at 120–21 (calling for "better constitutional argumentation"). Bork tried to draw the obvious distinction between ways of deriving constitutional arguments and substantive decisions. His questioners typically did not accept the distinction, prompting him repeatedly to reassert it.
24 Id. at 402.
25 Id. at 403.
26 See, Philip Bobbitt, "The Ninth, Tenth, and Fourteenth Amendments: Rules for Reading Constitutional Rights" (work in progress).
27 Id. at 130.
28 Id. at 248–9. See also, "If somebody shows me historical evidence of what they meant by the ninth amendment, I have no problem using it. I just don't know the historical evidence." Id. at 325.
29 "[Y]ou look at the founders and the ratifiers, and you look at the text of the Constitution, their words, what it was that was troubling them at the time, why they did this, and you look at the Federalist Papers and the Anti-Federalist Papers and so forth and so on and so on, to

get what the public understanding of the time was of what the evil was they wished to avert, what the freedom was they wished to protect. And once you have that, that is your major premise; and then the judge has to supply the minor premise to make sure to ask whether that value, that freedom, is being threatened by some new development in the law or in society or in technology today. And then he makes the old freedom effective today in these new circumstances." Id. at 402. See also this text, Book I, ch. 3, p. 13 above.

30 Id. at 132.

31 *Plessy* v. *Ferguson*, 163 U.S. 537 (1896) was the case upholding the constitutionality of segregation that was overruled by *Brown* v. *Board of Education*. *Plessy* involved a Louisiana statute requiring railway companies to provide "separate but equal" compartments for whites and blacks.

32 *Senate Hearings*, at 370, reprinted from a 1987 speech to the Federalist Society.

33 *Senate Hearings*, at 156.

34 Id. at 663.

35 *Senate Report*, at 23.

36 *Senate Hearings*, at 185.

37 Id. at 112–13. *The Legal Tender Cases*, 79 U.S. (12 Wall.) 457 (1870), upheld the Civil War statutes authorizing the issuance of paper money by holding that such notes were legal tender for debts, including those contracted before the enactment of the legislation. The Court later held that Congress had the power to issue paper money in time of peace as well as in time of war. *Legal Tender Case*, 110 U.S. 421 (1884).

38 *Senate Hearings*, at 264–5.

39 Id. at 265.

40 Id.

41 Justice Harlan was the sole dissenter in *Plessy*. The vote was seven to one.

42 *Senate Hearings*, at 265 (emphasis added).

43 A. Bickel, *The Least Dangerous Branch* (1962), 116.

44 *Senate Hearings*, at 292–3. For those interested in Prudential argument and its intellectual history, see Philip Bobbitt, *Constitutional Fate: Theory of the Constitution* (1982), ch. 5.

45 *Senate Hearings*, at 399.

46 Id. at 405. The passage Bork referred to is: "The principle now contested [whether Congress has the power to incorporate a bank] was introduced at a very early period of our history, has been recognised by many successive legislatures, and has been acted upon by the judicial department, in cases of peculiar delicacy as a law of undoubted obli-

gation. It will not be denied, that a bold and daring usurpation might be resisted, after an acquiescence still longer and more complete than this. But it is conceived that a doubtful question . . . if not put at rest by the practice of the government, ought to receive a considerable impression from that practice." *McCulloch* v. *Maryland*, 17 U.S. (4 Wheat.) 316, 401 (1819).

47 *Senate Hearings*, at 405.

48 Id.

49 Id. at 435.

50 Id. at 436. To which Bork replied, "Well, I have also said, Senator, that anybody who tries to follow original intent must also have a respect for precedent because some things it's too late to change. Now the application of the equal protection clause to all kinds of people other than racial groups is so settled and so many expectations have grown up around that, so many segments of our population have internalized that kind of protection, so many institutions are built on it, that it's an interpretation that should not be overturned."

51 Id. at 465.

52 Id. at 126–9.

53 A. Bickel, *The Least Dangerous Branch*, 111 ff.

54 G. Gunther, "The Subtle Vices of the Passive Virtues – a Comment on Principle and Expediency in Judicial Review," 64 Col. L. Rev. 1, 3 (1964).

55 Readers who are interested in this discussion may turn to Bobbitt, *Constitutional Fate*, at 68–9, from which it is taken.

56 *Senate Hearings*, at 153.

57 R. Bork, "Original Intent: The Only Legitimate Basis for Constitutional Decision Making," Judge's J. 13, 14 (Summer 1987).

58 *Senate Hearings*, at 448.

59 *Ashwander* v. *Tennessee Valley Authority*, 297 U.S. 288, 346–56) (Brandeis, J., concurring).

60 See, e.g., Frankfurter's dissent from the grant of certiorari in *Youngstown Sheet & Tube Co.* v. *Sawyer*, 343 U.S. 937, 938 (1952), also discussed in Bobbitt, *Constitutional Fate*, at 65–6.

61 The Fifth Annual Judicial Conference of the United States of Appeals for the Federal Circuit, May 8, 1987, 119 F.R.D. 45, 60–1.

62 "[T]o seek in historical materials relevant to the framing of the Constitution, or in the language of the Constitution itself, specific answers to specific present problems is to ask the wrong questions. With adequate scholarship, the answer that must emerge in the vast majority of cases is no answer. . . . No answer is what the wrong question begets, for the excellent reason that the Constitution was not framed to be a catalogue of answers to such questions." Bickel, *The Least Dangerous Branch*, 102–3.

63 Compare, "I cannot understand then why the precise words used in the 14th amendment, which are 'deny to any person within its jurisdiction the equal protection of the laws' creates the confusion that it does with you. It does not with me. What words of those words I just read are not precise? If the plain language of the amendment requires States to equally protect all within its jurisdiction, why would there ever need to be any analysis of the legislative history or intent of the Congress when those words are as precise as this person can read them?" *Senate Hearings*, at 254. See also, the description of the textualist's approach in Bobbitt, *Constitutional Fate*, at 25–38.

64 *Senate Hearings*, at 248–9.

65 *Barnes* v. *Kline*, 759 F.2d 21, 55 (1985) (Bork, J. dissenting).

66 As the opinions in *INS* v. *Chadha*, 462 U.S. 919 (1983) (legislative veto case); *Bowsher* v. *Synar*, 478 U.S. 714 (1986) (the Gramm–Rudman opinion) and *National League of Cities* v. *Usery*, 426 U.S. 833 (1976) (federal, structural limits on Congress's power) all amply demonstrate; see Book I, ch. 3, n. 11.

67 *Senate Hearings*, at 1004.

68 Id.

69 See *Harper* v. *Virginia Bd. of Elections*, 383 U.S. 663 (1966). *Harper* held a state poll tax unconstitutional as a violation of the equal protection clause of the Fourteenth Amendment because it required the payment of a tax as a precondition for voting, thus conditioning the right to vote on wealth.

70 *Debate on the Articles of Impeachment*, House Committee on the Judiciary, 93rd Cong., 2nd Sess. 110 (1974).

BOOK III

Introduction

1 "[C]an common-sense blaming coexist with those often counter-intuitive notions of justice which set the factually guilty criminal defendant free? Can common sense make sense of interpretive principles, deriving, say, from a constitutional text, which trump our 'natural' inclination to blame the factually guilty? Common sense probably would not surrender concrete evidentiary truth to abstract constitutional principle – whether that principle be a matter of construing fourteenth amendment due process or the fifth amendment privilege against self-incrimination." Richard K. Sherwin, "A Matter of Voice and Plot: Belief and Suspicion in Legal Storytelling," 87 Mich. L. Rev. 543, 595 (1988).

2 Philip Bobbitt, *Constitutional Fate: Theory of the Constitution* (1982).

3 Edwin Meese, "The Attorney General's View of the Supreme Court:

Toward a Jurisprudence of Original Intention," 45 Pub. Admin. Rev.
701 (1985); "Symposium, 'Construing the Constitution'", 19 U.C.
Davis L. Rev. 1–30 (1985) (reprinting addresses by Brennan, Justice
John Paul Stevens, and Meese). Among Kafka's notes was found this
sketch: a legend of Prometheus in which all are fed up with the
senseless story. The gods are tired, the eagles are tired, the wound
heals painfully.

4   For example, *Senator DeConcini*: "I cannot understand then why the
precise words used in the 14th amendment . . . create the confusion
it does with you. It does not with me. What words of those words I
just read are not precise? If the plain language of the amendment
requires States to equally protect all within its jurisdiction, why would
there ever need to be any analysis of the legislative history or intent
. . . when those words are as precise as this person can read them?"
45 CQ [Congressional Quarterly] Weekly 2263 (1987).
Senator Metzenbaum: "The basic problem as I see it, is that to you
[Judge Bork] the Constitution is not a living document; it is not a
charter of liberty. And if you cannot find protection for the individual
in the fine print, then the people of this country are out of luck." Id.
at 2330.
Senator Specter: "[I] think there is some difference of opinion as to
whether you can really find original intent, whether the tradition of
U.S. Constitutional interpretation looks to specific Constitutional
rights as, for example, privacy . . . Justices who advocate restraint,
like [Felix] Frankfurter, talk about values rooted in conscience and
tradition of the people, as I see it, has in many cases not been grounded
on original intent sometimes, yes, but frequently not." Id. at 2332.

5   Mark Tushnet, *Red, White and Blue: A Critical Analysis of Constitutional Law* (1988), 24.
6   Tom Stoppard, *Travesties* (1975).
7   Harry H. Wellington, "Common Law Rules and Constitutional Double Standards: Some Notes on Adjudication," 83 Yale L. J. 221, 267–71
(1973); R. Dworkin, *Laws Empire* (1986); R. Posner, *The Problems
of Jurisprudence* (1990).
8   Obviously, I am not using the technical definition of "meta-logic." I
mean only some rule whose generality purports to govern the choices
among the forms of argument.

*Chapter I   How Can the American System of Interpretation
be Just?*

1   John Rawls, *A Theory of Justice* (1971).
2   William H. Rehnquist, "The Notion of a Living Constitution," 54
Tex. L. Rev. 693 (1976).

3 Robert Bork, *The Tempting of America: The Political Seduction of the Law* (1990).

4 Mark Tushnet, *Red, White and Blue: A Critical Analysis of Constitutional Law* (1988).

5 Compare, William Ewald, "Unger's Philosophy: A Critical Legal Study," 97 Yale L. J. 665 (1988); Edwin Meese III, "The Supreme Court of the United States: Bulwark of a Limited Constitution," 27 S. Tex. L. J. 455, 466 (1986).

6 J. Singer, "The Player and the Cards; Nihilism and Legal Theory," 94 Yale L. J. 1, 11 (1984).

7 Daniel Boorstin, *The Genius of American Politics* (1953), 68–98.

8 Indeed, one could make a very strong case that it was the seventeenth century, and not the eighteenth century, that fundamentally rearranged pre-existing constitutional norms.

Chapter 2   Proposals to Correct the System

1 U.S. Const. art. I, sec. 8, cl. 15.

2 *Martin* v. *Mott*, 25 U.S. (12 Wheat.) 19 (1827).

3 Jefferson Powell, "The Original Understanding of Original Intent," 98 Harv. L. Rev. 885 (1985).

4 Philip Bobbitt, *Constitutional Fate: Theory of the Constitution* (1982), 10.

5 Raoul Berger, "The Founders' Views According to Jefferson Powell," 67 Tex. L. Rev. 1033 (1989).

6 Richard H. Fallon, Jr, "A Constructivist Coherence Theory of Constitutional Argumentation," 100 Harv. L. Rev. 1189 (1987).

7 Id. at 1286.

8 Id. at 1209.

9 Laurence H. Tribe, *Constitutional Choices* (1985).

10 Stanley Fish, "Working on the Chain Gang: Interpretation in Law and Literature," 60 Tex. L. Rev. 551 (1982).

11 Fallon, "Constructivist Coherence Theory," at 1223–1224.

12 Id. at 1230. Although there remains some controversy, I think it better to say that there are six types of constitutional argument (see the discussion of Tushnet in the following pages).

13 Mark Tushnet, *Red, White and Blue: A Critical Analysis of Constitutional Law* (1988).

14 Id. at 2.

15 Id. at 3.

16 Id. at 25.

17 The Convention was convened "for the sole purpose of revising the Articles." Resolve of Congress, passed February 21, 1787.

18   Bobbitt, *Constitutional Fate*, at 25 n. 15.
19   One would look to the intentions of the Civil War ratifiers to argue that the Privileges and Immunities Clause of the Fourteenth Amendment (No State shall make or enforce any law which shall abridge the privileges or immunities of citizens of the United States) was intended to apply the Bill of Rights against the states, the decision of the Slaughter-house Cases notwithstanding. In *The Slaughter-House Cases*, 83 U.S. (16 Wall.) 36 (1873), the Supreme Court held that the Privileges and Immunities Clause was inapplicable to a state's regulation of business matters.
20   Raoul Berger, *Government by Judiciary* (1977), 1–19, 36.
21   Tushnet, *Red, White and Blue*, at 32.
22   Id. at 36–7.
23   Id. at 37.
24   Id. at 37, n. 55.
25   *Whitney* v. *California*, 274 U.S. 357 (1927).
26   Tushnet, *Red, White and Blue*, at 40.
27   *Whitney* v. *California*, 274 U.S. 357, 375 (1927).
28   Tushnet, *Red, White and Blue*, at 46.
29   Id.
30   Henry M. Hart, Jr, "Foreward: The Time Chart of the Justices," 73 Harv. L. Rev. 84, 99 (1959).
31   Tushnet, *Red, White and Blue*, at 47 n. 79.
32   Id. at 49.
33   Id. at 57.
34   Id. at 60.
35   Id. at 61.
36   Id. at 68–9.
37   For two authors who do tell us a great deal about textualism, see the estimable Hans Linde's rightly influential "Due Process of Lawmaking," 55 Neb. L. Rev. 197 (1976); Frederick Schauer, "Easy Cases," 58 S. Cal. L. Rev. 399 (1985); Frederick Schauer, "The Constitution as Text and Rule," 29 Wm. and Mary L. Rev. 41 (1987).
38   John Hart Ely, *Democracy and Distrust: A Theory of Judicial Review* (1980), 71.
39   Tushnet, *Red, White and Blue*, at 89.
40   Id.
41   C. Black, *Structure and Relationship in Constitutional Law* (1969), 42–4.
42   Philip Bobbitt, "Is Law Politics?" (Book Review), 41 Stan. L. Rev. 1233, 1279–80 (1989).
43   Tushnet, *Red, White and Blue*, at 110–11.
44   Id. at 120.

45 Id. at 139–41.
46 Id. at 108.
47 Learned Hand, *The Spirit of Liberty* (3rd edn, 1960), 306–7.
48 Tushnet, *Red, White and Blue*, at 147–8.
49 Id. at 149–58.
50 Id. at 160, 162–3, 164 (quoting Owen Fiss, "Foreward: The Forms of Justice," 93 Harv. L. Rev. 1, 2 (1979)).
51 Id. at 175.
52 Id. at 186.
53 Id.
54 Id. at 187.
55 It has been suggested before that individual liberty can only be assured within a community of a certain sort or one possessing a certain public responsibility. Rousseau, for example, maintained that personal liberty depended on the performance of public services. See Jean-Jacques Rousseau, *The Social Contract* (1762) (M. Cranston trans., 1968). It has also been argued that the qualities required by each person in order to perform civic duties must be the civic virtues. See Quentin Skinner, "The Idea of Negative Liberty," in *Philosophy in History* (R. Rorty, J. B. Schneewind and Q. Skinner eds, 1984), 193.
56 Tushnet, *Red, White and Blue*, at 179.

Chapter 3   Why it was Thought such Proposals were Necessary

1 I. D. Davidson, *Essays on Actions and Events*, 3, 8 (Clarendon) (1980).
2 Ronald Dworkin's characterization of this rationalization is, I think, exemplary.
3 *Watkins* v. *U.S.*, 354 U.S. 178 (1957). Watkins was convicted to a violation of 2 U.S.C. sec. 192 which made it a misdemeanor for any person summoned as a witness before a Congressional committee to refuse to answer any question "pertinent to the subject under inquiry."
4 "No person shall be held to answer for a capital, or otherwise infamous crime . . . nor be deprived of life, liberty, or property without due process of law . . ." U.S. Const. amend. V.
5 C. G. Hempel, *Aspects of Scientific Explanation*, 300–1 (Free Press) (1965).
6 Fallon, "A Constructivist Coherence Theory of Constitutional Interpretation," 100 Harv. L. Rev. 1189 (1987).
7 Post, "Theories of Constitutional Interpretation (n.d.) (unpublished manuscript on file with the Stanford Law Review).
8 Powell, "The Original Understanding of Original Intent," 98 Harv. L. Rev. 885 (1985).

9   M. Tushnet, *Red, White and Blue: A Critical Analysis of Constitutional Law* (1988).
10 R. Dworkin, *Law's Empire* (1988).
11 H. L. A. Hart, *The Concept of Law* (1961).
12 Id.
13 Dworkin, *Law's Empire*.
14 P. B. Medawar and J. S. Medawar, *The Life Science* (1977), 116–17.
15 Learned Hand, *The Spirit of Liberty* (1954), 15.
16 Benjamin Cardozo, *The Nature of the Judicial Process* (1921), 40–41.
17 *Papers of Thomas Jefferson:1* (J. Boyd, ed.) (1950), 423.
18 Proclamation no. 17, 12 Stat. 1268 (1863); see, for example, James M. McPherson, *The Struggle for Equality: Abolitionists and the Negro in the Civil War and Reconstruction* (1964).
19 Pub. L. No. 93–148, 87 Stat. 555 (1973) (codified at 50 U.S.C. secs. 1541–48 (1982)).
20 Max Brod, Postscript to the First Edition (1925) of Franz Kafka's *The Trial* (1956), 326–35.
21 Id. at 332.

Chapter 4   The Possibility of Justice

1   Richard H. Fallon, Jr, "Constructive Coherence Theory of Constitutional Argumentation," 100 Harv. L. Rev. 1187, 1286 (1987).
2   *Bork*: "I was making the point that where the Constitution does not speak – there is no provision in the Constitution that applies to the case . . . All that means is that the judge may not choose."
    Biden: "Who does?"
    Bork: "The legislature." 45 *CQ Weekly* 2259 (1987).
3   Fallon, "Constructivist Coherence Theory," 1189.
4   *Griswold* v. *Connecticut*, 381 U.S. 479 (1965). The Court held that a state could not criminalize the use of contraceptives because it violated a married couple's privacy interest, which, although not specifically mentioned in the Constituion, was protected within the "penumbra" of the Bill of Rights. The First Amendment protects the right of free speech and the right to the free exercise of religion. U.S. Const. amend. I. The Third Amendment protects the security of an individual's home from the billeting of troops. U.S. Const. amend. III. The Fourth Amendment protects individuals, their papers, and their homes from unreasonable searches and seizures. U.S. Const. amend IV.
5   Id. at 527 (Stewart, J., dissenting).
6   Id. at 486 (Goldberg, J., dissenting).
7   Philip Bobbitt, *Constitutional Fate: Theory of the Constitution* (1982), 39–58.

8   *Furman* v. *Georgia*, 408 U.S. 238 (1972).
9   Id. at 270 (Brennan, J., concurring).
10 Id. at 358–60 (Marshall, J., concurring).
11 Id. at 257 (Douglas, J., concurring).
12 Id. at 310 and 312 (Stewart, J., and White, J., concurring respectively).
13 *Jurek* v. *Texas*, 428 U.S. 262 (1976). The Texas legislature had passed a capital sentencing procedure which required a jury to consider five categories of aggravating circumstances and which focussed on the particularized circumstances of the individual offense.
14 *Gregg* v. *Georgia*, 428 U.S. 153 (1976). The Georgia legislature established a system under which the guilt and punishment portions of the trial were bifurcated.
15 *Erie Railroad Co.* v. *Tompkins*, 304 U.S. 64 (1938).
16 *Swift* v. *Tyson*, 41 U.S. (16 Pet.) 1 (1842). The Supreme Court held that federal courts exercising jurisdiction on the ground of diversity of citizenship need not, in matters of general jurisprudence, apply the unwritten law of the state as declared by its highest court. Rather, they were free to exercise independent judgment as to what the common law of the state was.
17 *Erie Railroad Co.*, at 78; H. Friendly, *Benchmarks* 20 (1967).
18 *Erie Railroad Co.*, at 71.
19 Characteristially he cites recent research [Brandeis was relying on Warren, "New Light on the Federal Judiciary Act of 1789," 37 Harv. L. Rev. 49 (1923)] that cast doubt on Story's statutory construction of the Judiciary Act, but he makes clear that "If only a question of statutory construction were involved we should not be prepared to abandon a doctrine so widely applied throughout nearly a century. But the unconstitutionality of the course pursued has now been made clear, and compels us to do so." Id. at 77–8.
20 Judiciary Act of 1789, ch. 20 sec. 34 (current version at 28 U.S.C. sec. 1652 (1982)).
21 Bobbitt, *Constitutional Fate*, at 181.
22 Charles Black, *Decision According to Law* (1981), 77–8.
23 See G. Hunter, *Metalogic: An Introduction to the Metatheory of Standard First Order Logic* (1971). Hunter defines meta-logic as "the theory of sentences-used-to-express-truths-of-logic." Id. at 3.
24 But a state of affairs is a possible world only if it is *complete* or *maximal*. "*S*" is a complete state of affairs if and only if for every state of "*S*" either "*S*" includes or precludes "*S*". A state of affairs "*S*" includes a state of affairs "*S*" if it is not possible that "*S*" obtain and "*S*" not obtain. A state of affairs "*S*" precludes a state of affairs "*S*" if it is not possible that both obtain. (Inclusion among states of affairs is like entailment among propositions.)

25 In 1819, there was an equal number of slave and free states. Thus, when the issue of statehood arose for the Territory of Missouri, there was a fierce debate between the proponents and opponents of slavery. The House passed a bill on March 1, 1820 admitting Missouri as a free state. The Senate struck the antislavery position and replaced it with the Thomas Amendment which provided that Missouri would be admitted as a slave state but restricted slavery in a large portion of the Lousiana Purchase. Following additional debates, the Missouri constitutional convention proposed a second compromise on March 2, 1821 which stipulated that Missouri would not be admitted until it agreed that nothing in its constitution should be interpreted to abridge the privileges and immunities of citizens of the United States. The pledge was secured, and on August 10, 1821, Missouri became a state.

26 Cf Alvin Plantinga, *The Nature of Necessity*, 164–84 (1974).

27 V. Nabokov, Preface to Lolita (1955).

Chapter 5   Justifying and Deciding

1 See, e.g., R. Unger, *The Critical Legal Studies Movement* (1986); Frug, "The Ideology of Bureaucracy in American Law," 97 Harv. L. Rev. 1276 (1984); R. Unger, *Law in Modern Society* (1976); Duncan Kennedy, "The Structure of Blackstone's Commentaries," 28 Buffalo L. Rev., 209 (1979); Duncan Kennedy and P. Gabel, "Roll Over Beethoven," 36 Stan. L. Rev. 1 (1984); R. Unger, *Knowledge and Politics* (1975), 32; David Kennedy, "Critical Theory, Structuralism and Contemporary Legal Scholarship," 21 New Eng. L. Rev. 209 (1985–6); M. Tushnet, "Critical Legal Studies and Constitutional Law; An Essay in Deconstruction," 36 Stan. L. Rev. 623 (1984); Gordon, "Critical Legal Histories," 36 Stan. L. Rev. 57 (1984); Turley, "The Hitchhiker's Guide to CLS, Unger and Deep Thought," 81 Nw. U. L. Rev. 593 (1987); M. Kelman, *A Guide to Critical Legal Studies* (1987).

2 R. Unger, *The Critical Legal Studies Movement* (1986), 7–8.

3 Id. at 8.

4 See, e.g., *Report of the Congressional Committees Investigating the Iran–Contra Affair*, S. Rept. no. 216; H. Rept. no. 433, 100th Cong., 1st Sess. 22 (1987).

5 Judge Friendly told the author this story.

Chapter 6   The Role of Ideal Systems

1 P. Bator, P. Mishkin, D. Shapiro and H. Wechsler, *Hart & Wechsler's The Federal Courts and the Federal System* (2d edn, 1973); H. Hart

and A. Sacks, *The Legal Process: Basic Problems in the Making and Application of Law* (10th edn, 1958).

2 For example, A. Kronman and R. Posner, *The Economics of Contract Law* (1979); C. Goetz, *Cases and Materials on Law and Economics* (1984); "The Constitution as an Economic Document" (Symposium), 56 Geo. Wash. L. Rev. 1 (1987); "Symposium on the Theory of Public Choice," 74 Va. L. Rev. 167 (1988); S. Rose-Ackerman, "Progressive Law and Economics – And the New Administrative Law," 98 Yale L. J. 341 (1988).

3 See Book III, chapter 5, n. 1.

4 S. Levinson and S. Mailloux, *Interpreting Law and Literature: A Hermeneutic Reader* (1988); H. Dreyfus and P. Rabinow, *Michel Foucault: Beyond Structuralism and Hermeneutics* (1982); Hutchinson, "From Cultural Construction to Historical Deconstruction," 94 Yale L. J. 209 (1984); Bernstein, *Beyond Objectivism and Relativism: Science, Hermeneutics and Praxis* (1983); Hoy, "Interpreting the Law: Hermeneutical and Poststructurist Perspectives," 58 S. Cal. L. Rev. 135 (1985); Peller, "The Metaphysics of American Law," 73 Calif. L. Rev. 1151 (1985); J. M. Balkin, "Deconstructive Practice and Legal Theory," 96 Yale L. J. 743 (1987).

5 Coase, "The Market for Goods and the Market for Ideas," 64 Am. Econ. Rev. 384 (1974); Calabresi, "The Decision for Accidents: An Approach to Nonfault Allocation of Costs," 78 Harv. L. Rev. 713 (1965); K. Arrow, *Social Choice and Individual Values* (2nd edn, 1963); Coase, "The Problem of Social Cost," 3 J. L. & Econ. 1 (1960); J. Buchanan and G. Tullock, *The Calculus of Consent* (1962).

6 J. Habermas, *Communication and the Evolution of Society* (T. McCarthy trans., 1979); J. Habermas, *Knowledge and Human Interests* (J. Shapiro trans., 1971); J. Habermas, *Toward a Rational Society* (J. Shapiro trans., 1970); M. Horkheimer, *Eclipse of Reason* (1974); M. Horkheimer and T. Adorno, *Dialectic of Enlightenment* (J. Cummings trans., 1969), 27; T. Adorno, *Negative Dialectics* (E. Ashton trans., 1973); H. Marcuse, *One Dimensional Man* (1964); H. Marcuse, *The Aesthetic Dimension* (1972).

7 Derrida, *Of Grammatology* (G. Spivak trans., 1976); R. Barthes, *The Pleasure of the Text* (R. Miller trans., 1975); M. Foucault, *Power/Knowledge: Selected Interviews and Other Writings* (1980); H. Gadamer, *Philosophical Hermeneutics* (D. Linge ed., 1976).

8 For Critical Legal Studies, see Unger, Duncan Kennedy, Tushnet, and Gordon, Book III, chapter 5, n. 1 above. See also, M. Kelman, *A Guide to Critical Legal Studies* (1987); Duncan Kennedy, *Legal Education and the Reproduction of Hierarchy: A Polemic Against the System* (1983).

For law and hermeneutics, see R. Barthes, *The Pleasure of the Text* (R. Miller trans., 1975); Balkin, "Deconstructive Practice," S. Levinson, *Constitutional Faith* (1988).

For law and economics, see R. Posner, *Economic Analysis of Law* (3rd edn, 1986); R. Posner, *The Economics of Justice* (1981); Easterbrook, "The Supreme Court, 1983 Term – Foreward: The Court and the Economic System," 98 Harv. L. Rev. 4 (1984); Easterbrook, "Statutes' Domain," 50 U. Chi. L. Rev. 533 (1983); Easterbrook, "Ways of Criticizing the Court," 95 Harv. L. Rev. 802 (1982).

9 D'Amato, "Whither Jurisprudence?" 6 Cardozo L. Rev. 971 (1985); Diamond, "Not-so-Critical Legal Studies," 6 Cardozo L. Rev. 693 (1985); Kelman, "Consumption Theory, Production Theory and Ideology in the Coase Theorem," 52 S. Cal. L. Rev. 669 (1979); Leff, "Economic Analysis of Law: Some Realism About Nominalism," 60 Va. L. Rev. 451 (1974); Hansmann, "The Current State of Law & Economics Scholarship," 33 J. Legal Ed. 217 (1983).

10 Bruce Ackerman, *Private Property and the Constitution* (1977), 88–167.

11 The Fifth Amendment requires that just compensation be given to the owner of private property when that property is taken for public use. Two cases discussing this issue are *Hodel* v. *Irving*, 481 U.S. 704 (1987) and *Almota Farmers Elevator and Warehouse Company*, 409 U.S. 470 (1973).

12 Philip Bobbitt, "Is Law Politics?" (Book Review), 41 Stan. L. Rev. 1233, 1254 (1989).

13 John Rawls, *A Theory of Justice* (1971) and *Two Concepts of Rules* (1968). Two federal courts citing Ralws: *Memphis Development Foundation* v. *Factors Etc., Inc.*, 616 F. 2d 956, 958–9 (6th Cir. 1980) and *Runway 27 Coalition, Inc.* v. *Engen*, 679 F. Supp. 95, 105 (D. Mass. 1987).

14 In a similar vein regarding the fundamental nature of philosophy, Dworkin has written: "Even the debate about the nature of law, which has dominated legal philosophy for some decades, is, at bottom, a debate within the philosophy of language and metaphysics." R. Dworkin (ed.), *The Philosophy of Law*, 1, (Oxford) (1977).

15 Charles Fried, "The Artificial Reason of the Law or: What Lawyers Know?," 60 Tex. L. Rev. 35, 57 (1981).

16 Cleary, "Evidence as a Problem in Communicating," 5 Vand. L. Rev. 277 (1952); Stewart, "Perception, Memory, and Hearsay: A Criticism of Present Law and the Proposed Federal Rules of Evidence," 1970 Utah L. Rev. 1 (1970).

17 Minow, "Interpreting Rights: An Essay for Robert Cover," 96 Yale L. J. 1860, 1865 (1987).

18 Duncan Kennedy, "Legal Education as Training for Hierarchy," in *The Politics of Law: A Progressive Critique* (D. Kairys ed., 1982), 48.
19 See, e.g., R. Rorty, *Philosophy and the Mirror of Nature* (1979).
20 Boris Pasternak, *Dr Zhivago* (1958).

Chapter 7   The Role of Moral Decision

1 Chrétien de Troyes, *Le Chevalier de la Charrette* (1963 edn).
2 Henkin, "Foreign Affairs and the Constitution," 66 For. Aff. 284, 301–2 (1987).
3 R. Unger, *The Critical Legal Studies Movement* (1986), 7–8.
4 G. Calabresi and P. Bobbitt, *Tragic Choices* (1978).
5 Ronald Dworkin, "Introduction," *The Philosophy of Law* (ed. R. Dworkin) (1977), 8–9.
6 See, for example, the essay "Mind and Matter" reprinted in Bertrand Russell, *Portraits from Memory* (1951), 145–65.
7 Dworkin, "Introduction." See n. 14 *supra*.
8 Richard Rorty, "Science as Solidarity," Manuscript, November 1984, 8.
9 Mark Sagoff, "The Principles of Federal Pollution Control," 71 Minn. L. Rev. 19, 95 (1986).
10 See the excellent work by Stephen Hilmy, *The Later Wittgenstein* (1988).
11 And aren't all that way: simply self-containing,
   if self-containing means: To transform the world outside
   and the wind and the rain and the patience of spring
   and guilt and restlessness and muffled fate
   and the darkness of the evening earth
   and even the changing and flying and fleeing of the clouds
   and the vague influence of the distant stars
   into a handful of inwardness.
   R.M. Rilke, "The Bowl of Roses," *New Poems* (E. Snow trans., 1907).
12 C. Black, "Reflections on Teaching and Working in Constitutional Law," 66 Ore. L. Rev. 1, 16–17 (1987).
13 C. Black, *Decision According to Law* (1981).
14 T. Mann, *The Coming Victory of Democracy* 50 (1938).
15 J. A. Schumpeter, *Capitalism, Socialism and Democracy*, 243 (Harper) (1942).
16 Friedrich Nietzsche, *The Wanderer and His Shadow*, in Oscar Levy (ed.), *Complete Works of Friedrich Nietzsche:7*, 358 (1911).
17 M. Walzer, "Philosophy and Democracy," 9 Political Theory 379, 379 (1981).
18 F. Nietzsche, Preface to *The Gay Science* (2nd edn, 1887).

Index